Historical Problems:
Studies and Documents

Edited by
PROFESSOR G. R. ELTON
University of Cambridge

4
ENGLISH RURAL SOCIETY
1200–1350

In the same series

ENGLISH
RURAL SOCIETY
1200–1350

J. Z. Titow

Lecturer in Economic and Social History
in the University of Nottingham

LONDON · GEORGE ALLEN AND UNWIN LTD
NEW YORK · BARNES AND NOBLE INC

FIRST PUBLISHED IN 1969

This book is copyright under the Berne Convention. Apart from any fair dealing for the purposes of private study, research, criticism or review, as permitted under the Copyright Act 1956, no portion may be reproduced by any process without written permission. Enquiry should be made to the publisher

SBN 04 900014 4 *cloth*

SBN 04 900015 2 *paper*

PRINTED IN GREAT BRITAIN
in 10 *on* 11 *pt Plantin type*
BY WILLMER BROTHERS LIMITED
BIRKENHEAD

EDITOR'S FOREWORD

The reader and the teacher of history might be forgiven for thinking that there are now too many series of historical documents in existence, all claiming to offer light on particular problems and all able to fulfil their claims. At any rate, the general editor of yet another series feels obliged to explain why he is helping one more collection of such volumes into existence.

One purpose of this series is to put at the disposal of the student original materials illustrating historical problems, but this is no longer anything out of the way. A little less usual is the decision to admit every sort of historical question: there are no barriers of time or place or theme. However, what really distinguishes this enterprise is the fact that it combines generous collections of documents with introductory essays long enough to explore the theme widely and deeply. In the doctrine of educationalists, it is the original documents that should be given to the student; in the experience of teachers, documents thrown naked before the untrained mind turn from pearls to paste. The study of history cannot be confined either to the learning up of results without a consideration of the foundations, or to a review of those foundations without the assistance of the expert mind. The task of teaching involves explanation and instruction, and these volumes recognize this possibly unfashionable fact. Beyond that, they enable the writers to say new and important things about their subject matter: to write history of an exploratory kind, which is the only important historical writing there is.

As a result, each volume will be a historical monograph worth the attention which all such monographs deserve, and each volume will stand on its own. While the format of the series is uniform, the contents will vary according to need. Some problems require the reconsideration which makes the known enlighteningly new; others need the attention of original research; yet others will have to enter controversy because the prevailing notions on many historical questions are demonstrably wrong. The authors of this series are free to treat their subject in whatever manner it seems to them to require. They will present some of their evidence for inspection and help the learner to see how history is written, but they will themselves also write history.

G.R.E.

PREFACE

This book, primarily intended for the undergraduate student, hopes to provide an introduction to the study of English rural society between 1200 and 1350. The agrarian history of that period abounds in issues which are at present much debated and sometimes highly controversial. I have, therefore, thought it best to present the reader with the main points of discussion, to explain what evidence the historian has to help him determine the truth, and to some extent myself engage in controversy where I believe existing interpretations to be mistaken. In this, I have had to rely in part on unpublished researches and if some of my assertions may strike the reader, occasionally, as insufficiently substantiated this is because I thought it more important to provide, in the documents appended at the end, a representative cross-section of the basic material on which our knowledge of the rural society in this period rests, rather than sacrifice valuable space for a more generous selection of extracts illustrating specific points in some of the more controversial arguments.

I am grateful to Professor J. D. Chambers for valuable comments, and much encouragement, in connection with chapters I and III, and to Dr Alan Rogers for ploughing through my translations of all the documents, as well as reading much of the text, and making many helpful suggestions.

I would also like to record my gratitude to Mrs E. Cottrill, and her staff at the Hampshire Record Office in Winchester, for much kindness, help, and understanding, which I have always met with on my frequent visits there, not the least, while selecting documents for this book.

CONTENTS

INTRODUCTION

Introductory:
Sources and Problems

I

It is a well known fact that the population of England in the thirteenth century was predominantly rural and that rural population was predominantly peasant, yet a student of the rural society approaching the period for the first time may well wonder why it is that most of the studies he comes across deal mainly, if not exclusively, with great estates and their owners. The answer to this apparent paradox is a simple one.

In his reconstruction of the past the historian is circumscribed by the existing documentation, and the documents on which our reconstruction of medieval rural society rests emanate almost entirely from the great estates. This is quite understandable. The peasants have left no records behind. Even had they been literate, as most of them certainly were not, they would have found no need to keep a record of their activities; even had some of them managed to keep such records, their chances of survival would have been almost nil from the start. It is the great landlords, with estates too vast to be administered by them personally, who were in need of written records, who would have found the expenditure involved justified, and who would have taken steps to ensure that such records were kept and preserved. The extent to which such records were drawn up and preserved, and the amount of detail included in them, depended primarily on the degree to which the landlords themselves were involved in the administration of their estates. The thirteenth century was, as will be explained presently, a period of renewed interest on the part of the landlords in the exploitation of their estates, and this accounts for the fact that a vast volume of records was produced in this period.

The need to keep records would be greatest, and the chances of dispersal for estates, and documents, the least, when the landlord was an institution; this is particularly true of ecclesiastical (episcopal or monastic) landlords, for they did not, after all, have to provide for younger sons, nor find dowries for marriageable daughters, nor set aside portions for widows, nor could they die out in direct line as so many great lay families have done. But it is not only this permanence and continuity built into ecclesiastical ownership of land which is behind the survival of so many collections of documents of ecclesiastical estates; ecclesiastical landlords had also at their command the necessary skill for their creation and preservation. In medieval times the clerics were the only literate class in society, and ecclesiastical landlords had a vast army of clerics to draw upon in the administration of their estates. This is probably the main reason why documents of lay estates are frequently inferior to those of ecclesiastical ones, both in content and presentation. It is quite inconceivable, for instance, that an ecclesiastical landlord in the early fourteenth century, when preparing an extent of his estates, would have accepted a return that the 'demesne lands were not evaluated because they have not been measured', as did the landlord of a small lay estate in Nottinghamshire as late as 1324 (Doc. 6).

There is another important reason why studies of rural society and economy usually centre on the great estates. In spite of the myth which dies incredibly hard, medieval agrarian economy was not self-sufficient, self-contained, or 'natural'.[1] It was, of course, localized to a much greater extent than is the case nowadays, but it was influenced by many external factors of more than local character. Population changes could send prices up or down; disturbances of international trade could alter the balance of profitability between arable and sheep farming; plagues, famines, and epidemics could profoundly affect land values and wage levels. Over all such factors neither the lords nor the peasants had any real control, but the lords had the freedom, which the peasants frequently had not, to trim their sails to the wind of change. It is through the study of changes in their policies with regard to their estates that we can get at these broader economic influences and through them arrive at an understanding of why men behaved as they did.

Finally, the great estates were an integral, and a very important, part of the rural scene. Though peasant farming, speaking quantitatively, was much more important than landlord farming, (i.e. the

---

[1] See R. Lennard, 'Manorial Traffic and Agricultural Trade in Medieval England', *Journal of Proceedings of the Agricultural Economics Society*, V, 1938, and M. M. Postan, 'The Rise of Money Economy', *Economic History Review*, XIV, 1944.

area under peasant cultivation was much greater than the area in demesne cultivation), in one sense the great estates were the more important, for it was within the framework of the estate that the peasant cultivators operated. This is what historians mean when they talk of the manorial system.

How far back the institution of the manor goes is still debatable. The argument hinges on what one understands by the term; whether one sees the manor as a primarily legal, or primarily economic, entity—if the latter, as I incline to do, then one must agree with Dr Aston[2] that it is clearly a pre-Conquest institution. This is not the place to discuss the origins of the manor in England, nor the process of evolution whereby England came to be covered by manors; readers interested in this aspect of the problem are referred to Maitland, Round, Vinogradoff, Lennard, Aston, and Kosminsky.[3] But a few words of explanation must be said about manors and manorialism in general.

After the Conquest all land in England was held in estates; the lowest unit of estate administration in *all* its aspects—territorial, economic, and juridical—was the manor. In practice, manorial structure itself, and the degree of manorial control over the rural population, differed considerably as between different areas. It could be almost completely nominal in some areas, as for example, in those parts of the Danelaw where large concentrations of free tenants, called sokemen, existed—tenants whose only link with the manor to which they belonged was that they paid their rents there and owed their lord suit of court. Such concentrations of sokemen, known as territorial sokes, frequently lay miles away from the manorial centre to which they were attached.[4] Manorial control would also be weak in regions where scattered homesteads and isolated hamlets predominated,[5] and it was at its strongest in the nucleated villages of the Midlands, the South, and the West.

What made the manorial control a purely nominal link with an

[2] T. H. Aston, 'The Origins of the Manor in England', *Essays in Agrarian History I*, ed. W. E. Minchinton, London, 1968.

[3] F. W. Maitland, *Domesday Book and Beyond (1897)*, London, 1960, pp. 140–188; P. Vinogradoff *The Growth of the Manor*, London 1911; J. H. Round, 'The Domesday Manor', *English Historical Review*, XV, 1900; R. Lennard, *Rural England 1086–1135*, Oxford, 1959, pp. 211–236; E. A. Kosminsky, *Studies in the Agrarian History of England in the Thirteenth Century*, London, 1956, pp. 68–80.

[4] F. M. Stenton, 'Types of Manorial Structure in the Northern Danelaw', *Oxford Studies in Social and Legal History*, ed. P. Vinogradoff, II, Oxford, 1910.

[5] See, for example, M. Beresford, 'Dispersed and Group Settlement in Medieval Cornwall', *Agricultural History Review*, XII, 1964.

B

estate, or an all-pervading influence over the peasants' daily life, was the extent to which the manor had developed and retained its demesne (i.e. the home-farm retained by the landlord in direct cultivation) and the degree of interest in the direct exploitation of it on the part of the landlord.

To say that the manor was the lowest unit of estate organization does not, of course, mean that it had to be small; some manors were very large indeed, including a number of villages within their bounds (e.g. the bishop of Winchester's Somerset manor of Taunton, or his Berkshire manor of Wargrave), while others consisted only of a part of a village, or settlement, and were hardly bigger than a substantial tenant's holding. What made the difference between a small manor and a substantial holding was not the size but the way in which the land was held. Landed property[6] to be a manor had to be held as a manor.

There is no need to enter here into what is, to my mind, the somewhat sterile discussion of what constitutes a manor. I still think that essentially a manor is what the old 'classical' definition of it said it was: an estate comprising four essential elements—the demesne, land in the hands of the tenants, dependent peasantry, and the owner's right of lordship over the inhabitants of the manor. It is true that one can find examples of manors where one of these elements is missing, but in my view such instances represent a peculiar development which does not invalidate the definition of a manor as previously given.

We do find places described as manors in the documents with no demesne on them, but this probably means no more than that the always fluctuating ratio between demesne and tenant land had changed, over the course of time, or through a single letting out, to the complete disappearance of the former. Occasionally, too, existing manors could be broken up into new groupings, some of them without a demesne at all.

We also find manors with only demesne and no tenant land at all, though this is less common than the former case. They could, however, be looked upon as real manors in the sense that though tenants, and thus also lordship, are missing from their actual composition at the time, potentiality for them existed if the person

[6] I am using the word 'property' in the sense appropriate to the medieval context. Absolute ownership of land, as we understand it now, did not exist in the Middle Ages, all land was *held* of somebody (ultimately the King) though holders of freehold land enjoyed perpetual right of occupation subject to the limitations imposed by the feudal theory of land tenure. Holders of customary land also enjoyed hereditary rights of occupation though with a lower degree of security.

responsible for their creation was already vested with the rights pertaining to manorial lordship in virtue of his possessions elsewhere.

There are also cases on record of individuals who having accumulated considerable landed property began to call them manors and behave towards their own tenants as manorial lords; this occasionally went on long enough to acquire a measure of recognition.[7] On the whole, however, we must guard against regarding as the lord of a manor every freeholder with tenants of his own, and some land in direct cultivation. Even when the documents speak of land held *in demesne* this does not necessarily mean manorial demesne; it is simply the usual way of saying that the land is kept in direct cultivation instead of having been let out to tenants. Similarly the mere existence of tenants does not, *of itself*, create lordship, and where true lordship is lacking there can be no manor. Mere creation of tenancies does not create jurisdictional rights over the tenants; they can only be created by those who have the authority to do so, or delegated by those who already have them. This is why I strongly suspect that in Professor Kosminsky's classification of manors, many of his 'manors' in the 'small manors' category are no more than substantial holdings held of somebody else's manor, and not manors in their own right.[8]

If one is to have proper understanding of the manorial system, and life under it in the thirteenth century, it is essential to look at the traditional manor—the manor with both demesne and tenants—first and foremost, for it is the presence of the demesne which constitutes the *raison d'être* of the manorial system and which provides the key to the understanding of subsequent developments. This preoccupation with the 'classical' manor is more than a theoretically dictated preference; Professor Kosminsky's study of the Hundred Rolls (the only document allowing this to be done on more than a local scale) has shown that in 1279 the 'traditional' manor still was the dominant type over much of England.[9]

2

If being subject to manorial control imposed tenurial obligations and personal disabilities on the peasant, this was not the only source

[7] An interesting example can be found in: R. H. Hilton, ed. *Stonleigh Leger Book*, Dugdale Society Publication 24, Oxford 1960, pp. xxxiv–xxxv.

[8] Professor Kosminsky seems to have counted as a manor any complex of free tenements which in sum amounted to 120 acres or more and had some tenants on them besides the land cultivated directly. *Studies in the Agrarian History of England*, 96.

[9] Ibid. 69.

of restrictions on his freedom of action. In so far as the exploitation of his land was concerned he was also subject to restrictions arising out of the fact that he shared in a communal system of cultivation —what the historians came to call the Open-Field System. Two books are absolutely essential reading on this subject: Professor Gray's study of the distribution of various field systems in England and a detailed study of the operation of the Open-Field System by the Orwins.[10] Subsequent research has done little to invalidate the broad outline of their conclusions though it has shown that the Open-Field System was more widespread, and its geographical distribution less clear-cut, than Gray allowed, and far more adaptable and flexible than has sometimes been assumed.[11] There is one important exception to this generalization. In an article published in 1965 Dr Joan Thirsk expressed the view that the Open-Field System was not in full operation in England before the mid-thirteenth century or so.[12] Salutary as it may be at times to re-examine old-established orthodoxies, and useful as it is to have the Open-Field System discussed, not from the somewhat sterile standpoint of pre-occupation with its origins, but as a living and changing institution, I find it impossible to accept Dr Thirsk's main thesis for reasons which I have already stated elsewhere.[13] It is, perhaps, worth pointing out that the two leading authorities on the English medieval rural society—Professor Postan and Professor Hilton—in studies published well after Dr Thirsk's article, have not forsaken the traditional view.[14]

What, briefly, was the Open-Field System? It was a system of co-operative farming under which all the arable land of the village was divided into two or three sectors[15] (the 'fields' of the Open-Field System), with the holdings of individual villagers consisting of strips

[10] H. L. Gray, *The English Field System*, Cambridge, Mass. 1915; C. S. and C. S. Orwin, *The Open Fields*, 3rd edition, 1967.

[11] Two essays summarize most conveniently, the state of research at the time of publication: H. P. R. Finberg, 'Recent Progress in English Agrarian History', *Geografiska Annaler*, 43, 1961; and J. Thirsk's introduction to the 3rd edition of *The Open Fields*.

[12] J. Thirsk, 'The Common Fields', *Past and Present*, 29, 1964.

[13] J. Z. Titow, 'Medieval England and the Open Field System', *Past and Present*, 32, 1965; also Dr Thirsk's reply in *Past and Present*, 33, 1966.

[14] R. H. Hilton, *A Medieval Society*, London 1966. M. M. Postan, *The Cambridge Economic History of Europe*, 2nd edition, Cambridge 1966, Chapter VII, pt. 7.

[15] In this context I find the term 'sector', as suggested by Professor Homans, less misleading, and hence more preferable, than the term 'Field'. See: G. C. Homans, *English Villagers of the Thirteenth Century*, Cambridge, Mass. 1942, p. 17.

scattered, more or less equally, throughout them.[16] Under the two-field system, one field was under crop and the other lay fallow each year; under the three-field system, two of the fields were cropped and the third lay fallow in rotation. All villagers with land in the common fields had grazing rights over the fallow, pasturing rights over the commons and a share in the available meadowland. With this type of arrangement a considerable degree of communal control was necessary and the freedom of individuals to do with their land what they wanted, when they wanted, was severely curtailed. Communal regulations were usually agreed upon, and their enforcement secured, through the machinery of the manorial court.[17]

This is a somewhat theoretical scheme of things; in practice, the common fields never contained all the arable of the village since colonization had frequently created holdings held in separate crofts and closes outside the Open-Field System. The equal distribution of strips among the fields was also in practice disturbed by exchanges among peasants or occasional irregular alienation. It is also a moot point to what extent demesne lands were interspersed with peasant land in the common fields or whether they tended to lie apart altogether. Evidence on this point is usually lacking, though documented instances of either arrangement can occasionally be found.

Dr Thirsk has recently reiterated her plea to differentiate between the 'Common-Fields' and the 'Open-Fields'.[18] She argues that the term 'common-fields' should only properly be used when there is clear proof of communal control, and she goes on to say that evidence of holdings distributed in strips throughout the arable of the village does not constitute clear proof of the presence of communal control. One must reply that although, in the strictest sense, it does not constitute clear proof of communal control, it clearly constitutes a very strong presumption in its favour, for it is quite unrealistic to suggest that peasants whose land was scattered in strips all over the village fields 'could do with them what they pleased at all times of the year'. It is quite inconceivable that such a peasant could, for example, grow a spring crop on one of his strips in the middle of a furlong under winter crop, or plough it out of turn and without the co-operation of his neighbours, or let it go to weed which would contaminate their

[16] For a most interesting juxtapositioning of early maps of open fields with the aerial photographs of the same, see: M. W. Beresford and J. K. S. St. Joseph, *Medieval England: An Aerial Survey*, Cambridge 1958.

[17] Professor Ault has collected a large number of such regulations. See: W. O. Ault, 'Open-Field Husbandry and the Village Community: A Study of Agrarian By-Laws in Medieval England', *Transactions of the American Philosophical Society*, 55, pt. 7, 1965.

[18] Orwins, *The Open Fields*, 3rd edition, p. x.

crops, or graze his animals on it without hindrance. Common control is as much a *sine qua non* of what historians have always understood by the 'open fields' as it is of what Dr Thirsk would like to differentiate from them as the 'common-fields'. For the Middle Ages, the distinction is quite artificial. In the past historians have used the two terms interchangeably, and rightly so, for this seems the only interpretation consistent with the intention of the documents. This is clearly so for the medieval period whatever the position in the sixteenth or seventeenth century may have been.

Thirteenth-century manorial documents leave us in no doubt at all that from the point of view of the agrarian organization at the time the fundamental distinction was between land held 'in closes' and land held 'in the fields'. The former meant land held in severalty (i.e. outside communal control), the latter land subject to such control. There was no need for the documents to be more explicit on this point since the primary interest of the officials for whom, and by whom, these documents were drawn up was usually with the nature of the holding, not the method of its cultivation; in any case, to them, the latter would have been clearly implied in the former. Land held 'in closes' must, by definition, be enclosed; land not held 'in closes' must by implication be 'open'; since closes are always described as such in the documents there was no need to describe land 'in the fields' as 'open'—this is the reason why the term 'open' never appears in the documents. It is an invention of historians. Occasionally, when not concerned with the description of the holdings as such but with the way in which parcels of land were held, the documents would talk of land held 'in severalty' (*separalis*) or 'in the common fields' (*communis*). This merely makes explicit what is otherwise implied: the identity of 'several' with 'enclosed', and of 'common' with 'open'. This is why medievalists have always used the two phrases interchangeably. The essential difference, in medieval documents, between 'enclosed' land and 'open' land is not that the former had a hedge or a ditch around it and the other had not—after all, the open fields themselves were hedged or ditched around—but that the former was, and the latter was not, outside communal control. Dr Thirsk would like to emasculate the term 'open fields' precisely by denying it this essential connotation. To agree to this suggestion would be to concede a tactical victory by accepting, by re-definition, what has first to be proven. To admit that the open fields must not be regarded as common fields unless the documents state so explicitly would be contrary to the logic of the documents and would reduce at the stroke of a pen the vast area of England where the Open-Field System was practised in the thirteenth century to a few villages where the documents actually use the term 'common fields'. The burden of proof rests clearly on those who would argue that the '(open) fields' of the medieval documents are something else than the 'common fields', not the other way round.

There were, of course, in the medieval period regions where fields were 'open'—in the sense that they consisted of strips belonging to a number of tenants whose individual holdings were, thus, not held in severalty—and which, yet, did not add up to the Open-Field System because such fields formed independent units of cultivation instead of being a part of a system embracing all the tenants and all the arable of the village. But the very reason for our knowing that this was so is precisely that the documents express themselves in terms other than the dichotomy of 'close' and 'field' so characteristic of the typical Open-Field country.

Two outstanding examples of different arrangements are Kent and East Anglia. The former seems to have been an area where various systems met and overlapped, and the arrangements seem frequently to have been very intricate.[19] Typical of East Anglia seems to have been the 'tenemental' system[20] whereby the unit of co-operative cultivation was not the whole of the village arable divided into two, or three, great fields, but a number of larger fields called 'tenements' (*tenementum*), consisting of strip-holdings of a number of villagers, over which two or three-course rotation was practised independently of other similar units in some of which the very same tenants could be involved. These 'tenements' were usually called after an eponymous, or some past, tenant and other tenants within the same unit were said to hold of, or in, that tenement; this should by no means be confused with sub-tenancies (Doc. 7).

3

If one is to appreciate the shortcomings of our knowledge of medieval rural society and of its development over the course of time, it is essential to have some idea what the main documents are from which it is derived and what are their main limitations.

[19] The position in Kent is discussed by: J. E. A. Jolliffe, *Prefeudal England: the Jutes*, Oxford 1933; and in a series of articles by A. R. H. Baker, notably 'The Field System of an East Kent Parish', *Archaeologia Cantiana*, LXXVIII, 1963; 'Some Fields and Farms in Medieval Kent', ibid. LXXX, 1965; 'Open Fields and Partible Inheritance on a Kent Manor', *Economic History Review*, XVII, 1964.
[20] D. C. Douglas, 'The Social Structure of Medieval East Anglia', *Oxford Studies in Social and Legal History*, IX, Oxford 1927, pp. 17–67.

Few of the relevant documents are narrative or descriptive in the true sense of the term, though contemporary chronicles, preambles to Acts of Parliament, correspondence, bishops' registers, and similar narrative documents, do occasionally tell us something about social and economic conditions. Most of our knowledge however, is derived from documents which first have to be analysed and studied *in series* before information contained in them falls into a meaningful and coherent pattern. Another limitation following from this is that it is never apparent whether the information so obtained is of general or only local validity. Where a narrative source could make it clear in one sentence that something was true of the whole area: a village, an estate, a county, or the country, information extracted from non-narrative documents has to be compared with information for other localities, similarly obtained, before one can decide whether one is dealing with a purely local, or a more general, phenomenon, with something typical or something exceptional. This being so, the usefulness of any given collection of documents is governed primarily by two considerations: the completeness of the collection as a series, and the extent of the geographical coverage provided by it.

The two commonest pitfalls into which many beginners fall is to fail to distinguish what is typical from what is exceptional and, more seriously, to draw wrong conclusions from the absence of certain items of information from the documents. This latter point is worth stressing; for persons with only a passing acquaintance with medieval documents, when searching them for certain items of information and finding such information absent from the documents in question, only too frequently conclude that developments in which they are interested were, therefore, not present at the time or place. It cannot be emphasized too strongly that lack of evidence on any given point can be taken for evidence to the contrary only when it is the explicit purpose of the documents in question to record such information; there are many things which we, as historians, would like to know that were of no interest at the time to the persons responsible for the drawing up of a given document.

The bulk of documentation relevant to the study of rural conditions is manorial. They fall into three main categories: Accounts, Surveys, and Court Rolls.

Accounts are by far the most useful type of document for the study of the economy of an estate (Docs. 1 and 2). The earliest surviving series comes from the estates of the bishops of Winchester, and the first extant account in that series covers the year 1208/9, though there is internal evidence to the effect that they had been kept at least from 1187.[21] Surviving accounts for other estates begin about 1250, and become increasingly plentiful as the century progresses;[22] few collections however, provide such a good series as that for the Winchester estates. They accurately record, with varying amount of detail (the earliest accounts are far more laconic than the later ones; compare Docs. 1 and 2) all the items of manorial income and expenditure in cash or kind. They may also include, as the very last items, an inventory of tools and implements, and give an account of hay and labour services[23]—though the last two items are rare before the late fourteenth century.

The main limitation of the Account Rolls, from a historian's point of view, is that they are concerned exclusively with the landlord's economy, and any information they may contain (and they contain surprisingly much) on the peasants' economy is seen obliquely through payments to the lord, and through his expenditure in money or kind.

Many writers have pointed out, quite rightly, that medieval manorial accounts were not a balance sheet, a profit-and-loss account, but a record of obligations and their discharge.[24] On the incoming side the accounting official, usually the reeve or bailiff, presented a record of all items of revenue which were received, or should have been received but were not, and of everything (with a few notable exceptions, e.g. hay) which was bought, received, or produced on the manor. On the outgoing side, he accounted for money expenditure and for all out-going items (and losses sustained) of manorial produce or live-stock, whether sold, sent elsewhere, stolen, perished, given in taxes, or consumed on the manor. The balance left over was, in the case of money, paid over to the central treasury; in the case of produce or livestock, carried over into the next accounting year.

It is clear that under such system of accounting, the money paid over to the treasurer at the end of each accounting year, did not represent the manor's net profit for the year. From a historian's point

[21] E. Swift, 'The Machinery of Manorial Administration with Special Reference to the Lands of the Bishopric of Winchester 1208–1454'(unpublished thesis of the University of London), p. xviii.
[22] For a list of some of them, with dates of the earliest surviving account in each series, see: N. Denholm-Young, *Seignorial Administration in England*, Oxford 1937, p. 123, n. 5.
[23] See Doc. 2 for an account of week-work due from customary tenants; one has to wait till the late fourteenth century for regular accounts of all the services.
[24] Denholm-Young, pp. 126–130., J. S. Drew, 'Manorial Accounts of St. Swithun's Priory, Winchester', *English Historical Review*, LXII, 1947., E. Stone, 'Profit-and-Loss Accountancy at Norwich Cathedral Priory', *Transactions of the Royal Historical Society*, 1962.

of view, this method of accounting also has the disadvantage of recording as income items of revenue which may never have been received, which fact may not become apparent until one has read through the income and expenditure sections and reached the section 'Allowances', where such items would be found to have been forgiven or written off. Another disadvantage of this method of accounting is that loans contracted are entered as income and that certain items of information (e.g. lapsed rents) may be repeated *ad infinitum* in successive accounts.

Some historians[25] have seen in this method of accounting a reflection on the medieval landlords' ability, or an indication that a truly commercial attitude to estate management was lacking on their part. This I cannot agree with. These accounts were drawn up for the benefit of absentee landlords whose primary concern was, and must have been, to know how their officials on the spot had discharged their duties. It is relatively easy to calculate profits from the information as it is recorded, and there is some evidence that at least some landlords were regularly making such calculations.[26] Had the accounts been arranged merely as profit-and-loss accounts it would have been far more difficult to work out from such an arrangement what the manorial officers were up to.

As a historian I feel in fact grateful that the accounts survive in the form in which we have them, for had they been drawn up in a different way it might well have been impossible to retrace the steps by which the final profit figures would have been reached; and I would dread having to rely on recorded profit calculations without the means of rechecking them. Anybody familiar with manorial accounts knows only too well how inconsistent the manorial officials were in their treatment of various items of income, expenditure and deliveries. To give but one example of the inconsistency with which the same item of information could be treated over a period of time, one may cite the case of 'foreign' expenditure (that not connected with the running of the manor). There are periods in the thirteenth century when on the Winchester estates *all* unusually large items of expenditure were entered as 'foreign' irrespective of the fact that some of them were clearly necessary agricultural expenditure; at one time, for instance, all large purchases of livestock or large expendi-

---

[25] It seems to be implied, for example, in R. H. Hilton, 'Rent and Capital Formation in Feudal Society', *Second International Conference of Economic History, Aix-en-Provence*, II, 1962.

[26] Some accounts have profit calculations entered on the rolls; other estates kept profit-books. See: Denholm-Young, pp. 128–30; and Stone, pp. 26–29, 46–48.

ture on agricultural buildings, were regularly entered as 'foreign' by Winchester officials. Conversely, large, truly foreign, expenditure was sometimes entered among 'necessary' expenses. Since foreign expenditure must be disregarded when calculating the net profitability of an estate, inclusion of considerable foreign expenditure in total expenses, or exclusion of considerable necessary expenditure from them, would result in widely inaccurate net-profit calculations.

Three practical warnings could perhaps usefully be issued to the newcomers to the manorial accounts. When looking for *selected items only* over long periods of time, it is necessary not to rely exclusively on reading through the accustomed places; some items of income or expenditure can be entered in places other than the usual ones. For example, sales of pasture (or pasture rights) are usually entered in the section 'Issues of the Manor' (*Exitus Manerii*) but, later on, they may appear, in addition, under their own heading 'Pasture' or under 'Farms' (*Firme*), as well, if some pasture has been let out for a period of years. Similarly, to mention but one more example, purchase of animals may be recorded not in the usual places but outside the expenditure section altogether, among the 'Allowances'.

Secondly, since the accounts are basically a record of obligations and their discharge, certain items of income may be repeated *ad infinitum* from year to year. This is particularly true of the 'Lapsed Rents' (*Defectus Redditus*) section in which some items of the uncollected rents may be carried on, with an explanation why they have not been received, from year to year literally for centuries on end. It is thus essential when looking at *isolated* accounts not to jump to the conclusion that such entries date from the account under scrutiny.

Thirdly, there is the problem of dating information obtained from specific account rolls. In the Middle Ages the accounting year ran from Michaelmas to Michaelmas, that is, from September 29th to September 28th. Much of the information contained in the account rolls cannot be ascribed to any definite part of the accounting year and could thus refer to the calendar year of the first three months of the year of account or to the calendar year of the last nine months of the year of account. The only safe way in such cases is to specify both calendar years and say that, for instance, the price of wheat in 1315–1316 was 16s 8d a quarter. This is, however, not always convenient in practice, particularly when tabulating information year by year, and so such information is usually referred to by a single calendar year. This is where the difficulty arises; some scholars are in the habit of referring to such information by the calendar year of the opening Michaelmas of the account, while others date their information by the calendar year of the account's closing

Michaelmas. This frequently leads to apparent discrepancies. For example, when Dr Farmer states that the price of wheat in 1315 was 16s 8d a quarter, and I that it was 7s 4d, this does not mean that one of us is wrong, or that we have here a case of wide regional variations; we are simply following a different convention. Dr Farmer enters his data under the calendar year of the opening Michaelmas of the account; I under the calendar year of the closing Michaelmas of the account. Thus Dr Farmer's figure for 1315 comes from the account roll 1315–1316; mine from the account roll 1314–1315. My own figure for the period September 29, 1315–September 28, 1316, would be 15s 5½d, only I would refer to it as the price of wheat in 1316.

There is no doubt in my mind that the use of the closing Michaelmas is the more logical. After all, three quarters of the year of account fall into the calendar year of the account's closing Michaelmas as against only one quarter which falls into the calendar year of the account's opening Michaelmas. With information relating to transactions, or activities, which are not by their very nature identifiable with any specific part of the year, the chances of it coming from the period January–September, rather than October–December, are far greater. This problem arises particularly in connection with prices, wages, and harvest data.

Thorold Rogers in his great work on English agricultural prices, dates by the opening Michaelmas.[27] Lane Poole in his article on the early livestock prices[28] dates by the closing Michaelmas. Lord Beveridge in his numerous articles[29] on the Winchester estates, dates by the opening Michaelmas. Dr Farmer accepts dating by the closing Michaelmas as the more logical, but to keep in line with Lord Beveridge enters his own data under the calendar year of the opening Michaelmas.[30] I have consistently dated all my data by the calendar year of the closing Michaelmas. Professor Raftis in his important study of the estates of Ramsey Abbey dates by the opening Michaelmas.[31] With many other writers (e.g. the various contributors

[27] J. E. T. Rogers, *History of Agriculture and Prices in England*, Oxford 1866–92.

[28] A. L. Poole, 'Live Stock Prices in the Twelfth Century', *English Historical Review*, LV, 1940.

[29] Particularly, 'The Yield and Price of Corn in the Middle Ages', *Essays in Economic History*, ed. A. M. Carus-Wilson, I, London 1954. and 'A Statistical Crime of the Seventeenth Century', *Journal of Economic and Business History*, I, 1928.

[30] D. L. Farmer, 'Some Price Fluctuations in Angevin England', *Economic History Review*, IX, 1956; and 'Some Grain Price Movements in Thirteenth Century England', ibid, X, 1957.

[31] J. A. Raftis, *The Estates of Ramsey Abbey*, Toronto 1957, p. 132.

to the volumes of the *Cambridge Economic History of Europe*) it is frequently impossible to be sure which convention is being followed.

What I find particularly misleading is the practice, not so much of entering data under the calendar year of the opening Michaelmas, as of referring to years under which it is tabulated as 'harvest' years. Lord Beveridge did this in his articles, and much more recently a most important publication—*The Agrarian History of England and Wales*—did the same.[32] Thus, for example, according to the convention followed by it, information recorded under the 'harvest' year 1220 would refer to the period September 29, 1220–September 28, 1221. The only connection which the account roll 1220–1221 has with the harvest of 1220 is that it covers the period over which the produce of that harvest was sold, consumed, or otherwise expended. Anything mentioned in that roll in connection with growing or gathering the harvest refers to the harvest of 1221; everything connected with the growing or gathering of the harvest of 1220 will be found not in that roll but in the preceding one, i.e. that of 1219–1220. To record data from the roll 1220–1221 under 1220 seems to me the wrong choice; to call it the 'harvest' year 1220 is confusing and misleading.

The second major category of manorial documents, the Surveys (Docs. 4-7), need not detain us long since they present no special problems. It is possible to distinguish certain subdivisions of this genus according to how comprehensive they are in what they survey. The surveys proper give the account of both demesne and tenants' holdings and, if they enter valuations as well, they are known as Extents[33] (Docs. 5-7). Surveys of tenants' holdings alone, with all the services, dues and obligations accruing from them but without the description of the demesne, are known as Custumals. Surveys of tenants' holdings which give rents only, without the services or any other obligations, are known as Rentals.

Manorial surveys were compiled from the information provided on oath by a jury of villagers chosen for their 'worthiness' and knowledge of local custom. The preamble to the 1181 survey of the estates of Saint Paul's, London, provides an explicit statement of the principles governing the impanellment of such juries:

'For the more easy discovery of the truth, we have decreed, that, according to the extent of the Manors and the number of the inhabit-

[32] *The Agrarian History of England and Wales*, IV, ed. J. Thirsk, Cambridge 1967, p. 869.

[33] R. Lennard, 'What is a Manorial Extent?', *English Historical Review*, XLIV, 1929.

ants, a greater or lesser number be chosen and bound by the obligation of an oath administered to them, that, in answering the interrogatories they will not knowingly either suppress the truth or assert what is false but will together, according to their conscience, disclose it.'[34]

There are two main limitations on the usefulness of the surveys. Firstly, what they present is basically a picture of conditions as they were at one point of time and it is thus necessary to have consecutive surveys for the same place to arrive at some estimate of change over time. Secondly, the surveys give a picture of nominal conditions. They record, frequently in minute detail, the services and obligations due to the landlord but they do not tell us which of these services were actually exacted and who was, or was not, performing them at the time. They also give us a full list of tenancies but they do not normally take cognizance of temporary changes in the actual occupation of land resulting from sub-letting among peasants.

Surveys are the earliest surviving type of manorial documents. Some sixteen twelfth-century surveys have come down to us and there is a very large number of them dating from the mid-thirteenth, or late thirteenth century.[35] The twelfth-century surveys are much more sparing with detail than the thirteenth-century ones but it would be wrong to assume that the fuller enumeration of services in the latter mean necessarily an increased burden of services.

Apart from the manorial surveys, three other documents of a similar kind—the last one in fact not a single document but a type of document—must be mentioned, however briefly. The first of them, the Domesday Book of 1086 (Doc. 3), though falling well outside the chronological scope of this essay, is of such an outstanding importance that no student of the English medieval rural society can be ignorant of it. There is a vast body of literature devoted to Domesday Book and problems centred on it, but newcomers to the

---

[34] *The Domesday of St. Paul's of the Year MCC XXII*, ed. W. Hale, Camden Society 69, 1858, p. 112. I have used Hale's own translation from p. vi but expanded it by one line.

[35] Many thirteenth century surveys have been published (though few in translation), notably: M. Chibnall, ed., *Selected Documents of the English Lands of the Abbey of Bec*, Camden Society, 3rd series, LXXIII, 1951; C. I. Elton, ed., *Rentalia et Custumaria Michaelis de Ambresbury* (i.e. Glastonbury Abbey), Somerset Record Society 5, London 1891; M. Hollings ed., *The Red Book of Worcester*, Worcester Historical Society, 1937–51; A. E. Wilson, ed., *Custumals of the Manors of Loughton, Willingdon and Goring*, (in translation), Sussex Record Society, 60, 1961.

subject would probably find Dr Finn's and Professor Galbraith's studies of the most immediate usefulness.[36]

The second document is the government-instigated survey of 1279, known as the Hundred Rolls, even more ambitious in scope than Domesday Book itself, though unfortunately carried out for a few counties only. An excellent discussion of this document will be found in Professor Kosminsky's study of thirteenth-century England,[37] which is in fact based on it.

Finally there are in existence a large number of documents known as the Inquisitions Post Mortem, that is, surveys of the estates of the deceased tenants-in-chief of the Crown, drawn up for the benefit of the royal administration into whose hands their estates have reverted (Doc. 8). These are also discussed by Professor Kosminsky.[38]

Court Rolls form the third major type of manorial documents. The earliest surviving rolls date from about 1245, but afterwards they become quite numerous. Court Rolls are a veritable mine of information on all sorts of aspects of peasant life. Not only do they record activities in which the landlord was directly interested—land transactions, marriages, transgressions of all sorts against the lord's estate, etc.—but they also throw light on relations between the peasants themselves and on their activities in which the landlord had no direct interest but which came to be recorded because they gave rise to an opportunity to collect a fine from a litigant or an offender (Docs. 9–12).[39] Some idea of the scope of the business of the manorial courts can also be gained from the questions put to the tithings at the view of frankpledge (Doc. 15).[40]

The main trouble with court rolls as a source of information is that the majority of the recorded items are, in the nature of things, accidental, and unless the series is exceptionally good it is almost impossible to construct complete case histories, or to follow any case

[36] R. W. Finn, The Domesday Inquest and the making of Domesday Book, London 1961; V. H. Galbraith, The Making of Domesday Book, Oxford 1961. For a detailed study of Domesday conditions, Professor H. C. Darby's multi-volume work, The Domesday Geography of England, is indispensable.

[37] Kosminsky, Studies, 7–46.

[38] Ibid. 46–67.

[39] There is an excellent discussion of the working of the manorial court in H. S. Bennett, Life on the English Manor, Cambridge 1965, pp. 193–221; and in F. W. Maitland, Select Pleas in Manorial and Other Seignorial Courts, I, Selden Society II, London 1888, with many translated extracts.

[40] For the discussion of the frankpledge system see W. A. Morris, The Frankpledge System, London 1910. For the discussion of the hundredal jurisdiction see H. M. Cam, The Hundred and the Hundred Rolls, London 1930, and the same author's 'Manerium cum Hundredo', English Historical Review, XLVII, 1932.

of litigation to its end. Thus the information provided seldom lends itself to statistical treatment and one has to rely on impressions when trying to decide if there were any significant changes in the course of time. Frequently too, after having had one's appetite whetted by some particularly interesting case one is left tantalizingly in the dark as to the outcome, because some important link, frequently the verdict itself, was recorded in a court whose records are missing.

Court rolls are most useful when they can be used in conjunction with other manorial documents, particularly accounts. Unfortunately few estates have documents of both these kinds existing together, and those which do, normally present a fairly patchy series; this is true even of the best of them such as, for example, Glastonbury and Ramsey Abbeys or the Priory of St Swithun's, Winchester. But whatever their imperfections, as a source of information about peasant activities and attitudes, court rolls are unrivalled among medieval records and in many ways the most lively type of manorial documents to read.

Absence of court rolls can occasionally be compensated for by the fact that some account rolls give summaries of court fines and this can sometimes give a better series than the court rolls themselves do. The account rolls of the bishopric of Winchester (for which no thirteenth-century court rolls exist) are an outstanding example of this, for they give summaries, at first, of all fines, and later, of entry and marriage fines only (Doc. 13). Since the Winchester accounts are by far the best (and also the earliest) series of its kind in existence,[41] the inclusion of summaries of court fines in them enables us to reconstruct land transactions of individual peasants and to trace provenance of holdings over long periods of time (Doc. 14). In every respect, however, such summaries are clearly only the second best, since they frequently leave out bits of information vital for our analysis of change. Take, for example, the entry fines. To be able to analyse them properly over long periods of time it is necessary to have five items of information under each fine: the sum paid, the name of the in-coming tenant in a traceable form (John, or John son

---

[41] There are 22 accounts extent for the period 1208–1249

32	,,	,,	,,	,,	1250–1299
46	,,	,,	,,	,,	1300–1349 (incl. 5 part-accounts)
47	,,	,,	,,	,,	1350–1399
37	,,	,,	,,	,,	1400–1449
28	,,	,,	,,	,,	1450–1499

All these accounts are composite accounts, that is, they bring together, in one great roll (or book, after 1457) the individual accounts of all the manors of the bishopric.

of William, clearly will not do), the description of the holding involved, the name of the previous holder, and the mode of acquisition.
It is not until well into the second half of the thirteenth century that
the Winchester summaries give all these items fully. Similarly, where
the court rolls leave us in no doubt whether the previous holder had
died, or merely surrendered his holding, summaries in the account
rolls usually only imply the former.

4

Manorial documents present us with a wealth of detailed information but no coherent story of what took place in the course of time;
this can usually be obtained only after painstaking extracting, tabulating, and processing of various data which have then to be
compared with similar data for other regions to distinguish between
developments which were purely local and transitory and those
which were more general and lasting. Such a scrutiny of documents
available for the late twelfth and the thirteenth century discloses
that the first half of the latter was a period of great activity in the
countryside, which manifested itself in a variety of ways. For example,
the fact that some 3,000 grants of markets were obtained from the
Crown during the century[42] is a clear indication of the expansion of
the rural economy, and so is the planting of some 88 new towns, between 1154 and 1250,[43] many of them (as for example the 6 new
towns of the Bishops of Winchester)[44] by local landlords on their
estates. Above all, this increased activity can be seen in the reclamation of land; in fact this was so widespread and persistent a phenomenon that it is almost the only aspect of this increased activity
which is apparent from the documents without much analytical
examination.

This colonizing activity shows itself in innumerable ways in both
manorial and non-manorial documents. In manorial documents it
manifests itself mainly in two ways: in Account Rolls through rapidly
rising rent rolls (i.e. increased total revenue from rents due to the
creation of new holdings), and in Surveys through a steady increase
in the number of holdings of assart origin (Doc. 4). Among the non-

[42] E. M. Carus-Wilson, 'Towns and Trade', *Medieval England*, A. L. Poole
ed., Oxford 1958, I, 241.
[43] M. Beresford, *New Towns of the Middle Ages*, London 1967, Table XI/1,
p. 328.
[44] M. Beresford, 'The Six New Towns of the Bishops of Winchester,
1200–1255', *Medieval Archaeology*, III, 1959.

C

manorial documents the Exchequer Pipe Rolls (the earliest of which dates from 1130), and the eyre rolls of the Forest, offer ample evidence of the steady encroachment on the wastes in the royal vills and within the royal Forests.[45]

Charters are another fruitful source of information on the reclamation of land, and some of the most important studies of the subject have been based largely, or entirely, on this type of evidence.[46] Occasionally, too, in areas of exceptionally large-scale reclamation, like for instance the Fenland, local chronicles and other narrative sources tell a full, and frequently highly dramatic, story of the struggle against a difficult environment, treacherous elements and, not infrequently, other competitors.[47]

It is obviously impossible within the compass of a few pages to do justice to such an important topic as that of the twelfth and thirteenth century colonization; all one can hope to achieve is to point out certain important features of the movement, and leave it at that. It is generally agreed among historians that the cause of this expansion must be sought in the rapid growth of population, for indeed, though available direct demographic evidence points to no more than a considerable increase between 1086 and 1348 without indicating how this increase was spread over the intervening centuries,[48] it is difficult to account for the great colonizing activity of these two centuries in any other way. Furthermore, what we know of the movement of prices and wages over this period supports this interpretation (Appendix B).

Reclamation of land in the thirteenth century seems to have been a feature common to all of England. Documents of practically all the estates which have so far been studied, or made available—for example, those of Winchester, Glastonbury, Duchy of Lancaster, Ely, Ramsey, Canterbury, to mention but a few of the more important

[45] The Forest in this context is the legal Forest, that is, the area reserved for the King's hunting and protected by special law against encroachment on land, wood and beasts. The Forest law was administered by special courts, the records of which survive in considerable quantity. Some royal forests were very extensive and included whole villages within their bounds. For the legal and administrative aspects of the Forest, see: G. J. Turner, ed., *Select Pleas of the Forest*, Selden Society, London 1901, pp. ix–cxxxiv., and R. C. Shaw, *The Royal Forest of Lancaster*, Preston 1956, pp. 6–90.

[46] T. A. M. Bishop, 'Assarting and the Growth of the Open Fields', *Essays in Economic History*, E. M. Carus-Wilson, ed. London 1954, I, 26–40; H. E. Hallam, *Settlement and Society; a Study of the Early Agrarian History of South Lincolnshire*, Cambridge 1965.

[47] Hallam, p. 25, for the great invasion of the Precinct of Crowland by the Men of Holland in 1189.

[48] For a fuller discussion of demographic evidence see Chapter III.

ones[49]—all tell the same story of expanding settlement and more extensive arable cultivation. What must not be assumed, however, is that because this activity was so universal, its character, extent, and chronology, was necessarily the same everywhere; much more work on a comparative basis will have to be done before one could venture safely on a generalization with regard to the exact relative position of different areas in the overall picture of settlement and colonization. However, even at this stage, certain broad assertions can be made with reasonable safety.

In so far as the character of the thirteenth-century colonization is concerned, it was almost entirely a matter of extending the frontiers of existing settlements rather than of creating new ones; studies of the Domesday Book have revealed that the great majority of English settlements found in the later Middle Ages were already there in 1086[50] and those which were a later creation were, almost certainly in the majority of cases, of twelfth rather than thirteenth-century origin. It seems equally true that, with the exception of special areas such as, for example, the Fenlands, reclamation was more in the nature of a relatively constant stream of small additions than of large scale undertakings carried out at one point of time.

This stems from the fact that the outburst of colonizing activity which we witness at this time must be in fact regarded as the tail-end of a very long process whose beginnings lie far back in the past. Since most settlements were already in existence by 1086, subsequent colonization had, perforce, to be in the nature of extending the arable of existing settlements rather than of throwing out new ones. A very important corollary of this is that much of the thirteenth-century reclamation must have been of a (qualitatively speaking) marginal character, the best lands having been already occupied in the earlier stages of expansion. Professor Postan has argued that the logic of land usage, and topographical and documentary evidence when available, point inescapably to this conclusion.[51] This would go a long way towards explaining, among other things, why the Forest areas were under such great pressure in the thirteenth century, and why landlords and peasants alike were prepared to pay vast sums of money for disafforestation of some of the Forest land; such land prob-

[49] Postan, *Cambridge Ec. History of Europe*, I pp. 548–552; E. Miller, *The Abbey and Bishopric of Ely: the Social History of an Ecclesiastic Estate from the Tenth to the Early Fourteenth Century*, Cambridge 1951, pp. 95–99; Raftis, pp. 72–75; F. R. H. du Boulay, *The Lordship of Canterbury: an Essay on Medieval Society*, London 1966, pp. 136–139.

[50] Lennard, *Rural England*, pp. 3–9.

[51] Postan, *Cambridge Ec. History of Europe* I, pp. 551–552.

ably represented the last substantial[52] reserves of potentially fertile land. For instance, between 1189 and 1194 the freeholders within the Forest of Lancashire offered £500 to John, then Earl of Mortain, for the right to increase freely the area of tillage within the bounds of the Forest, and they paid another £200, and 10 chargers, to him for the confirmation of his charter on his accession to the throne in 1199.[53] In 1190 the knights of Surrey offered 200 marks for the disafforestation of certain parts of the county, while in 1204 men of Cornwall and men of Devon offered 2,200 marks and 5,000 marks respectively for the disafforestation of the whole county.[54]

What has been said so far applies equally to landlords and peasants, but an important distinction must be introduced at this point: whereas the peasant colonization in the thirteenth century must be regarded as the tail-end of a centuries-long reclamation drive (though its intensity naturally fluctuated over the whole span), for the landlords this was largely a new development almost entirely of late twelfth, or early thirteenth-century origin. The renewed interest on the part of the landlords in the direct exploitation of their estates led to the expansion of their demesnes and brought the interests of the peasantry into a head-on clash with those of the landlords, particularly in areas of ancient settlement where colonizable resources were already largely exhausted by earlier reclamation.

Reclamation by the landlords not only restricted the amount of new land available to the peasants; it also, in the very nature of things, reduced the area of the commons which formed such a vital adjunct of the arable economy of the village at the time. The measure of popular discontent which was engendered by the activities of the landlords can be seen in the relevant provisions of the Statute of Merton (Doc. 20) passed in 1236, which forbade landlords to encroach on the wastes if the freeholders of the manor were thereby to be left with insufficient pasture for their needs.[55]

Reclamation of land seems to have petered out over most of the country towards the end of the thirteenth century, though in a few exceptional areas it lingered on well into the fourteenth century. Since this slackening off does not coincide, in so far as we can judge on the basis of the rather meagre evidence available to us, with the

[52] At its peak the Forest may heve covered as much as one-third of the country See: M. L. Bazeley, 'The Extent of the English Forest in the Thirteenth Century', *Transactions of the Royal Historical Society*, 1921.

[53] Shaw, p. 92.

[54] D. M. Stenton, *English Society in the Early Middle Ages*, Harmondsworth 1952, p. 109.

[55] The Statute did not deign to concern itself with the needs of customary tenants.

downward turn of the demographic trend, one must conclude that the reason for this cessation is to be sought not in demographic causes, which had set reclamation in motion in the first place, but in the fact that the supply of land fit for cultivation had in the main run out. This had some dire consequences for the rural population at large, as I shall try to show in Chapter III.

5

Another general point which emerges from the study of manorial documents is the high level of agricultural know-how already reached well before the beginning of our period. The last major breakthrough occurred well before the eleventh century with the widespread adoption of the heavy wheeled-plough, equipped with plough-share, coulter and mould-board, which made it possible to attack heavy soils hitherto avoided by early settlers and frequently potentially the more fertile. It was the adoption of the heavy plough which made the clearance of forests and the occupation of heavy clays possible. The next major breakthrough did not come until many centuries later with the adoption of new revolutionary rotations,[56] which did away with the unproductive fallow, and later still, with the introduction of chemical fertilizers. In between there were, of course, considerable improvements but nothing of really revolutionary significance.

I am aware of the fact that this view is contrary to the opinions of some writers on technological progress. It is true that in the past, technological improvements have frequently been shamefully neglected by agrarian historians, but it seems equally regrettable that some of the more recent writers on technological change have been carried away by their enthusiasm for 'progress' to the point of forgetting the need for historical verification of their claims.

Take for instance, Lynn White's oft-quoted book on the subject of medieval technology. According to him, in the period roughly between the tenth and the thirteenth century, three revolutionary changes took place.[57]

[56] J. D. Chambers and G. E. Mingay, *The Agricultural Revolution 1750–1880*, London 1966, p. 4. However, Dr. E. Kerridge (*The Agricultural Revolution*, London 1967, pp. 328 and 347–8) would place all major revolutionary changes squarely in the period 1560–1670.

[57] L. White, *Medieval Technology and Social Change*, Oxford 1962. Mr White does not himself use the word 'revolutionary', but since he uses such phrases as 'epoch-making', etc., he clearly regards them as such.

The first is the supposed replacement of oxen by horses for ploughing. 'Once the world of scholars'—he tells us—'has realized that the widespread replacement of oxen by horses marked an epoch in the application of power to agriculture, examination of local records will enable us to tell how rapidly, and in exactly what regions, the change took place. The state of archives in England, for example, is such that much information should emerge...'[58] Then, after quoting—rather astonishingly—a few examples of how *infrequent* are the references to ploughing by horse-teams in England in the twelfth and thirteenth-century documents, he concludes rather unexpectedly: 'These are random notices to which many more will undoubtedly be added as time passes. But their tendency is clear: in late twelfth-century England, at least in some regions which cannot yet be defined, the horse was taking over the plough.'[59] Mr White seems to be guilty, if one may say so, of putting the plough before the horse; to my mind he comes dangerously near to saying: once the scholars realize what a revolutionary step this is, they will find that *it took place*. This is a dangerous doctrine. The proper procedure, of course, is for the conclusion to await the examination of documents. Whatever the position on the Continent may have been, the English documents—of which there is a great profusion—make it clear, beyond any possibility of doubt, that there had been no general change-over from ox-ploughing to horse-ploughing in England at the time. The ratio of plough-horses to oxen in heriot payments would seem to indicate that this is true not only of the demesnes, but also of the peasantry.

This preference for oxen is well documented and is also reflected throughout our period in prices; for whereas cart-horses (whenever the documents allow us to distinguish what type of horse is being meant) invariably fetched a much higher price than oxen, the plough-horse—the *affrus*—regularly fetched a lower price. True, in the thirteenth century horses were not infrequently yoked together with oxen, but a team of six oxen and two horses can hardly be looked upon as replacement of the former by the latter. It is also true that horses were usually used for all additional, or emergency, ploughing, but there can be no doubt at all, except in a few cases of a genuine change-over, that ploughing by oxen was the dominant form throughout the Middle Ages in England. This was so, no doubt, for the reasons which the leading contemporary authority on estate management, Walter of Henley, had fully explained in his *Husbandry*:

[58] ibid. p. 63.
[59] ibid. p. 65.

under medieval conditions horses were a far more expensive source of power than oxen.[60]

Mr White waxes enthusiastic over the introduction of the triennial system of rotation. While one must agree that under the right conditions, this represents an undoubted improvement on the biennial system, claims that its adoption led to all sorts of revolutionary consequences will not bear closer examination. In the thirteenth and fourteenth centuries, when the profusion of manorial documents allows us to speak of such matters with considerable assurance, England was divided about equally into areas of two-field and three-field systems.[61] There is no reason to believe that areas under the three-field system must represent instances of an earlier change-over from the original two-field system, and apart from instances where in the process of colonization a third field was added to the already existing fields, documented examples of a true change-over from the two- to the three-field system are, to my knowledge, very rare.

The English documents of the thirteenth and fourteenth centuries do not show any replacement of the biennial system by the triennial system of rotation, but show their co-existence side by side; to imply that this represents the contrast between the primitive and the progressive would be quite wrong. Furthermore, at least in so far as England is concerned, it is difficult to accept as valid Mr White's argument that adoption of the triennial system led to revolutionary consequences. Mr White argues that 'the spread of the triennial system gave a major impulse to assarting', that it led to greater cultivation of oats, and that 'the new supply of oats made available by the three-field system increased the numbers and prowess of horses', which in turn led to the eventual replacement of oxen by horses.[62]

What is wrong with this whole argument is that it is 'theoretical', i.e. one improvement is deduced from another. When looked at from the point of view of available documentary evidence the various stages of this argument are found lacking. There was nothing to stop people growing oats under the two-field system. If there is a correlation between later colonization and oats-growing on a large scale, this is not because of the triennial system of cultivation, but because later colonization was frequently at the expense of poorer soils on which nothing but oats could be grown profitably. The fact that ploughing in England was done almost universally by oxen in areas of both two- and three-field systems, makes the contention that by

[60] E. Lammond, ed., *Walter of Henley's Husbandry*, London 1890. p, 13.
[61] Gray, pp. 70–72.
[62] White, p. 72.

the end of the Middle Ages there appears to be a clear correlation between the triennial rotation and the use of horses in agriculture[63] clearly not valid.

Above all, I cannot accept the argument that adoption of the triennial system *of itself* gave impetus to colonization.[64] This impulse came with the expanding population and it would be possible to argue that it would have been even greater if all newly reclaimed land had to be cultivated on the two-field system, since more land would have to be taken into cultivation to accommodate a *given* increase in population on the two-field system than on the three-field system.

I also find Mr White's efforts to show what a great improvement the three-field system was not entirely convincing. His argument takes the form of cost-analysis but this is done exclusively in terms of ploughing. It is true of course, as Mr White shows, that for the same acreage under crop there is a considerable saving in ploughing under the three-field as against the two-field system.[65] He overlooks the fact, however, that there is also a corresponding loss in terms of other operations such as weeding or harvesting. The real advantage of the triennial over the biennial system is not so much the saving in costs but the fact that, *other factors permitting,* more can be produced from the same area under the former than under the latter.

The real-reason, however, why I consider the argument that the three-field system was a great revolutionary step forward fallacious, in the context of the twelfth and thirteenth centuries, is that it makes sense only on the assumption that the adoption (or retention) of the two-field system was a matter of ignorance—ignorance of better methods of cultivation. This might have been true of some distant past but it clearly is not true of the twelfth and thirteenth centuries. Since in the twelfth and thirteenth centuries both systems co-existed side by side, the reason for the non-adoption of the latter could not have been ignorance of it. The only difference between the two systems that is fundamental is the length of time the soil has to recuperate after cropping. Professor Gray's conclusion that soil conditions are the real explanation why some regions adopted the three-field system while others did not, seems to me convincing;[66] some soils are simply too poor to be cropped continually for two years and must rest every other year, otherwise their productivity

[63] White, p. 73.
[64] ibid. p. 72.
[65] ibid. p. 73.
[66] Gray, pp. 71 and 73.

would decline. If this assumption is valid then it would follow that non-adoption of the three-field system in certain areas, and not its adoption, was the progressive thing to do.

But among the alleged results of the widespread adoption of the three-field system, as listed by Mr White, the most pregnant in consequences for northern Europe was the alleged cultivation of legumes (i.e. beans, peas and vetches) on a vast scale. The consequences of this as catalogued by Mr White are marvellous to behold. This vast expansion in the growing of legumes, we are told, 'goes far towards explaining the startling expansion of population, the growth and multiplication of cities, the rise in industrial production, the outreach of commerce, and the new exuberance of spirits which enlivened that age. In the full sense of the vernacular, the Middle Ages, from the tenth century onward, were full of beans'.[67]

What are the facts of the case? Until manorial accounts become available (and the earliest extant dates from 1208) we have absolutely no means of estimating quantitatively the relative importance of legumes to cereals. Ordericus Vitalis' lament over the destruction of 'grain and pulses' in the drought of 1094 will not support Mr White's interpretation that this shows 'that by the end of the eleventh century these latter loomed *as large* as the cereals'.[68] The English evidence shows that while there was a steady increase in the proportion of the arable under legumes during the thirteenth and fourteenth centuries, and while on some individual manors it could occasionally reach a very high figure indeed, the proportion was still very low by the early fourteenth century, taking estates as a whole, and must have been even lower at the beginning of the thirteenth. We have no figures for the twelfth century but it is far more likely that the proportion then was lower, rather than higher, than at the beginning of the thirteenth century.

For example, on the estates of the bishop of Winchester—the only estate for which figures are available for the first half of the thirteenth century—the acreage under legumes in 1208 was only 0·5 per cent, or some 53 acres out of the total of some 10,800 acres.[69] What is even more significant is the fact that of the thirty-two manors which are included in this total, eighteen grew no legumes at all, and none of the fourteen manors which grew them had more than eight acres

[67] White, p. 76.
[68] ibid. p. 75, italics mine.
[69] Hampshire Record Office, MS. Eccl. Comm. 2/159270A. The figures are converted from customary acres to acres measured by the perch, and are thus approximate.

under them. By 1345 the proportion of legumes to other crops rose only to some 8·3 per cent, or 683 acres out of 8,257 acres.[70]

On the estates of Ramsey Abbey in mid-thirteenth century, on the seven eastern manors for which Professor Raftis gives figures, only 64 quarters 7 bushels of legumes were sown as against 1,144 quarters and 4 bushels of cereals.[71]

On the great lay estate of the Earldom of Cornwall on the nine manors (distributed among eight counties) which were not farmed out at the time, the acreage under legumes, as late as 1296, amounted to only 1·8 per cent, or 34 acres out of the total of 1,900 acres, with no legumes at all on four of them.[72]

Many other estates tell the same story. The estates of Christ Church, Canterbury, with their high ratio of some 18 per cent under legumes in 1322[73] are quite exceptional, but even there the proportion must have been very much lower at the beginning of the thirteenth century since, according to Dr Smith, the great increase in the growing of legumes on the estates of Christ Church dates only from the late thirteenth century.[74]

All these are demesne figures; we have no figures for peasant production but there are grounds for believing that it followed, on the whole, the pattern of demesne production. So much for the claims that legumes 'loomed as large as cereals by the end of the eleventh century', and the momentous consequences flowing from it.

[70] Eccl.Comm.2/159361; the figures are in measured acres and involve no conversions.

[71] Calculated by me from: Raftis, Table XXXVI, pp. 164–170.

[72] Calculated by me from: *Ministers' Accounts of the Earldom of Cornwall 1296–1297*, ed. L. M. Midgley, 2 vols. Camden 3rd series, LXVI and LXVIII, 1942 and 1945.

[73] R. A. L. Smith, *Canterbury Cathedral Priory*, Cambridge 1943, p. 141.

[74] ibid., p. 139

Landlords and Peasants

I

'Farming out', that is leasing the whole manor as a going concern to a 'farmer' for a fixed rent in money or kind, seems to have been the typical way in which great estates were exploited by their owners in the twelfth century; at least this is the impression one gets from the Pipe Rolls and the surviving twelfth-century Surveys, and there are reasons to believe that, though the number of the latter is relatively small, the situation they depict is representative of the country at large.[1] This disengagement from direct cultivation on the part of the landlords was usually also accompanied by the actual contraction of the area of the demesne itself.

Since farming means opting for a fixed income, as against the fluctuating, and therefore uncertain, profits of direct cultivation, one has to assume that the great landlords of the time either did not think much of existing agricultural opportunities or were too preoccupied with other matters to find time for the administration of their estates. Professor Postan has, in fact, suggested that both these considerations were behind the landlords' choice; a low level of prices coupled with political anarchy over the middle years of the century clearly constituted an unfavourable climate for agricultural enterprise.[2]

With the end of the Civil War and the return of more normal conditions, the landlords turned their attention once more to their estates and could have hardly failed to notice that the economic situation in the latter part of the century was looking distinctly more promising. In so far as we can judge, there was a continuous upward

[1] For a fuller discussion of 'farming', 'farmers', and 'farms', see Lennard, *Rural England*, pp. 105–175. For an example of how the system operated on a specific estate, see Raftis, *Estates of Ramsey Abbey*, pp. 76–85.
[2] Postan, *Cambridge Ec. History of Europe*, I, p, 585.

movement of prices of agricultural produce from about 1160 onwards which was particularly pronounced between *c.* 1180 and *c.* 1220 (Appendix B). This clearly meant that the 'farming out' of estates was preventing the landlords from taking advantage of this upward movement of prices; the 'farmer', the person who leased their estates from them, was the person to reap the full benefit of the rising demand for foodstuffs. In fact, the 'farmer' stood to gain twice over: through higher prices which the produce of the demesne itself was fetching on the local markets,[3] and from the new rents which he pocketed due to the creation of a large number of new holdings by assarting.

I have already tried to indicate that the late twelfth century, and the first half of the thirteenth century, was a period of rapidly expanding cultivation and growing demand for foodstuffs, induced by expanding population; the rise in prices of agricultural produce over the same period is but the other side of the same coin. Whether, earlier on, the landlords were unable to see the opportunities inherent in the situation, or whether they were prevented by other considerations (i.e. political considerations, general lack of interest, or merely the fact that existing leases had to run out before they could be revoked) from taking action sooner than they did, is really immaterial here, the fact remains that by the beginning of the thirteenth century, or thereabouts, they turned again, *en masse* to direct exploitation of their estates, and 'farming out' became quite exceptional. Not only did the landlords resume direct control over their estates but this was usually also accompanied by the expansion of the arable area of the demesne itself (Doc. 18) and by concerted efforts to maximize the profitability of their estates by various means, primarily by introducing better methods of cultivation and a more efficient organization of their administration.[4]

The expansion in demesne production led almost at once to a great increase in the total revenues of the great estates. Professor Painter estimated, on the basis of some 272 baronial estates, that by 1220 'the revenue from the average English manor expressed in terms of money had increased 60 per cent over its Domesday

---

[3] It is still not appreciated widely enough what a high proportion of demesne produce went onto the market even at the time when, as in early thirteenth century, baronial households were still largely perpipatetic and living off their demesnes. See Lennard, 'Manorial Traffic'.

[4] Proliferation of treatises on estate management in the thirteenth century and the great flow of manorial documents themselves are a vivid testimony to this new revival of interest on the part of the landlords. See: D. Oschinsky, 'Medieval Treatises on Estate Accounting', *Economic History Review* XVII, 1947, and the same author's 'Medieval Treatises on Estate Management', ibid. 2nd series, VIII, 1956.

valuation. By 1250 an approximately equal increase had taken place
—between 51 per cent and 64 per cent. Between 1250 and 1350
the growth in revenue amounted to only 28–32 per cent'.[5] Though
comparisons with Domesday valuations (Docs. 3 and 4) must be
accepted with the greatest caution, there can be no doubt at all as
to the great increase over the first half of the thirteenth century;
practically every estate studied so far tells the same story.

The increase in manorial revenues, in the period with which we
are concerned here, was not due to the expanding arable cultivation
alone. A considerable increase in the production of wool also took
place on many estates, particularly those of the Cistercians. Towards
the end of the thirteenth century the total number of sheep in the
country could have been as high as some 15–18 million.[6] The export
of wool alone (running towards the end of the century and in the
early fourteenth century at some 30–40 thousand sacks a year[7]) must
have, at the official conversion rate of 240 fleeces to a sack, represented a total flock of some $7\frac{1}{2}$ to $9\frac{1}{2}$ million sheep and allowance
must, of course, be made for the home consumption of wool and for
the fact that the multiplier of 240 is valid only for fully grown
animals, whereas wool exports included lamb's wool which obviously
represented a higher number of animals per sack.

The increase in manorial incomes over this period was also due
to the fact that expanding population, the motive force behind the
new favourable situation, affected simultaneously all the major
components of manorial revenues:[8] produce sold through rising
prices, land values (rents and entry fines) through growing demand
for land, and seignorial profits (profits of court and seignorial mon-
opolies, chiefly mills) through the increased volume of business

[5] S. Painter, *Studies in the History of the English Feudal Barony*, Baltimore
1943, p. 160. See also, G. A. Holmes, *The Estates of the Higher Nobility in
XIV Century England*, Cambridge 1957, Ch. IV.

[6] M. M. Postan, *The Medieval Wool Trade*, The Wool Education Society,
London 1952, p. 4; this figure assumes home consumption of about the same
order of magnitude as the exports. For some examples of flocks on individual
estates, and discussion of peasant production, see: E. Power, *The Wool Trade in
English Medieval History*, Oxford 1941, pp. 30–35.

[7] For export of wool see graphs and tables in E. M. Carus-Wilson and O.
Coleman, *England's Export Trade 1275–1547*, Oxford 1963.

[8] Practically every study of individual estates includes a break-down of
manorial revenues; these usually show the dominant role of rents and produce
followed, a long way behind, by seignorial profits. On some estates however,
usually lay ones, rents could account for the bulk of the revenues and, very
occasionally, one can even find estates on which the demesne was farmed out
almost entirely in the thirteenth century, as for example, on the estates of the
Earldom of Cornwall. See also Painter, pp. 121–123 and 152–154.

handled by the manorial courts and the greater frequency of certain types of offences as shortage of land and pasture became progressively more acute (Docs. 9, 11, 12). The very same population pressure kept wages at a steady level (in fact falling in real terms) well into the fourteenth century, thus contributing indirectly to the increased profitability of direct cultivation; this, at least, is my own reading of the Winchester evidence on wages, though Lord Beveridge has found it otherwise.[9]

A number of important caveats must be entered at this point. Firstly, there were landlords and landlords; some managed their affairs better than others. The great ecclesiastical estates seem to have been doing particularly well in this respect which was, in no small measure, due to the fact that some of the abbots and bishops in this period were men of outstanding administrative ability.[10]

Secondly, there were estates and estates; they differed tremendously in size and also, though this is on the whole less important, in type. Particular mention must, however, be made here of the Cistercians who, because of the peculiar character of the Order whose rule required it to live apart from ordinary communities, created a type of estate which, in the medieval world, came nearest to a modern farm: the so-called 'granges'—all demesne, with no tenant land and no tenants, cultivated by the labour of the lay brethren, the *conversi*.[11]

Thirdly, we must not let our modern notions of values distort our appreciation of what an increase, or decrease, of a few pounds a year meant to the person experiencing it, at the time when only a handful of the richest men in the land enjoyed an annual income in excess of £2,000[12] when an annual income of £10–£20 was deemed sufficient to maintain a knight in the state appropriate to his rank; when a bailiff of a large estate, with a number of manors under his

[9] Sir William Beveridge, 'Wages in the Winchester Manors', *Economic History Review*, VII, 1936; so far as I can see, the trends shown in Table I, p. 38, are largely fictitious, particularly the steadily rising trend in the last column of the table. See also, E. H. Phelps-Brown and S. V. Hopkins, 'Seven Centuries of Wages and Prices', *Economica* XXVIII, 1961.

[10] Postan, *Cambridge Ec. History of Europe*, I, p. 582.

[11] For the discussion of different types of estates and the consequences following therefrom see Postan, ibid., pp. 577–581. For the Cistercian estates see R. A. Donkin, 'The Cistercian Order in Medieval England: Some Conclusions', *Transactions of the Institute of British Geographers*, XXXIII, 1963, and C. V. Graves, 'The Economic Activities of the Cistercians in Medieval England, 1128–1307', *Analecta Sancti Ordinis Cisterciensis*, 1957.

[12] No single study of incomes of thirteenth-century landlords exists to my knowledge, but all studies of individual estates concern themselves with this problem. See: Painter, pp. 173–175 for some examples of baronial incomes.

care, received a fee of £10 a year, and when a labourer's wage for a full day's work fluctuated between 1d and 1½d according to the season and the urgency of the work to be done.

Finally, we must not confuse changes in the profitability of landed estates with the financial standing of their owners. Anyone, in any century, can live beyond his means, and many medieval landlords did just that. While there can be no doubt at all that the thirteenth century was a period of 'high farming' for most estates, with their revenues steadily rising, or maintained at a high level, it is equally obvious that many landlords were in a state of chronic indebtedness which, at times, reached alarming proportions.

Thus, after investigating the affairs of the baronage, Professor Painter came to the conclusion that 'in all probability throughout our period a fair proportion of the English baronage was always in debt to the crown', though the debts 'do not appear to have been so out of proportion to the revenues of the baronies that there was little or no hope that they would be paid'.[13]

Two eminent medievalists have argued recently that the very smallest lay landlords (whom we could, perhaps, anachronistically, call the gentry for lack of a better word—that is, those above the peasantry socially and below the great landlords economically) were, as a class, getting rapidly into difficulties, debt and not infrequently penury.[14] It must be pointed out, however, that this is the most elusive group of all in so far as documentary evidence is concerned, and that the argument loses some of its impact from the fact that the bias of survival of the documents on which it rests (charters, in this case) is in its favour. Since it was the buyer of land who received a charter we can see the larger institutions as buyers of land of lesser men, whereas the latter, with no muniment rooms to preserve their charters, appear thereby almost exclusively in the guise of sellers of land.

The financial affairs of many of the monastic houses too, appear to have been in a shocking state. In the words of Bishop Moorman who has studied the subject extensively: 'all the evidence which we possess—and which is considerable—goes to prove that almost every English religious house in the thirteenth century was deeply in debt'.[15] He cites instances which are so telling that some of them are worth quoting in full by way of illustration:

---

[13] Painter, p. 187

[14] Postan, *Cambridge Ec. History of Europe*, I, pp. 593–595, and Hilton, *A Medieval Society*, pp. 51–52.

[15] J. R. H. Moorman, *Church Life in England in the Thirteenth Century*, Cambridge 1955, p. 294.

'Matthew Paris tell us that the monks of Christ Church, Canterbury, in spite of the great financial asset of the "holy blissful martyr" were over £2,500 in debt in 1255, while at Rochester the debts were "inestimable". Gloucester and Peterborough each had a debt of £2,000 about the middle of the century, while St Mary's Abbey at York in 1300 owed no less than ten thousand marks (£6,666) to the Earl of Lincoln. Even the small priory of Dover, a cell to Canterbury, ran up a debt of nearly £88. Pecham, on visiting Reading Abbey in 1281, found what he called "an intolerable burden of debt", and at Winchester in 1286 the prior was so heavily involved in debt that he could not meet the demands of his monks. Eynsham and both the Canterbury houses were, like Bury St Edmunds, in toils of Jewish moneylenders, while the monks of Bath were reduced to borrowing from the local clergy. At Ramsey in 1300 the abbot had got into such financial difficulties that the monks refused to accept any responsibility for his debts and, knowing his love for music, threatened to cut off the singing in the choir until the abbot got himself out of "Queer Street".

'The Cistercians, in spite of their flourishing trade in wool, were no better off than the Benedictines. Bruerne in 1284 owed over 2,000 marks; Meaux in 1270 had debts of £3,678; Kirkstall in 1284 was in debt to the tune of £5,248, while Fountains was in such a bad way at this time that the Archbishop of York had to report to the Abbot of Clairvaux to inform him that the monks of Fountains were "temporarily ruined", "in a desperate condition", "a cause of scandal and derision to the whole kingdom", "in dire need and lamentable poverty".

'The Cluniac houses visited in 1262 and 1275 were almost all in debt, Lewes to the extent of 4,000 marks and Pontefract of 3,200. Bermondsey became deeply involved in debt through foolishness of Abbot John, who allowed himself to get into the toils of Adam de Stratton, a notorious moneylender.

'The Augustinians fared no better. In 1267 the canon of Bolton had borrowed £324 from their neighbours, and by 1300 their debts were £445. Dunstable owed 400 marks in 1262, Newburgh was over £700 in debt in 1275. Nostell by 1328 had contracted debts to a sum of more than £1,000, and in 1231 some of the canons of St Oswald's at Gloucester were sent into exile because they had pledged their house to the Jews.'[16]

Indeed, Walter of Henley had good cause to warn his readers to live by the Extent (i.e. according to their expected incomes as assessed

---

[16] Moorman, pp. 303–304.

in the extents of their estates) and he did so, no doubt, with the
example of the many who went to the wall through extravagant
living, bad management, or political embroilment, ever before his
eyes.[17]

2

How far can the increase in profits of the landlords in the thirteenth
century be ascribed to their own efforts rather than to the confluence,
during this period, of a number of trends favourable to them though
external to their control? There can be no doubt that the majority
of landlords whose activities we can study in the records they left
behind were eager to maximize their profits and improve the productivity of their estates according to the best advice available at the
time. If their efforts to increase the productivity of their demesnes
did not always produce results commensurable with their efforts,
this was usually due to the deficiencies of contemporary methods,
or resources, rather than to lack of trying. In so far as arable farming
is concerned, extensive marling (a very costly operation) and a more
extensive use of leguminous crops[18] were probably the only major
improvements open to them. In so far as animal farming is concerned, expansion of wool production, selective breeding to improve
stock, and attempts to combat animal diseases by large expenditure
on various medicaments,[19] would again almost exhaust the list of
major improvements open to medieval farmers.

Were the landlords doing enough within the framework of what
they could do? In an important article, Professor Hilton has argued
that while the average thirteenth-century landlord took out a lot in
cash income from his estates, what he put in by way of expenditure
on capital formation was not all that much; probably not more than
5 per cent of the total income, on average.[20] While I cannot but
admire the fairness and thoroughness with which Professor Hilton
examines all aspects of the problem and presents his conclusions, and
while I am quite certain on the basis of my own experience that the

[17] Lammond, *Walter of Henley's Husbandry*, p. 3.
[18] For an example of these practices on a specific estate, see Smith, pp. 135–139.
[19] In 1310 for example, (a year of unusually large expenditure) £25 5s 0¾d
were spent at Crawley, £11 11s 4½d at Overton, and £15 18s 2¾d at Downton.
These were among the largest wool-producing manors of the Winchester estates.
[20] Hilton, 'Capital Formation . . .', p. 45 and 53; this figure of 5 per cent would
be considerably higher if it were calculated as a percentage not of the total
income but of the production income only, though even then it would not be
very impressive.

D

figures obtained by him are of the right order of magnitude, I am far less willing to accept the implied censure on the business acumen of the medieval landlords at large. As I see it, the crucial point is not *how much* the thirteenth-century landlords ploughed back into their estates, but whether they ploughed back *enough* to expand production, or to maintain it at as high a level as was possible in the circumstances.

My impression is that they did plough back enough (at least the more progressive among them did), that they were not, in fact, running down their estates through excessive withdrawal of funds. Unlike the position nowadays, the technical limitations of medieval husbandry seem to me to have imposed their own ceiling on what could be usefully spent on an estate; after all, no useful purpose would have been served by buying two ploughs or putting up two barns, where one would have sufficed; the supply of purchaseable fertilizers was very limited, if it existed at all, and investment in additional land or livestock may well have been—as Professor Hilton himself has pointed out—prevented by the exhaustion of available colonizable resources and the general shortage of pasture. This is why, while I wholeheartedly welcome Professor Hilton's pioneering study of this important aspect of the exploitation of their estates by medieval landlords, I am not at all sure that the proportion of the total income spent on capital formation is a valid yardstick with which to measure the competence and progressiveness of medieval landlords.

Though I have not attempted to approach the problem statistically, the impression I get from the study of the accounts of such estates as I have seen, is that medieval landlords were spending as much as was necessary on the upkeep of farm buildings and implements. Incidentally, the great increase in building all over the countryside, consequent on the expansion of manorial production, is an important aspect of this expansion which so far has escaped the attention it deserves. Some of these truly magnificent buildings do survive to our own days,[21] and the records of many medieval estates (e.g. Winchester Account Rolls) are full of detailed descriptions (though unfortunately they seldom give dimensions) of costs and expenditures incurred in connection with almost every type of building, residential or farm, imaginable (Doc. 19).

Mention must also be made of two rather special aspects of the rural economy in this period. Many landlords tried to increase their

---

[21] As, for example, the two great barns of the Abbey of Beaulieu, excellently photographed, and illustrated with drawings, in W. Horn and E. Born, *The Barns of the Abbey of Baeulieu at its Granges of Great Coxwell and Beaulieu-St. Leonards*, University of California Press, 1965.

revenues even further by creating new market towns on their land, or by obtaining market rights for some of their manors.[22] Some of the luckier ones have even managed to obtain control of important local fairs which could be a most valuable asset to them (Doc. 16)[23]

The Forest must also be mentioned in this connection, for it occupied a very important place in the economy of the countryside. To the landlord (almost always the king) it brought considerable additional revenue from assarts made within its bounds, from sale of wood and timber, and from sale of grazing rights; it also provided him with an opportunity to establish vaccaries and stud-farms on a large scale.[24] To the peasantry it presented a means of eking out what otherwise might have been a most precarious existence, by expanding their animal husbandry and occasionally by extending their arable acreage a little.[25]

3

The period of 'high farming' did not last for very long; by the end of the thirteenth century, sometimes a little earlier, sometimes a little later, the period of expansion (or stability at a high level) came to an end and a progressive contraction set in. This contraction is far more apparent when the basis of production (arable acreage and the number of animals) is examined then when one looks at the total profitability of the estates in terms of cash revenues. This is so because while income from production was falling off, income from rents and seignorial profits could still be rising; frequently too, the high level of prices compensated for the falling quantity of produce sold. The situation was aggravated in the second half of the four-teenth century by acute labour shortage and rising costs generally, consequent on the outbreak of the plague in 1349 and in later years. Since, however, it is quite clear that the contraction of the arable production on most estates set in well before the advent of the Black Death, its causes must be sought elsewhere.

There is far less agreement among historians about the causes of

[22] See Beresford, *New Towns*.
[23] E.g. the fair of St Ives in the case of Ramsey Abbey, and the fair of St Giles in the case of the bishopric of Winchester; unfortunately when the records of the latter became available from 1287 onwards, the fair was already on the decline.
[24] Shaw, pp. 353–391; and C. E. Hart, *Royal Forest; A Study of Dean's Woods as Producers of Timber*, Oxford 1966.
[25] Shaw, pp. 397–410, and J. R. Birrell, 'The Forest Economy of the Honor of Tutbury in the Fourteenth and Fifteenth Century', *University of Birmingham Historical Journal*, VIII, 1962.

this recession than about the causes of the earlier expansion. One fact stands out clearly, however, the timing of this recession differed widely not only as between estates, but also as between different manors of one and the same estate. For instance, the period of 'high farming' *par excellence* on the estates of Canterbury Cathedral Priory (1306–1324)[26] coincides almost exactly with the period of the greatest contraction on the estates of the bishop of Winchester; and some of the manors of the latter started contracting their demesne as early as the middle years of the thirteenth century, while others show hardly any traces of contraction until well into the fourteenth century,[27] It would seem, therefore, that any explanation in terms of a sudden change in the general economic situation, such as for instance a change in the demand for foodstuffs, must be ruled out. It is true that on some estates this contraction coincided with the periods when prices were temporarily depressed and costs (mainly wages) already rising,[28] but it is equally true that on other estates the contraction set in while prices were still buoyant and costs stable (Appendix A).

And yet, this phenomenon of contracting demesnes is so widespread in its appearance that one is perforce driven to look for some overriding general consideration, operating on a sliding time-scale perhaps, but nevertheless of an almost universal application. Can an explanation of this kind be found? Professor Postan has been arguing for a long time now that the contraction of demesne cultivation was due mainly (for there were of course, other contributory factors operating at the same time) to previous overcultivation; that the taking in of too much marginal land at the peak of the thirteenth century reclamation had to be paid for later on by a fall in productivity, once the stored-up fertility of such lands was exhausted.[29] Since the phase of marginal reclamation had been reached on different estates at different points of time, one would expect to find considerable differences in the time by which the stage of diminishing returns was reached on different estates—hence the differences in the timing of the contraction of arable cultivation from one estate to another.

My own study of the estates of the bishopric of Winchester has convinced me that Professor Postan's hypothesis must be the right one. Since on some Winchester manors contraction set in as early

[26] Smith, p. 143.
[27] All references to Winchester estates are based on work done by me for a forthcoming study of the Winchester estates between 1208 and 1475; I have already covered the period up to 1350 in my unpublished Ph.D. thesis lodged in the Cambridge University Library.
[28] An upward readjustment of certain wage-rates took place on some Winchester manors following the great famine of 1316–1317.
[29] Postan, *Cambridge Ec. History of Europe*, I, pp. 556–559.

as the middle years of the thirteenth century we cannot be dealing here with some general change in agricultural prospects and opportunities. Since on some manors no contraction can be detected until the mid-fourteenth century, clearly we cannot be dealing here with a change in a particular landlord's general policy, his preference for the ease and safety of income from rents as against the risks and tribulations attaching to direct cultivation. Since the level of animal population on the Winchester estates at no time before 1350 exceeded its peak level reached in the 1220s and 1250s, clearly we are not dealing here with a change-over to a different type of economy either; if some 30,000 sheep and some 3,500 cattle and horses could be accommodated at the time when the arable demesne was at its most extensive (over 13,000 acres under seed) there was surely no need to convert arable land to pasture to accommodate a lower number of animals, and yet the total area under seed on the Winchester estates was reduced between 1270 and 1330 by some 5,000 acres.

This left Professor Postan's hypothesis to be investigated, and I realized from the very beginning that the first step must be a re-calculation of yields for the Winchester manors. I had no faith in Lord Beveridge's handling of Winchester evidence and even had it been otherwise, his calculations of Winchester yields were limited to a handful of manors only.[30] Having calculated the yields for all the major crops and all the manors of the estate for which this could be done between 1208 and 1350, I then tried, by a process of elimination, to arrive at some explanation of the emerging patterns of productivity changes.

The results have convinced me that Professor Postan's suggested explanation must be the right one, at least in so far as the Winchester estates are concerned. My analysis of the Winchester yield data shows that on the great majority of manors a fall in productivity had occurred in the last quarter of the thirteenth and/or the first quarter of the fourteenth century, and the very considerable contraction of the area under seed over the same period appears to have been a conscious countermeasure, but for which this fall may have been even more pronounced.[31]

An objection could be raised at this point that it is wrong to argue from the experience of a particular estate to the general situation.

[30] Beveridge, 'Yield and Price of Corn . . .'.

[31] The foregoing is based on an unpublished study of the productivity of corn on the Winchester estates. I have so far refused to have it published without full tabulation of, at least, the yield figures themselves, and as these run to some 80 pages, as against some 30 pages of text, this makes the whole study too long for an article, and too short for a book. I am still looking for a way out of this dilemma.

The objection is valid, but up to a point only. Most of us come to the study of rural economy via some particular estate and we all must be on our guard against a perfectly natural inclination to assume that what is true of our own estate must also necessarily be true of others. However, it would be equally wrong to go, in a fit of diffidence, to the other extreme and accept that what is true of one estate cannot necessarily be valid for any other; especially when lack of relevant documentation forces upon us the choice of studying a given problem on the basis of a single collection of documents, or not at all. While not necessarily claiming any general validity for conclusions based on the evidence of the Winchester estates alone, it would clearly be foolish to disregard the possibility that similar conditions may have been responsible for similar developments elsewhere.

4

While the fortunes of landlords moved up and down, between 1200 and 1350, those of the peasantry likewise did not remain stationary. A great deal has been written in the last twenty years or so on the position of the peasantry in medieval England, and I see no need to duplicate here what others have done so much better elsewhere. I shall, therefore, refrain from discussing a number of, largely matter-of-fact, topics and shall concentrate on the two controversial issues concerning the peasantry; the problem of freedom and the problem of prosperity, the latter in Chapter III.

Of the major topics which I do not propose to discuss here, the following deserve special mention. I shall not discuss the various rules, traditional attitudes, and memories of how things were done in the past—which collectively formed what was known at the time as the Custom of the Manor, and which regulated the life of the villagers in such vital matters as inheritance, the rights of widows, provision for minors, marriages, acquisition and forfeiture of land, etc.—for Professor Homans has dealt with such sociological factors very extensively in his inavaluable study of thirteenth-century villagers.[32]

I shall also not consider the daily routine of a peasant's life, nor the *minutiae* of peasant services and obligations (Docs. 4–7, 9–14),

[32] Homans, *The English Villagers of the Thirteenth Century*. See also J. A. Raftis, *Tenure and Mobility*, Toronto 1964, for a discussion of similar topics for the manors of Ramsey Abbey and a very generous selection of translated extracts from manorial court rolls illustrating the various points raised. For a recent discussion of the rules of inheritance, and the consequences flowing therefrom, see R. J. Faith, 'Peasant Families and Inheritance Customs in Medieval England', *Agricultural History Review*, XIV, 1966.

since the former has been admirably reconstructed by Mr Bennett and the latter conveniently summarized by the late A. L. Poole.[33] Neither shall I attempt to describe the physical environment in which the peasant community operated, nor their living conditions (particularly housing), since these too, have been described by others.[34]

Finally, I do not intend to discuss the role of the Church in the life of the peasantry, though I would like to point out in this connection, since it is usually passed over lightly in histories of the period, that the only regular taxation with which the population was burdened at the time was that imposed for the benefit of the Church —tithe. Because of this there does not seem to have been much love lost between the peasantry and the parish clergy.[35] Not all parish priests, of course, were as grasping as that parish priest of the Abbey of Glastonbury village of Merkesbury who was hauled before the manorial court in 1340 to answer the charge that he has 'appropriated to himself John son of William Henry, a villein of the lord, asserting him to be his, as the due of his church, as the tenth son of his father',[36] but the payment of the great tithes (corn and animals) alone must have constituted a real hardship, and a constant irritant, to the poorer sections of the rural community; the more so since all the major services required of the village priest (marriages, baptisms and funerals) had to be paid for separately, and since the parish churches already had their glebe lands to support their incumbents.

It is usual with many historians to begin their discussion of the peasantry by drawing a line between the free and the unfree and discussing them accordingly. The problem is not as simple as all that, for the definition of freedom in the medieval period is not as straightforward as might appear at first sight, and the focus may change as one looks at the problem from the personal, tenurial, or legal standpoint. This complexity of the problem is easy to overlook

[33] Bennett, *Life on the English Manor*, and A. L. Poole, *Obligations of Society in the Twelvth and Thirteenth Century*, Oxford 1946; the latter deals with all classes of society, not only the peasantry.

[34] W. G. Hoskins, *The Making of the English Landscape*, London 1955; M. W. Barley, *The English Farmhouse and Cottage*, London 1961; R. H. Hilton, *A Medieval Society*, pp. 93–105.

[35] H. G. Richardson, 'The Parish Clergy of the Thirteenth and Fourteenth Century', *Transactions of the Royal History Society*, 1912. See also Bennett, pp. 321–336.

[36] Longleat, MS. 10773: '*Johannes de Pykesleghe persona ecclesie de Merkesbury assumpsit sibi Johannem filium Willelmi Henry nativum domini asserens ipsum esse suum eo quod est decimus puer patris sui quem idem persona clamat ut ius ecclesie sue etc.*' I have this reference by courtesy of Professor Postan.

and even some distinguished historians have fallen into the trap; for example, the frequently met division of the peasantry into three groups: (i) the freeholders, (ii) the villeins, and (iii) the cottars, when looked at more closely, turns out to be totally inadequate, for it is not based on a uniform criterion of classification.[37] Type of tenure is the criterion behind the first category, personal status behind that of the second, and size of holding behind the third; in fact, villeins could also be freeholders (though this was rather rare), and cottars were usually villeins (though they could also be free men, and/or freeholders if they happened to hold freehold cottages) except in the terminology of Domesday Book, which no longer applied in the thirteenth century.

In an article which deserves to be widely read—for it emphasizes what badly needed emphasizing and what should be realized more widely—Professor Hilton has pointed out that in the context of manorial documents 'freedom' invariably means freedom from the more onerous labour services, particularly the week-work (*opera*).[38] It is quite understandable that this should have been so. From a practical point of view, a man who for the best part of the week has to work for somebody else, as his duty, is clearly not free; by comparison, a man whose time is entirely his own is in a very real sense freer, even though he may be prevented from doing certain things without permission.

If we look at the position of the thirteenth-century peasant we find that he could be 'unfree' in two respects: with regard to his time and the necessity of working for another, and with regard to his inability to do certain things (such as leave the manor, or marry his daughter, or send his son to school, or make a cleric out of him) without his lord's permission. The first type of 'unfreedom' is tenurial in character, that is, it arose only when a person held land burdened with labour services, or, as contemporaries would have said, when he held land in villeinage. The second type of 'unfreedom' was not tenurial but personal, that is, it applied even if the person concerned held no land at all—or he may even have held free land—and it applied because the person concerned was deemed to have been born into servile condition.

It is very necessary to distinguish these two aspects of 'freedom' when discussing conditions in the thirteenth century; it is necessary, because by that time the two had ceased to coincide, if they ever

[37] e.g. G. O. Sayles, *The Medieval Foundations of England*, University Paperbacks 1966, p. 432.
[38] R. H. Hilton, 'Freedom and Villeinage in England', *Past and Present*, 31, 1965.

did completely. We do find peasants of free personal status (*liberi*) holding villein land and we do find villeins (*villani* or *nativi*) holding freehold land, though both these occurrences are rare and both were frowned upon, or prohibited, by the landlords for fear of various complications.

Students must be warned at this point not to take the writings of the contemporary lawyers on the subject of freedom too literally. Lawyers naturally like to sort everything into neat compartments, and their writings may suggest a situation much more clear-cut than was in fact the case. If one follows the legal aspect of the problem as it developed historically, the position appears to have been somewhat as follows. As long as slavery existed, the legal dividing line between the free and unfree was the line separating the slaves from the rest; it would thus appear that all men except slaves were legally free. Slavery seems to have disappeared soon after the compilation of Domesday Book, and it would seem that all men would then have been looked upon as free *de jure*. However, it was patently obvious at the time that men differed tremendously in the degree to which they were *de facto* free, and what the twelfth and thirteenth-century lawyers seem to have done, in effect, was to say: certain persons are clearly less free than others and we should not any longer treat them as equal in the courts of law; those who are restricted in their freedom in a way which is either incompatible with the dignity of a free man (i.e. specific personal disabilities), or who have submitted themselves to another man to the extent of having to put up with his demands for services which are both base in character (manual labour) and oppressive in extent (week-work), must henceforth be given different treatment from those who have not been so restricted, and to whom the term 'free' would henceforth be exclusively applied; the former, that is the villeins, would henceforth, in the eyes of the law (they may have already been so for some time in popular estimation) be looked upon as the exclusive concern of their lords, and the royal courts would no longer entertain pleas from such persons against their landlords in matters concerning their lands or the conditions of their tenure. It must, however, be emphasized that in any other matter the villeins were to receive, at the hands of the law, the same treatment as free men, even against their own lords.

To the extent to which this theory was acted upon by the courts, this turn in legal thinking was clearly to the disadvantage of a very considerable proportion of the English peasantry;[39] on the other

[39] The proportion of villeins to freemen differed considerably from one part to another; the latter were particularly numerous in the Danelaw where sokeman formed a large proportion of the population. See Kosminsky, pp. 203–206 for

hand, it was not always easy in practice to decide whether a given person was a villein or not, and it would appear that there was a progressive tendency on the part of the royal courts to side against the landlords in doubtful cases—to that extent, the harshness of the new legal doctrine was somewhat mitigated as time went on. In any case, the outbreak of the plague in 1349 changed the position radically in favour of the peasantry and accelerated greatly the economic trends which led to the almost complete disappearance of villeinage in England by the early fifteenth century.

However, we should not be unduly preoccupied with the legal position; this mattered only when a peasant wanted to get redress, against his own landlord, in matters affecting his holding or his services. Thirteenth-century villeinage was neither arbitrary nor unpredictable, even though it was deprived of the protection of the royal courts; the lord knew what he was entitled to and the peasants knew what to expect, since such matters were governed by the Custom of the Manor which was binding on landlords and peasants alike.

Professor Hilton, in a pioneering study of peasant discontent, has assembled an impressive array of instances in which peasants resorted to action, legal or otherwise, against acts of arbitrary oppression by their landlords.[40] While not disputing the facts of the case I doubt if such instances can be taken as representative; looking at the evidence of the royal court is, in this context, like looking at hospital records to find out the state of the nation's health—one would hardly find a healthy person anywhere. It should be remembered that for every peasant who sued his landlord in the royal courts there were hundreds who did not, and even among the plaintiffs there must have been many who may have been mistaken in their belief that they had a legitimate grievance; for instance, insistence on the performance of labour services from a hitherto commuted holding was perfectly within any landlord's right, and yet it could easily have seemed an injustice to a peasant who had not rendered such services for a long time. I am strengthened in my views by the fact that the overwhelming impression one gets from the perusal of the records of the manorial courts is not one of arbitrary landlords settling disputed issues by their own

estimates of freehold land and villein land; F. M. Powicke, 'Observations on the English Freeholder in the Thirteenth Century', *Wirtschaft und Kultur: Festschrift zum 70. Geburtstag von Afons Dopsch*, Baden-bei-Wien 1938; R. H. Hilton, *Social Structure of Rural Warwickshire in the Middle Ages*, Dugdale Society occasional papers 9, 1950; and Sir Frank Stenton, 'Free Peasantry of the Northern Danelaw', *Bulletin de la Société Royale des Lettres de Lund*, 1926.

[40] R. H. Hilton, 'Peasant Movements in England before 1381', *Economic History Review*, 2nd series, II, 1949, (also in Carus-Wilson, *Essays*, II).

fiat, but of men respectful, on the whole, of the manorial custom
and willing to leave the decision to the verdict of a sworn jury of
villagers. In fact, it seems to me that it is possible to put a different
interpretation on the examples assembled by Professor Hilton and
regard them, not so much as evidence that acts of arbitrary
oppression were widespread, as of evidence that the English peasantry
was neither cowed into submission nor oblivious of their rights, and
that they were prepared to defend them in those, relatively infrequent,
instances when they were disregarded by overbearing landlords.

The main reason, however, why we should not pay too much
attention to the legal aspect of freedom is that to the thirteenth-
century peasantry the problem must have been much more one of
practical considerations than of legal theory; and in this the emphasis
placed upon the problem of labour services by manorial records
seems to represent a realistic assessment of what mattered most to
the persons involved. It is not the legal, nor the personal, but the
tenurial aspect of villeinage which, in practice, must have represented the really significant difference between freedom and the lack
of it.

It is not difficult to see why the personal aspect of villeinage would
be overshadowed by the problem of labour services in the minds of
the peasants themselves. Disabilities arising out of unfree status
would come into operation only sporadically, if at all, for few peasants
would normally consider emigration, or sending their sons to school,
and one did not, after all, marry off one's daughters all the time. In
any case, even when one of these contingencies arose, payments for
permission ran at a low level throughout the thirteenth and early
fourteenth century, and I have yet to come across a single instance of
the lord's permission being witheld. Not so with labour services, particularly week-work, which obliged a man to work for his landlord
so many days a week, every week, in addition to rendering other
occasional services.

Accepting the view that the problem of labour services must be
placed squarely at the centre of any discussion of freedom of the
thirteenth-century English peasantry will not only, in my view,
bring us nearer to the realities of the situation; it will also, incidentally, lay bare an additional weakness involved in approaching the
subject via the legal definition. Even if we agree that for all practical
purposes it is permissible to identify freemen with freeholders, and
villeins with tenants in villeinage, the legal approach will still be
found lacking in one important respect: it ignores the presence of
a third category of tenants—the villeins who have commuted their
labour services for a money rent. *De jure* such tenants are in a fund-

amentally different position from freeholders, whereas *de facto* there is very little difference between the two (except that the former pay a higher rent) as long as the landlord does not revoke the commutation agreement. Similarly, the ever increasing number of assart holdings, and holdings created by piecemeal letting out of the demesne, do not really fit into the bipartite division of tenant land into freehold and villeinage, since they are strictly speaking neither one nor the other.

The amount of labour services required of the peasantry at any given time was clearly linked to the extent of the demesne at that time. In an article, which no student of English medieval rural society can afford to ignore, Professor Postan has demonstrated that the twelfth-century 'farming out' of manors was accompanied by an increase in the commutation of labour services and that the subsequent return, on the part of the landlords, to direct cultivation led to the reversal of this trend: new commutation was refused, revocation of previous commutation took place, redefinition of services to the advantage of the landlords was attempted, and new services were arbitrarily imposed on holdings which did not owe them previously.[41] It would seem that Professor Postan has subsequently modified his original position, for the latest exposition of his views puts far less emphasis on the arbitrary imposition of services by the landlords;[42] this modification agrees well with my own impressions, for I tend to regard known instances of such arbitrary impositions as exceptional rather than typical.

Though the fact of the 'manorial reaction' in the thirteenth century cannot be disputed we should not, I feel, overestimate its extent and significance for a number of reasons. Firstly, many manors (particularly, on the old-established ecclesiastical estates) were overprovided with labour services in relation to the needs of their demesnes at the time when the new expansion took place. Secondly, the rapidly rising population made hiring of labourers more attractive, in many instances, than embarking upon the unpopular policy of imposing new services; this is certainly true of the Winchester estates, for example. Thirdly, the expansion of demesnes was not all that long-lasting and, once it ceased, the need for increased labour services disappeared. When the contraction of demesnes set in again towards the end of the thirteenth century (or early in the fourteenth)

[41] M. M. Postan, 'The Chronology of Labour Services', *Transactions of the Royal Historical Society*, 4th series, XX, 1937; it is also reprinted in *Essays in Agrarian History*, I, 75–91.

[42] *Cambridge Economic History of Europe*, I, pp. 605–609.

the flow of commutation increased again,[43] though it now usually took the form of the sale of superfluous week-works (*opera*) rather than of permanent commutation incorporated into the rent (Doc. 2). Finally, even at the height of the 'manorial reaction' the proportion of money rents to labour rents was very considerable. Professor Kosminsky has shown, in what is the most authoritative study of the subject so far, that in the second half of the thirteenth century, even in those parts of England which were heavily manorialized, money rents represented a higher proportion of total rents than did labour services.[44]

If the temporary cessation of commutation in the early thirteenth century can be looked upon as a movement away from a previous liberalization of the peasants' position, the ever-increasing number of assarts, and eventually of holdings carved out of the demesne as well, must be regarded as a force acting in the opposite direction. Since assarts and holdings of demesne origin were practically never in the thirteenth century held otherwise than for a money rent (with at most a few boon-works thrown in) their increased number clearly strengthened the free, as against the servile, element in the land-holding situation. The growing activity of the village land market, under the pressure of expanding population and progressive scarcity of land, should also probably be considered as a factor contributing to the greater liberalization of conditions in the course of the thirteenth century.[45]

All in all, except for the short period of 'reaction' at the beginning, the thirteenth century should be regarded as a period of gradual improvement—in practice though not in theory—so far as the freedom of the peasantry is concerned, though it was also, at the same time, a period of progressive deterioration in their economic position, as I shall try to show in the next chapter.

5

Finally, though here I am rather out of my depth, reference must be made to certain changes in legal theory and practice, social con-

---

[43] On the Winchester estates, for example, the total amount realized from commutation (excluding the very insignificant amount incorporated into the rents) rose from £14 14s 6d in 1221 to £255 15s 4½d in 1348.

[44] Kosminsky, p. 191.

[45] For the discussion of the village land market see: M. M. Postan, 'The Charters of the Villeins', *Carte Nativorum*, C.N.L. Brooke and M. M. Postan ed. Northamptonshire Record Society, XX, 1960, chapter II, pp. xxviii–lx.

cepts, and fiscal measures, all of which had considerable effect on the position of landlords and peasants alike.

The period under our consideration witnessed a tremendous amount of legislative activity which seems to have run, broadly, in three channels:[46] much of the new legislation was concerned with the curtailment of private jurisdiction and transference of the administration of justice from baronial to royal courts; much of the new legislation was concerned with preserving the rights, and inheritance, of the great landlords (the king included) by regulating rules of inheritance (Statute *De donis conditionalibus*, 1285) by ending sub-infeudation by the existing feoffees (Statute *Quia emptores terrarum*, 1290), and by stopping unauthorized alienation of land to the Church in free alms (Statute of Mortmain, 1279); some of the new legislation was aimed at protecting the lesser freeholders against encroachment by the landlords, in particular by restraining the latter from occupying common wastes (The Provisions of Merton, 1236 Doc. 20) and limiting their right of distraint on the goods of their tenants (Statute of Marlborough, 1267).[47]

The thirteenth and fourteenth centuries also saw a gradual change in the social standing of the knightly class which by a process of evolution diversified itself eventually into the gentry and the aristocracy. Anybody interested in this aspect of social change should read Professor McFarlane's stimulating essay and follow up the references given there.[48]

Finally, the subject of taxation must be touched upon, however briefly. The thirteenth century was a period during which a completely novel type of national taxation was introduced—parliamentary taxes on personal property.[49] Collected as a proportion of the total value of movables, theoretically always in the nature of an extraordinary grant, levied at first only intermittently, the new taxes increased in frequency as time went on to become almost annual with the outbreak of the Hundred Years War. The years 1290–1334 were the

---

[46] See: Sir Maurice Powicke, *The Thirteenth Century, 1216–1307*, Oxford 1953, pp. 350–380, and T. F. T. Plucknett, *Legislation of Edward I*, Oxford 1949; also any good constitutional history or a general history of law.

[47] This continued the work of protecting the lesser freeholders, against arbitrary acts on the part of their landlords, going back to the possessory assizes of Henry II's reign, particularly the Assize of Novel Disseisin and Assize of Mort D'ancestor.

[48] K. B. McFarlane, 'The English Nobility in the Later Middle Ages', *Twelfth International Congress of Historical Sciences*, Vienna, 1965, I, 337.

[49] See J. F. Willard, *Parliamentary Taxes on Personal Property 1290–1334*, Cambridge (Mass.) 1934; and S. K. Mitchell, *Taxation in Medieval England*, New Haven 1951.

crucial period in their development; by the latter date they were fixed at one-fifteenth for rural and one-tenth for urban communities, and the machinery for their collection had become fully developed.

To the historian of rural society the new experiment in taxation is more important for the documents it left behind than for the taxes themselves. Although it is common for many text books to bewail these taxes as representing a great hardship to both landlords and peasants, it seems to me that this aspect of the problem can easily be exaggerated. Even when they had become virtually annual, the burden they imposed was less heavy than that represented by the tithe, and yet one finds few historians bemoaning the imposition of the latter.

Moreover, in so far as the landlords are concerned, there is a considerable body of evidence to suggest that the movable wealth of the landlords was greatly under-assessed by the tax assessors. Dr Harvey, in his study of the village of Cuxham, has a table showing the very close correlation between expenses arising in connection with the arrival of the tax assessors (bribery, in plain language) and the fluctuations in the assessed value of the landlords' property.[50] Some of the Winchester evidence also shows clearly that the landlords' property was under-assessed, in fact, twice over: by valuing the movables at a rate fixed well below their market value (about 50 per cent below it in the instances which I have come across) and by greatly underestimating their total number (animals) or quantity (grain). But the new taxation left in its wake a vast body of taxation returns which have been put by historians to a variety of uses, some quite sound, others less so. Of these, by far the most important ones are the light these documents throw on the vexed question of peasant livestock[51] (Doc. 17), and on the more general problem of the distribution of wealth and changes in local prosperity over periods of time;[52] but for the taxation returns, speculation concerning these most important aspects of the economic situation would belong almost entirely to the realm of make-believe.

[50] P. D. A. Harvey, *A Medieval Oxfordshire Village: Cuxham 1240–1400*, Oxford 1965, Table X, p. 106.
[51] See for instance, Postan, 'The Village Livestock'.
[52] See for instance, R. E. Glasscock, 'The Distribution of Wealth in East Anglia in the Early Fourteenth Century', *Transactions of the Institute of British Geographers*, XXXII, 1963.

The Standard of Living Controversy

'What this means in human terms is that about one-half of the peasant population had holdings insufficient to maintain their families at the bare minimum of subsistence'. M. M. Postan[1]

'Far from suffering from over-population England was a prosperous country in all but the worst years.' J. C. Russell[2]

I

One of the most important, and most controversial, debates at present occupying historians of the English medieval rural society is the problem of change in the standard of living of the rural population. Some historians believe that towards the end of the thirteenth century it had reached an extremely low level; others deny this.

The view that conditions deteriorated to such a point that by the end of the thirteenth century a high proportion of the peasantry was living on, or below, subsistence level was first formulated some years ago, and subsequently elaborated, by Professor Postan in lectures, discussions and articles. Reduced to essentials his interpretation runs as follows. The thirteenth century was a period of rapidly expanding population. This was at first accompanied by extensive reclamation of land which, however, came to an end by the end of the thirteenth century. When this happened, and since population was still expanding, a progressive lowering of the standard of living of the rural population took place, reaching, by the end of the century, a stage which can be described as one of 'over-population'. The term 'over-population' in this context is clearly relative and means no more than that, in relation to available sources, the population of the country-

---

[1] *Cambridge Ec. History of Europe*, I, p. 624.

[2] J. C. Russell, 'The Pre-plague Population of England,' *Journal of British Studies*, V, 1966, p.1.

side had reached a level at which a very high proportion of that population existed on, or below, subsistence level. Some time in the early fourteenth century the upward demographic trend seems to have been halted and the situation eased off a bit. No precise dating for this turning point can be offered though it could be argued that the great famine of 1315–1317 could well be the decisive factor here.[3]

Professor Postan's interpretation has gained widespread acceptance among historians working in the same field either because they were swayed by his arguments or because their own independent investigations have led them to very much the same conclusions. There are, however, some notable exceptions. Among those who have expressed their views in print, Professor Russell seems to be the only person to have persistently voiced his opposition to this interpretation. Quite recently, Miss Barbara Harvey has ranged herself on the same side of the controversy;[4] so it could be that we are now witnessing the beginning of the swing of the pendulum in the opposite direction.

This issue is obviously so crucial to the study of the rural society in this period that it seems worthwhile to examine the evidence, and the arguments, on both sides, in some detail. In this I shall endeavour to be as objective as I possibly can be, but since I am arguing from a partisan position I can only urge readers to acquaint themselves, as soon as possible, at first hand, with the arguments of the various protagonists in the debate.

The proposition that the economic position of the English peasantry was progressively worsening over the latter half of the thirteenth century seems to be generally accepted; this is but an inevitable logical consequence of the general acceptance by historians of the belief that the rural population was expanding throughout the century and into the fourteenth century, and of the fact that reclamation of land had petered out almost completely well before the end of the century.

The debate is frequently presented—usually by the opponents of Professor Postan's views—as one centred on the problem of over-population. This is, I think, unfortunate for it shifts the centre of gravity of the debate from what is essentially a debate about a human situation to what might appear to be one on a purely academic

---

[3] M. M. Postan, 'The Fifteenth Century', *Economic History Review*, IX, 1939; 'Some Economic Evidence of Declining Population in the Later Middle Ages', ibid. 2nd series, II, 1950; and *Cambridge Ec. History of Europe*, I, particularly pp. 551–552 and 557–561.

[4] B. F. Harvey, 'The Population Trend in England between 1300 and 1348', *Transactions of the Royal Historical Society*, 1966.

E

plane of demographic speculation. Demographic speculation does, of course, play a vital part in the debate but it would be quite wrong to exclude other, frequently very important, considerations from it. Furthermore, many discussions of the problem which approach it purely from the demographic point of view tend to fall into a very common pitfall of operating with aggregates—i.e. seeing the problem in terms of total population and total resources—and overlooking completely the necessity of taking very real inequalities in the distribution of wealth into consideration. Some of them also tend to shift the emphasis from the historian's preoccupation with the human situation to an academic wrangle about the precise dating of the end of demographic expansion, or the beginning of demographic decline.

The real issue at stake, which we historians must not lose sight of, is the degree of impoverishment—if there had been widespread impoverishment—to which the rural population had sunk by the end of the thirteenth century as a result of a long and continuous expansion of population unaccompanied by a simultaneous, and matching, increase in resources and aggravated by other factors brought about by that very same population expansion; higher prices, low wages, and progressive shortage of land.

The problem can be approached in two ways. On a national level, by attempting to construct 'global' estimates of population and national resources; on a local level, by collecting, collating, and fitting into a comprehensive pattern all pieces of information, or impressions, obtained from documents depicting the position of the peasantry over a narrow area—a manor, an estate, or a region.

There is no doubt in my mind that, from a historian's point of view, the latter method is preferable, for it is far more intimately linked with the documentary evidence. The almost complete absence of any demographic data for the period under consideration makes purely demographic arguments based on more-or-less hypothetical calculations of aggregates and on highly speculative statistical exercises involving various 'vital' statistics (sex ratios, rates of birth and deaths, expectation of life, etc.) obtained in various devious ways, highly unsatisfactory.

2

Let us first look at the problem of population changes. The estimates which seem to have the widest currency at present are those of Professor Russell. He estimates the population of England at the time of Domesday Book at about 1·1 million, and in 1377 at about 2¼ million.[5] Both these estimates must be regarded as the lowest possible estimates.

The main hypothetical element in calculating population in 1086 on the basis of Domesday Book is the multiplier used to convert the number of tenancies enumerated in that document into total population. Professor Russell has constantly, and persistently, advocated the use of the 3·5 multiplier and he has used this in his calculations. This multiplier is regarded by many historians, and in my view must be regarded, as far too low. Late medieval evidence seems to point to a multiplier of between 4·5 and 5·0 and there is no reason to believe the number of persons represented by each tenancy to have been smaller in 1086—rather the contrary. When Professor Russell's figures are recalculated on the basis of the 5·0 multiplier the total population of some 1·6 million is obtained for 1086.

Calculations of the total population in 1377 are relevant to the discussion only in so far as they serve as the basis for calculating population before the Black Death of 1349, that is, at its highest medieval level. Such calculations are based on the returns of the Poll Tax of 1377. This was a tax of fourpence on each person, male or female, of fourteen years of age or more. It was followed by two other Poll Taxes, somewhat differently assessed, in 1379 and 1381. The returns for these taxes are the only documents since Domesday Book on which national calculations can be based. Since the comparison of the returns of the 1379 and 1381 Poll Taxes with those of the 1377 Poll Tax show a very considerable rate of evasion, and because the rate of survival of these returns is also very much better for 1377, the figures obtainable from the returns of the 1377 Tax have been found far more suitable for population estimates than those of its two successors.

As in the case of Domesday population, Professor Russell's estimates of the total population in 1377 must be considered a minimum estimate, because at various stages of the calculation he is using much lower figures than other historians think proper. The main hypothetical elements in this calculation are: the extent of the evasion in the Poll Tax returns, the percentage of the total population represented by the under-fourteens, and the aggregate mortality of all the pre-1377 plagues.

Most recently Professor Postan has suggested that Russell's figures must be upgraded on all these points. He suggested 40 to 50 per cent for under-fourteens as against Russell's 33⅓ per cent; per-

[5] J. C. Russell, *British Medieval Population*, Albuquerque 1948, pp. 54 and 146.

haps as much as 25 per cent for under-enumeration (evasion, exemptions and errors) as against Russell's 5 per cent; and 50 per cent for the aggregate mortality of all the pre-1377 plagues as against Russell's 40 per cent. Professor Russell arrived at the figure of some $3\frac{3}{4}$ million for the population of England on the eve of the Black Death; Professor Postan's corrections would bring that figure to just over 6 million.[6]

I have no views of my own on the question of evasion though to assume that there had been practically none, as Professor Russell does, seems to me quite unacceptable in view of my experience of various other fourteenth and thirteenth-century taxation returns.[7] But, perhaps, Professor Postan's suggested 25 per cent is too high. Since I reject Russell's multiplier of 3·5 per household I must also reject his estimate of $33\frac{1}{3}$ per cent for the under-fourteens as too low. I have no doubt at all in my mind that the aggregate mortality of 40 per cent for all the pre-1377 plagues is far too low; even Postan's 50 per cent seem to me on the low side.

There were at least two very serious and general outbreaks of plague before 1377: the Black Death itself in 1349-1350 and the plague of 1361–1362, and two other, though less serious and probably also less general, outbreaks in 1369 and 1374. The mortality of the Black Death is usually, in historical textbooks, assumed to have been in the region of 33 per cent, but such estimates seem to me to be too low. Professor Russell's own estimate is even lower than this and it offers one of the best examples of his refusal to accept any evidence other than his own calculations; if he considers such evidence at all it is merely to find reasons why it should be rejected as inaccurate.

Professor Russell's own calculations are based on a small sample of heirs and heiresses of the tenants-in-chief who came into their inheritance before 1349 and died in, or survived, the plague of 1349–1350. Of the 505 such heirs constituting the sample 138, or some 27 per cent, died in the plague.[8] This is in striking contrast to the other figures which Russell considers; the clerical mortality of well over 40 per cent, 43 per cent for rural mortality calculated on the basis of frankpledge payments on three Essex manors, and 56 per cent for rural mortality calculated for the estates of Crowland Abbey on the basis of manorial documents.[9] The figure for clerical mor-

---

[6] *Cambridge Ec. History*, I, pp. 561–562.

[7] The unreliability of taxation returns as a source for population calculations is brought out quite well in Willard, *Parliamentary Taxes on Personal Property*, pp. 174–182.

[8] Russell, *British Medieval Population*, p. 216.

[9] After Russell, ibid., pp. 221, 226 and 227.

tality is probably much too low but Russell dismisses as 'sensational' all literary evidence of high mortality among monks. But perhaps the most striking feature of these figures, which Russell considers only to reject them as inaccurate, is the great disproportion between his own calculations on the one hand, and all the other evidence on the other hand.

When evidence derived from different types of documents conflicts with each other to this extent the decision which figures to accept and which to reject must rest on the answer to two questions: which set of figures is likely to be more accurate, and which set of figures is likely to be more representative. Anybody looking at the problem of plague mortality objectively, and historically, must come to the conclusion that on both these counts Russell's own figures should be the first to be discarded. From the point of view of accuracy the Inquisitions Post Mortem are no better than the manorial records on which the higher estimate of the Black Death mortality are based; and the figures of mortality among heirs and heiresses to the great estates are the least likely to represent mortality of the population at large. Clerical mortality is probably the next in the declining order of preference and figures relating to ordinary people the most acceptable. Those for the latter are of course hard to come by, but such calculations as I have been able to make indicate a mortality above 50 per cent for the rural population and it seems generally agreed that mortality was higher in towns than in the countryside. What is my evidence?

The account rolls of the bishopric of Winchester contain a complete transcript of entry fines imposed in the manorial courts, as well as a transcript of marriage fines, and heriots. Some time ago, using the records of the Hampshire manor of Bishop's Waltham, I constructed an index of marriages, heriots, and transfers of land, arranged under individuals to whom they relate for the period c. 1245–1500. I have incorporated into this index entries from the custumal of 1259–1260, the rental of c.1331–1332 and the rental of 1464,[10] and I have also reconstructed the provenance of most of the virgated holdings over the same period of time (Doc. 14). Because of the existence of the rental of 1332, and of an almost unbroken series of annual accounts for the period 1325–1403,[11] it was possible by working from the rental, and using the evidence of entry

---

[10] Br. Mus. MS. Egerton 2418, Hampshire Record Office, MS. Eccl. Comm. Var. 159512$\frac{1}{9}$, and Eccl. Comm. Var. 158819$\frac{1}{10}$.

[11] Only one year (1333–4) is missing before the Black Death and two other account rolls do not cover the whole year, though this probably did not affect the recording of entry fines.

fines, to reconstruct fairly accurately a list of tenants on the eve of the Black Death and the number of casualties due to it. This reconstruction makes it clear that there were no significant changes in the total number of holdings between 1331 and the Black Death or between the Black Death and the second outbreak of 1361–1362 since there were no holdings left vacant after the first outbreak and very little duplication of holdings before 1362. By tracing the provenance of holdings it was also possible to reconstruct the number of tenants in the tithing of Burseldon, the only tithing omitted from the rental of 1332, thus making the record complete.

The mortality was as follows: for the Black Death (Michaelmas 1348 to Michaelmas 1349) 264 deaths, for the second outbreak (Michaelmas 1361 to Michaelmas 1362) 53 deaths. The total number of tenants in the rental of 1332 was 363 which, if some 41 tenants are added for Burseldon, would bring the total to 404 tenants. Thus the Black Death mortality represents some 65 per cent of the total and that of the second great outbreak some 13 per cent.

Another strong argument for rejecting Russell's estimate of the Black Death mortality as too low is the order of magnitude of the mortality of 1349–1350 and 1361–1362 in his calculations. On Russell's showing the mortality of both these outbreaks was almost the same: 27 per cent for the former and 22·7 per cent for the latter.[12] This is contrary to all available evidence, literary or manorial, which leaves us in no doubt at all that the Black Death itself was a far more serious outbreak than that of 1362. On the manor of Waltham the mortality of the Black Death was some 26 times greater than the average mortality of the preceeding two years (264 deaths in 1349 as against 7 in 1347 and 14 in 1348). The mortality of the second outbreak was only some 7 times greater than the average mortality of the two preceding years (53 deaths in 1362 as against 8 in 1360 and 6 in 1361). Although Waltham is the only Winchester manor for which I have been able to make a thorough study of heriots, fines, and provenance of holdings, it appears manifestly on the basis of crude heriot figures for other manors that the respective mortalities of these two major outbreaks were very much of the same order of magnitude elsewhere on the Winchester estates. Incidentally, a thorough examination of Waltham fines has also revealed a very large number of deaths where the manorial officials failed to record, and presumably also to collect, a heriot.

My other attempt to estimate the mortality of the Black Death statistically is based on the *chevagia* lists in the court rolls of the

[12] Russell, *British Medieval Population*, pp. 216 and 217.

estates of Glastonbury Abbey. As Professor Postan has pointed out,[13] the manors of Glastonbury Abbey are remarkable for the astoundingly large number of villeins absenting themselves, year after year, from the manor with the landlord's permission on a payment of a small sum of money known as *chevagium*: on the larger manors the figures can be well over a hundred. In the year of the Black Death these lists have numerous names crossed out with the explanation 'because he is dead' superimposed. The average mortality for the twenty-two manors for which I have the figures[14] was 54·6 per cent; the lowest figure was 33·3 per cent and the highest 69·4 per cent. This again suggests a level of mortality much higher than that commonly assumed and very much higher than Russell's 27 per cent.

In view of all this the overall mortality of some 40 per cent for all the pre-1377 outbreaks of plague (and there were at least two others besides the ones I have discussed so far) suggested by Professor Russell seems to me unacceptably low.

Professor Postan's suggested figure of *c.* 6¼ million for the total population on the eve of the Black Death must clearly be regarded as a maximum figure just as Professor Russell's estimate must be regarded as a minimum figure; the real figures would lie somewhere between, though on the basis of such evidence as we do possess so far it seems that it would, in all probability, be much nearer Postan's than Russell's estimate.

However, what matters far more than the exact figure itself is the order of magnitude of the changes which took place between 1086 and 1348. Even if we take the higher Domesday estimate and the lower pre-1349 estimate, it is clear that the population of England between 1086 and 1348 had increased at least by some two-and-a-half times. If we take the higher pre-1349 estimate the increase might have been as great as fourfold. What also strengthens the impression of a large population on the eve of the Black Death is the fact that on so many manors all holdings vacated through the Black Death were taken up at once without any apparent difficulty and without that doubling up of holdings which is so noticeable thereafter; and this suggests a countryside teaming with people rather than one starved of them.

Estimates of the area under the plough in 1086 are, of course, highly hypothetical since Domesday Book records the arable in terms

---

[13] *Cambridge Ec. History of Europe*, I, p. 624.

[14] I am grateful to Professor Postan for permission to use his transcripts of Glastonbury documents; responsibility for the correctness of the transcripts themselves, and of the calculations based on them, is entirely my own. Longleat, MS. 11179.

of 'plough-teams'. Two points, however, can be made with certainty. The area under the plough in 1086 was already very extensive. Using Professor Darby's and Maitland's estimates, Lennard reckoned the total arable in the twenty-eight counties of Domesday England to be 71,785 'plough-teams'. At the traditional figure of 120 acres to a 'plough-team' this would give the area of 8·6 million acres, or at the more cautious estimate of 100 acres to a 'plough-team', a total of 7·2 million acres; the official Agricultural Statistics give the total of arable acreage for the same area on 4 June 1914 as 7·7 million acres.[15]

The second point which is equally certain is that there could not possibly have been anything like the doubling of that area between 1086 and the end of the thirteenth century. It must therefore follow that the amount of cultivated land must have been progressively declining on a per capita basis, and that in view of the absence of any decisive technological advance over this period the quantity of food produced per head of population must have also been declining.

A total population of some 6 million persons—that is, if we accept the highest possible estimate for the sake of argument—may seem to us, when compared with the total size of the country, far too low to warrant talking in terms of overpopulation, and this may be one of the reasons why writers approaching the problem through the calculation of aggregates frequently find the notion of rural over-population towards the end of the thirteenth century hard to accept. But it must be remembered that the level of medieval productivity of land was extremely low, at least three times lower than in modern times. It must also be remembered that perhaps as much as one third of the country was under the forest law and thus effectively removed from systematic exploitation.[16] Finally, it must not be overlooked that any discussion of the problem in terms of aggregates and overall averages takes no account whatsoever of great inequalities in the distribution of land; it must not be forgotten that a very high proportion of the arable land, and possibly the best part of it as well, was under the direct cultivation of the great landlords and did not contribute to the material well-being of the rural population at large.

Since we lack any national series of population figures and do not possess any series for the area under cultivation we can neither trace the decline in prosperity over time nor pin-point the period from which the turn for the worse dates, nor be precise about the rate of this deterioration; but the conclusion seems inescapable that there must have been a deterioration. The only series of figures, known to me, which can be equated with population is unfortunately a local

[15] Lennard, *Rural England*, Appendix I, p. 393.
[16] Bazeley, 'The Extent of the English Forest'.

one. It is the record of the collection of payments known as 'hundred-penny' on the bishop of Winchester's Somerset manor of Taunton. This was a payment of a penny collected at the view of frankpledge from each male villein over twelve years of age. The series begins in 1208 and shows a steady and progressive increase until the early years of the fourteenth century when, unfortunately, the payment became standardized at a fixed sum. It would obviously be quite improper to claim any national validity for this locally documented trend but in view of the complete lack of any other series of figures, local or national, the possibility must not be ruled out that it constitutes an example of more than purely local validity.[17]

3

However, most adherents of the view that widespread distress, rather than general prosperity, was characteristic of the position of the English peasantry towards the end of the thirteenth century, came to that view not through the study of aggregate and demographic change as such but through the study of local conditions as depicted in countless manorial documents from all parts of the country. What, briefly, is the main evidence for their views? It falls under three heads: evidence of the growing shortage of land, evidence that rural population was becoming largely one of smallholders, and miscellaneous evidence of rural poverty.

The argument that land shortage was rapidly developing over the latter part of the thirteenth century rests mainly on the evidence of the rapid increase in land values. Since in the Middle Ages sales of freehold land took the form of grants of land by charter, and sales of villein land of surrender and re-granting in the manorial court, we have no record of the price of land and cannot plot its changes. There is, however, another way of getting at land values: by examining the movement of rents. Since, however, rents in this period were customary rents (i.e. they were fixed by custom and could not easily be changed) the best way of getting at the real changes in land value is not through the rent proper (redditus assisus) but through entry fines.

Since medieval landlords found it difficult to adjust rents to the real, market, value of the holdings involved, they reacted to this predicament exactly in the same way in which present-day landlords in periods of rent controls reacted to theirs: by charging key-money. In

[17] J. Z. Titow, 'Some Evidence of the Thirteenth Century Population Increase', *Economic History Review*, 2nd series, XIV, 1961.

the period under our consideration every new tenant, before he could enter upon his holding, had to pay an entry fine (or a relief if the land was freehold). It is the very steep and progressive rise in the level of entry fines which is our main argument in support of the view that there must have been progressive land shortage over the thirteenth century. It is the very high level of these fines at times as high as £80 per virgate—which leads us to believe that in some localities this land shortage reached the state of an acute land hunger.

In the article which I have already mentioned Miss Harvey has argued that this view is not valid. It seems to me that she has misunderstood the very argument she attacks.

Miss Harvey succeeds in showing that on most manors entry fines were not very heavy in the late thirteenth and early fourteenth century, and she argues that the evidence of entry fines does not, therefore, support the view that land shortage was developing over the thirteenth century. Miss Harvey is quite right in her statement that entry fines were generally fairly low; I could in fact add a large number of examples of my own in support of this assertion. But this is not the crux of the matter. I know of no medievalist of repute— certainly not Professor Postan—to have claimed that entry fines were high *everywhere*. What has been claimed by those who support the view of growing land shortage is that a *rising* level of entry fines must be regarded as evidence of growing scarcity of land, and a *very high level* of fines must indicate an acute land shortage. The crux of the matter is not that entry fines were at a low level on most estates but that they were at a high level on some. Professor Postan and those of us who hold similar views on the subject have always been aware of the former.

The real problem is how to reconcile the existence of some places with a high level of entry fines with the presence of a relatively low level of fines elsewhere. As I see it there are two alternatives:

(i) We could regard the low level of fines as representing the real value of land and regard instances to the contrary as artificially inflated. Or

(ii) We could regard the high level of fines as representing the real land value and regard instances to the contrary as artificially depressed.

Let us look at the arguments for and against each of these alternatives. We must guard, however, against attaching undue importance to the fact of mere numerical preponderance of places with a low level of fines over places with a high level of fines. The problem is primarily one of logic. I can think of no way at all in which a landlord could artificially push entry fines to an exorbitant level well above the market value of land, impose it successfully on the unwilling peasantry, and maintain it at this high level over a large area for at least three-quarters of a century. On the other hand, it is easy to find reasons why the general level of entry fines could remain low in spite of the rising demand for land.

Apart from the difficulty of envisaging the mechanism through which entry fines could be artificially maintained above the level of the market value of land, there are at least two good reasons to regard this as most unlikely. We do know what form taking up of land under compulsion took in the thirteenth and fourteenth centuries. Late thirteenth and early fourteenth-century accounts on various Winchester manors offer many examples of peasants being compelled to take up vacant holdings for which no takers could be found in the ordinary way. In every case the new, and reluctant, tenant was elected to the holding by the community of the villagers (*homagium*) and the entry fine was either waived altogether or fixed at a purely nominal sum.[18]

Secondly, the very marked drop in the level of entry fines both on the manors of Glastonbury Abbey and at Taunton—our main areas of high fines—after the Black Death suggests that they were determined by economic factors and not by the *fiat* of the landlord. After all, the landlords in question can be safely assumed to have been as powerful, and as greedy, after 1348 as they were before that date.

One could quote many examples of high fines on the Glastonbury estates and at Taunton. At Taunton the highest fine per virgate was £40 and fines of over £10 were very frequent. A convenient illustration of the level of fines on the Glastonbury manors—convenient for it comes ready-made, so to speak—occurs in the 1348 court roll. On the composite manor of Brent the Abbot's officials have drawn up what can only be described as an inventory of widows. The widows were assessed on their customary holdings and those too old to remarry had no values entered against them. Of the 21 widows listed with values given:[19]

1 was assessed at the rate of £2 per virgate

---

[18] e.g. Hampshire Record Office, MS. Eccl. Comm. 2/159343, Ivinghoe: '*Et memorandum. Johannes filius Roisie de Hanecombe pro 1 messuagio et 1 virgata terre in Hanecombe que fuerunt in manus domini et ad que electus est per totum homagium habendis, ideo finis nullus*'. (1330/31).

[19] Longleat MS. 11179. I am grateful to Professor Postan for allowing me to use his transcript of this document. The rates are calculated on the basis of a 40-acre virgate and ignore additional meadow; the valuations used are those of the Cellarer.

2 at the rate of £13 6s 8d (20 marks)

1 at the rate of about £17 15s 6d (6 marks for 1 messuage, 9 acres)

1 at the rate of about £20 (10 marks for 1 fardel of 13 acres)

1 at the rate of about £20 16s 8d. (25 marks for ½ virgate of 32 acres)

1 at the rate of £21 16s 8d (32 marks)

6 at the rate of £26 13s 4d (40 marks)

1 at the rate of about £25 (£10 for 1 fardel of 16 acres)

1 at the rate of about £30 9s 6d (20 marks for 1 messuage, 17½ acres)

1 at the rate of about £30 13s 4d (£10 for 1 messuage, 13 acres)

1 at the rate of about £33 6s 8d (£5 for 1 messuage, 6 acres)

2 at the rate of £40

1 at the rate of £42 13s 4d (64 marks)

1 at the rate of £80

No widow ever fetched anything like these high fines on the Glastonbury manors after 1349; are we to assume that they had suddenly lost all their charms? Obviously not. What happened is that the bottom fell out of the land market.

Another very significant fact to notice about these entry fines charged for widows with their land is that the assessment was done by sworn jurors who were to give their verdict on oath as to the names of widows, their holdings, and 'reasonable fines' which could be expected for them.[20] Only in two instances did the jurors disagree with the Cellarer's valuation and returned a lower assessment; in all the remaining cases the high fines, far from representing an arbitrary exaction of a rapacious landlord, represent the villagers' own assessment of what was 'reasonable' in the circumstances: In one instance, in fact, the Cellarer agreed to lower his own assessment, to that proposed by the villagers.

Are there any obstacles to the acceptance of the view that a relatively low level of entry fines on so many manors could have been artificially depressed rather than representing the real market value of the land? I do not think so. Such an assumption would be, in fact, in keeping with the general tendency, clearly visible throughout the Middle Ages, for various payments and obligations to become standardized and fixed under the influence of custom. Over the twelfth and thirteenth centuries we can see this happening to rents (*redditus assisus*), tithingpenny payments, tallages, marriage fines,

---

[20] '*Jurati et quesiti de nominibus viduarum huius manerii et tenuris earundem et de finibus rationabiliter pro tenuris earum factis*'.

and even to heriots. There is no reason to believe that entry fines were the only payments to escape this general tendency. The fact that on the manors with a low level of fines escheated holdings invariably commanded fines well above the average run of fines for those manors seems to add support to this assumption. One should rather wonder how was it that on some manors the landlords seem to have succeeded in staving off this development.

Apart from the standarizing influence of custom which may have exerted its influence on the level of fines there are, as well, other factors which could keep the level of fines low in spite of the rising demand for land. Entry fines, after all, are like key-money in our own times; they must be related to the quality of the accommodation offered. In the medieval conditions which we are considering, the desirability of the holding, and thus the magnitude of the fine which could be expected for it, would be affected by a variety of factors. The quality of the land itself, the size of the virgate, the extent of obligations, and whether the tenant's resources were already being tapped through tallage—all these would play a leading part in deter-mining the magnitude of the fine asked for a given holding in a given locality. The age of the settlement itself and the presence, or absence, of colonizable resources in the early thirteenth century would be yet another important consideration; if opportunity for large scale reclamation existed in the early thirteenth century this would have kept fines for customary holdings at a low level.[21]

But there is one very important consideration overlooked by Miss Harvey, though she could hardly have done otherwise since the Winchester documents are the only ones sufficiently early to illustrate the point. Low as the general level of entry fines may seem to have been in the late thirteenth and early fourteenth cen-turies, there is a very strong possibility that this represents, nevertheless, a considerable increase on the level prevailing at the beginning of the thirteenth century. It is clearly so on all the Winchester manors and could well have been the case elsewhere.

The upward trend of fines between the very beginning and the later part of the thirteenth century is unfortunately difficult to demonstrate satisfactorily. No court rolls exist for the Winchester estates and all we have are the summaries of court fines in the account rolls. These summaries are, at first, very laconic and over the first half of the thirteenth century do not normally specify the size of the hold-ing for which a fine is recorded; it is thus impossible to graph changes

[21] J. Z. Titow, 'Some Differences between Manors and their Effects on the Condition of the Peasant in the Thirteenth Century', *Essays in Agrarian History*, I, 39–51.

in the rate charged per virgate. However, the unspecified holdings in the early part of the century must have included the usual scattering of virgated holdings, very much in the same way as they did later on when descriptions are given. Since all entry fines in the early thirteenth century are very low the rate per virgate could not have been very much higher, and the increase between the early and the closing decades of the century is both unmistakable and clearly greater than the general increase in prices over the same period. It must therefore, be regarded as something more than merely a cost-of-living adjustment on the part of the landlord.

Very occasionally a comparison in terms of fines per virgate is possible. For example, the average fines per virgate on the bishop of Winchester's Wiltshire manor of Fonthill, for the period 1277–1348, was only 24s 4d with the fines ranging from 8s to 46s 8d.[22] This may seem very low indeed; but in 1219, one of those rare instances in the early thirteenth century when the size of the holding was specified, three virgated holdings were acquired at the rate per virgate of 1s 8d, 1s, and 1s respectively.[23]

4

While it might be possible to regard the presence of a high level of entry fines on some estates as perhaps no more than indicative of the worsening of the situation with regard to availability of land, the presence of a large number of smallholders in almost every thirteenth-century survey, custumal or rental known to us, must be looked upon as a virtually conclusive evidence of widespread hardship. There can be no doubt that smallholders constituted a very high proportion of the peasant population by the middle of the thirteenth century. The figures recently published by Professor Postan show that tenants with a quarter-virgate or less constituted some 45 per cent of the total tenant population on a sample embracing some 104 manors taken from eight estates in different parts of the country.[24]

On the twenty-five Winchester manors for which such calculations can be made on the basis of mid-thirteenth century custumals, tenants with 10 acres or less accounted for just over 50 per cent of the total tenant population, the figure on some individual manors

---

[22] This excludes holdings to which new tenants were elected.

[23] Hampshire Record Office, MS. Eccl. Comm. 2/159275; the fines were: 10d. for a half-virgate, 1s. for 1 virgate, and 6d. for a half-virgate.

[24] *Cambridge Ec. History of Europe*, I, p. 619.

being as high as 85·9 per cent in the most extreme case.[25] It is perhaps worth pointing out in this connection that on the manor of Bishop's Waltham the proportion of smallholders with less than ten acres each had risen between the custumal of 1259 and the rental of 1332 from 42·6 per cent to 51·5 per cent. Since most of the figures relating to smallholders are usually based on mid-thirteenth century surveys they may not reflect fully the severity of the situation towards the end of the century or in the early fourteenth century.

Using the non-manorial evidence from the Hundred Rolls, Professor Kosminsky has estimated that tenants with a quarter-virgate or less accounted for 46 per cent of the total tenant population[26] which, again, is almost exactly the figure obtained by Professor Postan from quite different sources and for quite different parts of the country.

An objection could perhaps be raised at this point that the upper limit of a quarter-virgate (that is between $7\frac{1}{2}$ acres and 10 acres) is too high to qualify for the designation 'smallholder'. The answer must be that the term 'smallholding' must be understood relatively. In the context of the standard of living debate the significant entity is the holding representing subsistence level in the conditions prevailing at the time, and anybody having such a holding or less must clearly be considered as living on or below subsistence level. The reason why historians nowadays seldom bother to differentiate among tenants with less than a quarter-virgate, and begin with the quarter-virgate as their lowest category, is that it is now generally recognized by historians of medieval rural society that the lowest significant demarcation line is that dividing those on or below subsistence level from those above it, and because of the widespread realization that this dividing line cannot be placed lower than the quarter-virgate.

Professor Russell is quite wrong when he states 'that on the question of subsistence there is apparent agreement that a tenant and his family needed five to ten acres, preferably nearer ten' and that 'since those who have so calculated had a family of five in mind, the subsistence base was one or two acres to a person, preferably nearer two'.[27] Some leading authorities on medieval agrarian society place it in fact even higher than the quarter-virgate, or ten acres, mentioned above. Professor Hilton, for example, talks of the half-virgater 'as living on the very edge of subsistence'.[28] I also strongly

[25] Calculated from the custumals in Br. Mus. MS. Egerton 2418.

[26] Kosminsky, p. 288. See also Professor Hallam's findings on the amount of land per head of population in some Fenland areas: H. E. Hallam, 'Population Density in Medieval Fenland', *Economic History Review*, 2nd series, XIV, 1961.

[27] Russell, 'Pre-plague Population', p. 20.

[28] Hilton, *A Medieval Society*, p. 114.

suspect that Professor Postan has lowered his dividing line to the quarter-virgate only to strengthen his own case by arguing from the position least favourable to his argument. I have no doubt on my own part that it should not be drawn lower than the quarter-virgate at the lowest.

What are the reasons behind this conviction? We have no figures which would allow us to reconstruct peasant budgets. We can, however, attempt some estimate of the order of magnitudes involved both, on the side of his income and his out-goings. There are four basic elements entering into any such analysis: (i) estimate of the productivity of peasant land, (ii) estimate of the total commitments *vis-à-vis* the landlord which have to be met before the peasant's own needs are satisfied, (iii) estimate of the minimum subsistence requirements of a single person in terms of a purely cereal diet, and (iv) estimate of the average size of the peasant household for which his holding had to provide.

The problem of determining the minimum size of a 'subsistence' holding for a peasant household can thus be expressed in the form of two equations:

$$\frac{C + S}{Y} \times F = A, \text{ and } A \times H = TA$$

where: C=compulsory out-goings, in terms of the quantity of grain which had to be surrendered to the landlord before the peasant's own needs could be met.

S=minimum subsistence requirement per year for one person.
Y=average yield per acre.
F=allowance for the fallow ($\times 2$ on the two-field basis, $\times 1\cdot5$ on the three-field basis).
A=minimum number of acres needed per person.
H=the household mutiplier (i.e. the average number of persons per household).
TA=total acreage required for subsistence of a peasant household.

The problem of productivity of peasant land need not occupy us long. I know of no instance in which productivity of peasant land can be calculated, but we have very precise knowledge of the productivity of demesne land and there is every reason to believe that the productivity of peasant holdings was, if anything, lower.

The average net yield (i.e. after deduction of tithe and seed for the next year's sowing) per acre, on the Winchester estates taken as a whole for the period 1209–1350, was as follows:

wheat: about 7 bushels
barley: about 10 bushels
oats: about 5 bushels

The medieval peasant would have grown all these three crops:
wheat as his cash crop, barley for his own consumption, and oats to
feed his animals, if he had any, in winter. It is difficult to speculate
what proportion of each he would grow but assuming that he grew
more barley than oats or wheat we can assume that his net yield per
acre would have been of the order of some 8 bushels of mixed grain.

His compulsory out-goings—compulsory for he would forfeit his
holding, and his means of livelihood, if he defaulted on his payments
to the lord—are probably the most difficult item to generalize about,
since the severity of burdens incumbent on holdings differed from
place to place, and since some of them, like entry fines for example,
had to be spread over an unknown number of years representing the
total duration of his tenancy. All one can say with certainty is that
such payments represented a heavy drain on a peasant's resources.
Professor Postan reached the conclusion that 'even without ... extra-
manorial obligations (tithes, taxes) the money dues of a villein
tenant would absorb a very large proportion of his gross output', and
he goes on to say 'that the proportion varied a great deal, but the
average was very frequently near or above 50 per cent mark'.[29]
Professor Hilton came to the conclusion that a half-virgater com-
muting his services in full would not have had enough left over for
his own, and his family's sustenance.[30] These seem fair assessments
for villein holdings burdened with the usual assortment of dues
(rents, tallage, entry fines, and various miscellaneous amercements)
and commutation payments; on holdings not burdened with commutation payments, and on free holdings, the proportion representing compulsory outgoings should be brought down to perhaps some
25 per cent of gross output.

Contemporary documents do not make it clear how much grain
per person, per year, must be regarded as the barest minimum for survival, but they do contain information which seems to indicate what
quantity, in terms of a purely cereal diet,[31] the contemporaries seemed
to have regarded as such. There are three ways in which the problem can, or has been, approached: through liveries given to manorial

[29] *Cambridge Ec. History of Europe*, I, p. 603.
[30] *A Medieval Society*, p. 114.
[31] One must fully endorse Professor Hilton's statement that 'there can be
little doubt that the mass of the population lived primarily on a carbohydrate
diet consisting mainly of foodstuffs and drink made from barley and oats',
A Medieval Society, p. 111.

F

servants, through purchase of corrodies (i.e. annuities in kind), and through surrenders of holdings recorded with details of maintenance agreements.

Manorial liveries on the Winchester estates were given at the rate of one quarter every eight weeks in the early thirteenth century, and one quarter every ten weeks later on. On other estates the rate was often one quarter every twelve weeks. I do not, however, think the use of this type of evidence very helpful. The scale of such liveries is clearly more than sufficient for the needs of one person and must therefore be regarded as a family allowance; on the other hand, since such liveries were additional to a stipend in cash, reduction in rent, and the produce of the servant's own holding, they clearly cannot be regarded as the minimum necessary for the sustenance of a household.

Corrodies and maintenance agreements offer better guidance to what must be regarded as the minimum requirement, but the trouble with using this type of evidence is that the quantity allowed is clearly linked to the purchasing price, in the case of corrodies, and the size of the holding, in the case of surrenders. Persons purchasing corrodies at a high price and tenants surrendering substantial holdings, could both expect provisions allowing for a comfortable retirement. On the other hand many surrenders involving small holdings made it possible for the recipient to give only so much and no more in return.

A modest corrody purchased from Winchcombe Abbey in the 1270s consisted of one monk's loaf (2½lb or about 2 qr 5 bushels a year) daily, a gallon of beer, and a dish from the Abbot's kitchen, a robe a year and 6s 8d for linen and shoes. Modest as it is it clearly represents more than the minimum and was recorded as being on the same scale as the middling servants of the Abbey. A corrody probably approaching the bare minimum of existence was that purchased from the priory at Worcester in 1317 consisting of 'a weekly allowance of four servants' loaves, six gallons of beer and an allowance from the kitchen ... probably a *Ferculum* (a dish of mixed pottage)[32] The rule laid down for the tenants of Worcester Cathedral Priory required the heir taking over his mother's holding to provide her with 12 bushels of rye, one of barley and 8 of oats annually.[33] On the Ramsey Abbey manor of Upwood, in a dispute concerning the rights of a widow who had surrendered her one-virgate holding, the jurors declared that by the custom of the manor she was entitled to receive 1½ quarters of mixed grain a year.[34]

[32] Hilton, *A Medieval Society*, p. 112.
[33] ibid., p. 112.
[34] Raftis, *Tenure and Mobility*, p. 46.

Manorial court rolls are full of surrenders of holdings and it is quite clear that all cases of *total* surrender must have involved provisions for the support of the surrendering person, but the number of such agreements recorded in full is not very great. A sufficient number, however, is available to give us a good idea of the quantities usually involved.

Professor Raftis gives details of eight such agreements on Ramsey Abbey manors. Two of these should probably be disregarded since they are instances of provisions made for non-inheriting brothers and sisters, and one clearly represents a very comfortable allowance; the remaining cases make provision at the rate of 2½ quarters, 2 quarters, 1½ quarters, and 1 quarter annually.[35]

Winchester records provide details of over thirty such agreements. If we disregard those which clearly make provisions on a very comfortable scale, as well as those which relate to tiny holdings and obviously represent the holder's capacity to pay rather than the true level of the recipient's needs, it would appear that an allowance of about 1 quarter of wheat or barley a year plus a cash payment of about 2s 6d (an equivalent of an additional half a quarter of grain) for shoes and clothing was regarded as the barest minimum. This agrees well with the evidence of Ramsey Abbey estates.

The final, and greatest, difficulty connected with estimating the size of a 'subsistence' holding concerns the size of the peasant household. Among contemporary scholars Professor Russell is the only one to have persistently maintained that a multiplier of 3·5 is the most likely figure for converting tenants into households,[36] in spite of mounting criticisms of his view, and the general rejection of his index as too low, by leading medievalists specializing in manorial history,[37] and in spite of direct contemporary evidence to the contrary. His considered view has recently been stated in an article which neatly summarizes all the important points in his argument.[38]

Professor Russell justifies his choice mainly on two grounds: (i) by a statistical argument involving a large number of frequently devious calculations of such variables as sex ratios, marriage rates, expectation of life tables, etc., which he had constructed on the basis of information concerning heirs and heiresses to the estates of the tenants-in-chief contained in the Inquisitions Post Mortem, and (ii)

[35] Raftis, *Tenure and Mobility*, pp. 42–46.
[36] Russell, *British Medieval Population*, pp. 22–31.
[37] e.g. Postan, *Cambridge Ec. History of Europe*, I, p. 562; Hilton, *A Medieval Society*, p. 92; H. E. Hallam, 'Some Thirteenth-Century Censuses', *Economic History Review*, 2nd series, X, 1958. See also: J. Krause, 'The Medieval Household: Large or Small', *Economic History Review*, 2nd series, IX, 1957.
[38] Russell, 'Pre-plague Population'.

by reference to the alleged arrangement of taxpayers by households in the poll tax returns of 1337.

This is obviously not the place to discuss all his assertions fully, one by one and point by point, but some indication must be given why they cannot be accepted as they stand. The first objection is this. If the purpose of the exercise is to find out whether there had, or had not, been chronic poverty among a large section of the peasantry, the use of highly speculative statistics relating to a group which was socially and economically quite different from the peasantry—a group which is, in fact, by definition not likely ever to have suffered privation—is clearly quite inadmissible. Secondly, to a person trained as a historian, to use such indirect hypothetical data to correct impressions obtained from contemporary (though non-statistical) evidence directly related to the group under investigation, is equally wrong; it is the latter which should be used to correct the former.

What makes Professor Russell's arguments particularly objectionable at times, from a historian's point of view, is that what is pure supposition in one place invariably turns up in another as the statistical basis from which yet another supposition is deduced and, in the end, the highly sophisticated statistical jugglery involved in this method frequently hides from the reader the meagre factual basis of the many-tiered final conclusion.

For example, when discussing manorial surveys Russell notices a high proportion of women among the tenants (17·3 per cent); he assumes that they were all unmarried; and he then suggests that an equal number of men among the tenants must also have been unmarried. This is strengthened by an assertion that 'the percentage of married folk was low before the plague' and that 'young men entered their holdings rather early in life which must mean that older men surrendered theirs for cottage-life'. All this leads to the conclusion that 'nearly 35 per cent of tenants were unmarried' and that, therefore, 'one may anticipate a low index number for the tenant'.[39] In fact, only the first proposition—that women represent a high proportion of the tenant population and that they would have been unmarried—is based on direct evidence. There is not a shred of direct evidence to support the remaining assumptions which could, at best, be described as no more than likely guesses—appeals to Russell's own expectation of life tables, sex ratios, etc., notwithstanding.

The same is true of the other mainstay of Professor Russell's

[39] Russell, 'Pre-plague Population', p. 3.

argument concerning the index figures for converting tenants into households—the alleged evidence on the size of the households in the poll tax returns of 1377.

We do not know how the tax was collected but Professor Russell is probably right when he suggests that a house canvass would have been the most likely way. The assumption which Professor Russell has no right to make, however, is that the size of households can be ascertained on the basis of the poll tax returns. There is nothing explicit or implicit in these documents to indicate that the taxpayers listed in them are grouped together by households or, more important still, to indicate where one household ends and another begins, if they were arranged by households. All we are given is a list of persons on whom the tax was levied. True, some persons are linked together in payment but this is only to have been expected; after all, it is only natural that the husband would have paid for his wife and their children. What is utterly unwarranted is to assume that persons linked together in payment represent necessarily separate and complete households, and persons not visibly linked to anybody must necessarily represent separate single-person households. Russell himself recognizes this difficulty when he says that 'in identifying occupants of one habitation the chief difficulty is caused by the appearance of single persons who may either be staying alone in a cottage or be sharing the dwelling with persons mentioned just above'.[40] They could have equally well been one or the other; there is absolutely nothing in the tax returns themselves to justify a decision either way. Since it makes a tremendous difference to the index figure whether one assumes one or the other, the only legitimate conclusion must be that so far as the size of the households is concerned the evidence of the poll tax returns is no evidence at all. There is no reason to assume that medieval peasant households were restricted to parents and their children alone; they could equally well have included other relatives, servants, and farm-hands living in with the family. Yet Russell presents his *assumptions* concerning the groupings of taxpayers into households as something done by the documents themselves[41] and uses the index figure so obtained as a criterion in deciding the veracity of other evidence.

From a historian's point of view, all discussion of the position of the peasantry in the thirteenth century must start with the documents relating directly to the peasantry—manorial surveys (custumals,

---

[40] Russell, *British Medieval Population*, p. 122.

[41] This seems to me a fair comment since Professor Russell clearly considers the evidence of the poll tax returns the best available on the size of the household; see *British Medieval Population*, p. 26.

rentals and extents) and manorial court rolls. Professor Russell's handling of such material is in my view at fault.

His argument runs somewhat like this. Since our index figure for converting tenants into total population is an average figure by which all tenants are multiplied indiscriminately, the effect of large house-holds will be countered by the effect of single-person households, and he contends that the very high proportion of the latter will bring the index figure down to about 3·5. In this connection it is really necessary to distinguish, as Russell does not, between two distinct though closely related, issues: what is the proper multiplier for converting tenants into total population and what is the most likely size of a medieval peasant household. Or, to put the question somewhat differently, how far is it correct to equate tenants with single households and what is the average size of a household. I find Russell's argument unacceptable on two counts; he underestimates the high element in the multiplier and he grossly overestimates the low element.

Manorial surveys list holdings rather than tenants; that is, the number of the latter is always smaller than of the former since one and the same tenant frequently holds more than one holding. When the number of holdings is reduced to tenants practically every survey will produce its crop of tenants with more than one holding and more than one dwelling. Since such multi-dwelling tenants are not likely to have been moving their residence from house to house in progression it seems reasonable to assume that they sub-let such dwellings to other villagers or settled their own relatives in them. Some surveys have few such tenants but others a large number. For example, on the bishop of Winchester's Hampshire manor of Waltham the total of 705 holdings entered in the rental of c.1331–1332 is reduceable to 363 tenants of whom nineteen held between them holdings involving some 70 dwellings (i.e. cottages or mess-uages). Such tenants must be looked upon as representing not a single household each but as many households as there are dwell-ings on their holdings. The number of such multi-household tenants vary from manor to manor and can be small on many of them, but, on the other hand, I have yet to see one completely without them. In fact, surveys with a very small number of multi-household tenants are frequently the surveys with suspiciously low number of cottages; it could be that the latter are concealed behind the main tenancies in the survey. There are instances when this is explicitly stated to have been so. For example, a mid-thirteenth century custumal of the Glastonbury Abbey manor of Damerham under one of its sub-divisions where only virgates are recorded states bluntly: 'there are also

32 cottagers holding of the villeins.[42] The effect of such multi-household tenancies, whether explicit or concealed, on the multiplier used to convert tenants into total population must clearly be taken into consideration. Russell seems completely unaware of their existence.

Secondly, Professor Russell greatly overestimates the numerical significance of the single-person households. In the context of the standard of living controversy this is, of course, the only significant issue since smallholders would, by definition, be in the single-household category of tenants. Russell argues that women represent some 17·3 per cent of tenants in manorial surveys and that most of them would be widows living on their own in a cottage to which they had moved after surrendering their holdings to the heirs, and that they would thus constitute single-person households. He then assumes that a similar number of men would be widowers (why, for symmetry's sake?) who have done exactly the same thing. This is virtually the whole extent of his analysis of the evidence of the manorial surveys. The position in fact is more complex and far less favourable to Russell's argument.

Though some of the women tenants were probably unmarried girls and thus clearly constituted single-person households, Russell is undoubtedly right in assuming that most of them were widows. I do think, however, that his 17·3 per cent is far too high a figure on average. On a random sample of thirteen manors chosen from the estates of the bishop of Winchester, Glastonbury Abbey and the bishopric of Worcester, the overall percentage was only 12·1 per cent, though the figures ranged from the very low figure of 6·4 per cent (Taunton) to the very high figure of 21·6 per cent (Bishopstone); most manors, however, fell between 9 and 15 per cent.[43]

The second, and more important, point is that by no means all of the widows were cottagers, as Russell assumes; on my sample of thirteen manors 66·2 per cent of women tenants were tenants of standard customary holdings of 5 acres or more (i.e. I have counted any holding below 5 acres among cottages), and some were very substantial indeed. Only 33·8 per cent were cottagers (or slightly better than cottagers) and even then this figure would have been much lower but for the fact that my sample included the manor of Bishop's Waltham on which there was an unusually large concentra-

---

[42] Br. Mus. MS. Additional 17450, f. 190b.

[43] The manors are; Winchester: Bishop's Waltham, Taunton, Bishopstone, North Waltham, Alresford, Downton, and Mardon, Br. Mus. MS. Egerton 2418. Glastonbury: Wringtone, Ashbury, Damerham, and Brent (comprising: East Brent, South Brent, Burghes and Lymplesham), Br. Mus. MS. Additional 17450. Worcester: Bishop's Cleeve 1299, Blockley 1299, Hollings, *The Red Book of Worcester*, pp. 327 and 295.

tion of cottages around the market place in Waltham itself. While the assumption that widows occupying cottages could, in some cases, represent single-person households may be acceptable, such an assumption is clearly less likely to hold good in the case of more substantial widows and must be invalid in the case of widows who were multi-dwelling tenants.

The assumption that an equal percentage of men tenants must be widowers and should be considered as representing single-person households is pure guesswork and has no basis in documentary evidence.

The most serious objection to Russell's assumption that widows and widowers must represent single-person households concerns the mechanism through which, according to Russell, they came to occupy their cottages. Russell argues that the reason why such tenants must be considered as single-person households is because they were settled in their cottages by the new tenants (usually sons) to whom they have surrendered their holdings. On this point Russell is, in my view, entirely at fault.

Manorial surveys show the position at one point of time only, they do not indicate how the tenants came into possession of their holdings; this can be ascertained only by a systematic investigation of entry fines. Such a systematic study of the provenance of holdings clearly reveals that this method of providing for the aged was quite exceptional, it happened only in the case of multi-dwelling tenancies and even then only occasionally. What happened in most cases was that the parent surrendered his holding to the heir and either retained a part *of it* for the duration of his life, or was provided with a room or a cottage by the new heir *out of what the heir had received from him or what he already had*. Thus, far from being set up as independent tenants, the aged were provided for out of the existing tenancies and swelled the number of dependents of the nominal tenant —the heir. Thus, such widows and widowers—the true single-person households, if they had a full cottage to themselves—would not have appeared as tenants, at all, had a survey been drawn at the time.

The vast majority of widows and widowers who do appear in the surveys are there either as tenants of holdings acquired in the normal way (in the case of widowers), or (in the case of widows) because they had obtained them on the death of their husbands. This creates a very strong presumption, almost a certainty, that in most cases— far from being the sole occupiers of their holdings—they represent the normal-size households minus one spouse. This assumption is further strengthened by the fact that widows and widowers frequently marry off their daughters, settle land on their children, or pass it on eventually by inheritance or surrender to sons and daughters who suddenly materialize out of the thin air; quite clearly they have been there all the time concealed from view as dependents of the nominal tenant.

All the above considerations, particularly the presence in the surveys of multi-household tenants and the fact that the aged were provided for within existing tenancies, makes the acceptance of Russell's view that a large proportion of tenants enumerated in the surveys were the sole occupiers of their holdings unacceptable. If Russell's argument needed some 36 per cent of single-person households to counteract the effect of large families and bring the index figure down to 3·5 on average, the reduction of that percentage to a far lower figure must obviously have the effect of raising the index figure considerably.

But we do have direct, contemporary evidence that the index figure must be higher than 3·5. Professor Hallam has discovered and analysed what is so far the only known English census of medieval peasant households. It was drawn up for the benefit of the Prior of Spalding on his three manors of Spalding, Moulton and Weston, in the second half of the thirteenth century. In each case the average size of the household was far above Russell's proposed 3·5: it was 4·37 in Weston, 4·72 in Moulton, and 4·81 in Spalding. The overall average for the three manors taken together was 4·68.[44] Russell refused to accept these figures arguing that they are inaccurate; but I do not find his arguments convincing.[45]

If we accept the index figure of 4·5 as the right one—and it seems to me that we must—then the total acreage representing subsistence level of a household, in terms of land alone will be:[46]

on the two-field system:

$$\frac{8 \text{ bushels } + c. \ 4 \text{ bushels}}{8} \times 2 = 3 \text{ acres per person}$$

$$\times 4 \cdot 5 = 13\tfrac{1}{2} \text{ acres per household}$$

on the three-field system:

$$\frac{8 \text{ bushels } + c. \ 4 \text{ bushels}}{8} \times 1 \cdot 5 = 2\tfrac{1}{2} \text{ acres per person}$$

$$\times 4 \cdot 5 = 10 \text{ acres per household}$$

[44] Hallam, 'Some Thirteenth-Century Censuses' p. 340.
[45] J. C. Russell, 'Demographic Limitations of the Spalding Serf Lists', *Economic History Review*, 2nd series, XV, 1962. See also Hallam's reply ibid., XVI, 1963.
[46] See p. 80 above.

This is a minimum estimate since both the eight bushels required per person, and the assessment of the out-goings as only 33 per cent of the gross output, must be regarded as very low estimates, and the calculation makes no allowance for clothing, repairs or replacement of farm tools, or fodder for the tenant's animals. It is because, in the conditions of medieval agriculture and land-holding, for reasons outlined above, a fairly substantial holding was required to support a family at the barest minimum of subsistence that the very high proportion of smallholders in medieval England assumes such sinister significance.

The opponents of the view that there had been widespread poverty and hardship in the late thirteenth and early fourteenth century England, are of course aware of the difficulty created by the un-disputed presence, all over the country, of a very large number of peasants with thoroughly inadequate holdings. They deal with this difficulty in different ways.

The way in which Professor Russell disposes of the problem is, frankly, astonishing. He accepts Professor Kosminsky's sample of 13,504 landholders, with its 4,929 smallholders, as representative and as illustrative of the problem at large. The smallholders in this sample average two acres each; this means that 36.5 per cent of peasant households had no more than two acres each to support at least 3.5 persons (to use Russell's own multiplier for the sake of argument). Nobody familiar with medieval conditions can accept that amount of land per household as even approaching the barest subsistence level. According to Professor Russell, however, this is not the case. Why? Because the *average* number of acres per household for the group represented by the *whole sample* is some fifteen acres.[47] This is as if somebody today had said: 'We know that there are some 5000 slum families in the city living on £5 assistance money a week, but they are really quite well-off because the *average* weekly income per family for the *whole city* works out at £40 a week.' In such a context overall averages are quite meaningless since they do not take into account the inequalities—real life inequalities—in the distri-bution of wealth. Ten medieval peasants of whom one had ninety-one acres and the remaining nine one acre each, would not constitute a group of ten peasants well off on ten average acres each, but one village Croesus and nine wretched small-holders struggling to sur-vive on inadequate resources.

Miss Harvey is also aware of the problem of the smallholders, and her attempt to tackle it is far more sensible. She queries, in effect, the propriety of discussing the problem exclusively in terms of land.

[47] Russell, 'Pre-plague Population', p. 20.

This is a very traditional line of argument though her reasons for being sceptical about the alleged widespread poverty among the smallholders appear novel. 'What makes it difficult (she tells us) to accept the prevalence of small-holdings as index of overpopulation is the failure of the regions where they had truly proliferated to show signs of distress in the early fourteenth century.'[48] But signs of distress are plainly there if only one has the eyes to see them. The very examples which Miss Harvey adduces to support her claim seem to me to prove the opposite case. Miss Harvey seems to be arguing two points: that the inclusion of a large number of smallholders in the subsidy returns of 1332 show that many smallholders were not poverty-stricken, and that the appearance of the same individual smallholders in consecutive documents indicates the same thing. Neither argument seems to me particularly valid. Even if one accepts the evidence of the subsidy rolls at its face value—and they are notoriously unreliable in respect of whom they include and whom they exclude—the samples cited by Miss Harvey all show that the great majority of the smallholders was too poor to be taxed, even though a number of them was taxed. Secondly, it seems quite wrong, unless the amounts paid clearly indicate this, to regard mere inclusion as a sign of being well-off. To qualify for inclusion in the Subsidy of 1332 a peasant had to possess goods to the value of 10s or more, but this represents no more than an ox or a horse (at current market values) and possession of such an animal is quite compatible with chronic poverty. As for the argument that presence of the same smallholders in consecutive documents implies that they were doing fine, one can only reply that this is a *non sequitur*; it certainly does indicate survival, and the persons in question may have been doing fine, but they could have, equally well, died of starvation the day after the second document was drawn up.

I take it as axiomatic that for the peasantry of medieval England land was the main basis of wealth. There were, of course, exceptions: there were exceptional areas, and there were exceptional individuals, but on the whole, most of the smallholders must have led a very precarious existence.[49] All that we know of medieval productivity, of the burdens incumbent on peasant holdings, of the size of peasant

[48] Harvey, p. 27.

[49] See: M. M. Postan and J. Z. Titow, 'Heriots and Prices on Winchester Manors', *Economic History Review*, 2nd series, XI, 1959. In view of more extensive examination of heriots *inter vivos*, which I have carried out subsequently, some figures in this article need revising, but the corrections are not of the magnitude to invalidate any of our main arguments. See also a critical appraisal of the article by G. Ohlin in *Industrialization in Two Systems: Essays in Honour of Alexander Gerschenkron*, H. Rosovsky ed., New York 1966, pp. 84-89.

families, must make this conclusion inescapable. If one is to argue that the lot of the smallholder was not a bad one, the proper way to do is to show that there existed *widespread* and adequate opportunities for eking out their meagre livelihood from the land. Miss Harvey does realize this. She considers two, out of the three usually suggested alternatives. She looks at wage-earning and she looks at industrial employment. I do not think that either of these offers a satisfactory alternative, though it must be pointed out, in fairness to Miss Harvey, that it is as difficult to demonstrate that these opportunities were not adequate as it is to show that they were.

Wage-earning at best is but a seasonal remedy. But this is not the main objection. Wage-earning could be the solution to the economic difficulties of the great mass of smallholders only if there existed a correspondingly large body of men in need of their services. I do not think that this condition was satisfied until well after 1348. Before the Black Death the potentially largest employers of wage labour—the manorial demesnes—were still largely relying on customary labour. On the other hand, if one looks at the late thirteenth century custumals one finds that the very substantial tenants—so substantial that they would have to rely regularly on hired labour—are simply not there in sufficiently large numbers.

Neither, except perhaps in a few very special cases, can increased industrial employment be regarded as being of more than a marginal significance.[50] The striking expansion of the rural cloth industry came much later,[51] and there is nothing in the first available (i.e. mid-fourteenth century) figures of cloth exports to suggest a rapidly expanding rural cloth industry at the turn of the thirteenth century.

In the past, the favourite argument of those historians who believed in the Merry England of the thirteenth century, was to improve the lot of the smallholders by crediting them with a considerable income from their livestock.[52] What the smallholders could not get out of their few acres they were said to have made up for by keeping animals. This view, though never convincing to me, was at least tenable when we knew next to nothing about peasant animals. When nothing could be disproved anything was possible. Recently, however, Professor Postan's study of peasant animals[53] has lifted the whole argument from the realm of wishful-thinking into one of

[50] Postan, 'Some Economic Evidence of Declining Population', p. 232.
[51] See: E. M. Carus-Wilson, 'Evidence of Industrial Growth on Some Fifteenth-Century Manors', *Economic History Review*, 2nd series, XII, 1959.
[52] See: Kosminsky, pp. 230–237, for a critical review of J. T. Rogers', I. I. Granat's, N. S. B. Gras', and H. S. Bennett's estimates of a medieval peasant's budget.
[53] Postan, 'Village Livestock'.

documented investigation. His study clearly shows, what one would have expected to have been the case on logical grounds alone, that the peasants who were rich in terms of animals were the very same peasants who were rich in terms of land. Professor Hilton's recent study of the Midlands makes the same point[54] and, even more recently, Dr Bowden has shown, by analysing costs and profits, that the view that the smallholders could find a profitable way out of their difficulties by investing in animals is fallacious.[55]

5

If this picture of the thirteenth-century English peasantry, as consisting largely of smallholders leading a wretched existence on an inadequate number of acres, has any validity at all, would we not expect to find in our documents constant references to poverty and distress? Well, in fact, we do find such references in considerable number but they do not lend themselves to statistical treatment. No medieval documents, manorial or extra-manorial, were interested in recording paupers as such. Obviously, too, any peasant society, in any century, is likely to contain its quota of paupers. What we cannot, unfortunately, prove or disprove is whether the number of paupers in our period was progressively increasing, or that it was greater than one would normally expect to find in a reasonably prosperous peasant society. All one can say is that references to poverty, direct or indirect, in manorial documents of the late thirteenth and early fourteenth century are frequent.

The most telling piece of indirect evidence are indications of the poor quality of much of peasant land and of a possible deterioration in its quality. Miss Harvey argues that there is no evidence of widespread abandoning of land by the peasants and that, therefore, the theory of soil exhaustion finds no support in available evidence.[56] What Miss Harvey says is perfectly true but it is true only in terms of *total abandonment* of holdings. My contention is that this is precisely the way in which one should not approach the problem. Land was the main source of livelihood to the vast majority of the medieval peasantry and it is precisely the smallholder to whom his few acres would be far more precious than they would have been to a very substantial peasant. To give them up altogether would have

[54] Hilton, *A Medieval Society*, p. 110.
[55] *The Agrarian History of England and Wales*, IV, p. 671. Though Dr Bowden's analysis is concerned with sixteenth century prices and values, the argument is valid for the thirteenth century as well.
[56] Harvey, pp. 33–34.

been the most drastic step a smallholder could take; even if the land was quite exhausted the holding would still have provided him with a roof over his head and guaranteed him certain communal rights. It must be emphasized, at this point, that our documents would not record partial abandonment of tenants' land (though they might of demesne land); it is either all or nothing, the tenant either appears to have retained his holding intact or has given it up altogether. But why should we discuss the problem in terms of total abandonment only, of utter soil exhaustion, or none at all? Surely, a wide range of gradation is possible. I certainly disagree with Miss Harvey that there is no evidence of soil exhaustion—quite the contrary. Though again it must be emphasized that all evidence on this point is fortuitous and that the silence of so many documents on this point must not be construed as evidence to the contrary.

While it is perfectly true that there is little manorial evidence of total abandonment of peasant land before 1348, there is considerable evidence of some abandonment and of the difficulty of finding tenants for a large number of holdings. The best known, though probably also the least reliable, evidence of abandonment of peasant land comes from the *Nonarum Inquisitiones*—a document of 1341 connected with royal taxation.[57] The evidence of the difficulty in finding tenants comes from manorial sources. Once again the Winchester accounts, because of their far greater inclusion of incidental matter than is the case with other manorial collections, are our main source of information. On the Winchester estates in the early fourteenth century instances of purely nominal, or completely waived, entry fines become very frequent and they are accompanied in many cases by explanatory statements indicating that, either the previous tenant has given up the holding because of poverty, or that the new tenant could not be found for it in the ordinary way and had to be compelled to take it up. The number of such entries seems to have been on the increase though it must be pointed out that this could be illusory; it may represent no more than the growing willingness of the manorial clerks to be more liberal with incidental information. The frequency of such explicit cases is such as to imply that they were not merely isolated instances. On the small manor of North Waltham, for instance, to cite but an extreme case, in the period 1330 to 1348 over 50 per cent of all transactions involving standard customary holdings belonged to the category of 'unwanted' holdings.[58]

[57] In particular, see A. R. H. Baker, 'Evidence in the *Nonarum Inquisitiones* of Contracting Arable Lands in England during the Early Fourteenth Century', *Economic History Review*, 2nd series, XIX, 1966.

[58] Hampshire Record Office, MSS. Eccl. Comm. 2/159342–357.

There are two ways of looking at such entries: either one sees in them evidence of a slackening demand for land generally, or one sees them as evidence of lack of demand for specific holdings and thus, indirectly of their deterioration. The fact that there is no evidence of general abandoning of holdings, and that other holdings still command the usual—frequently quite high—entry fines seems to indicate that the latter interpretation is the right one.[59]

The acceptance of such an interpretation also finds support in what we know of demesne land. We cannot measure yields on peasant land but we can measure them on demesne land, given the right documents. Examination of full Winchester evidence leaves me in no doubt at all that the last quarter of the thirteenth century and the early part of the fourteenth century witnessed a considerable decline in the productivity of demesne land on most manors of the Winchester estates.[60] In view of the manifestly superior ability of the great landlords to maintain the productivity of their land, as against the peasants' ability to do so, is it really so presumptuous to expect some deterioration to have occurred also on peasant land? The evidence for the demesne shows that such deterioration was not necessarily restricted to the most recent acquisitions alone and the evidence of 'unwanted' holdings suggests that the same was true of peasant land.

The most common type of explicit references to poverty are court fines which were forgiven on account of the poverty of the person involved. Court rolls of various estates are full of such references and they occur with monotonous regularity in the late thirteenth and early fourteenth centuries. Apart from this one type of reference however, one is entirely at the mercy of chance. There are many other pieces of information indicating poverty but since they are utterly fortuitous they defy any attempt at statistical presentation. In one sense they are all unusual, but this does not mean that the situation they depict is necessarily untypical. Let me give but two illustrations of the sort of information I have in mind.

In 1266, on the bishop of Winchester's Oxfordshire manor of Witney, the sum of 4s 3d representing 'the residue of Peter's pence' was entered with an explanation that it was not greater 'because there were many paupers who did not possess an animal to the value

---

[59] For example, on the manor of Twyford, in 1301, John Frewyne paid a fine of 40s. for half a virgate of land while, at the same time, Robert Dygon paid only 6d. for the holding of the same size to which he had been elected by the whole tithing. Hampshire Record Office, MS. Eccl. Comm. 2/159319. Such examples could be multiplied almost *ad infinitum*.

[60] See Chapter II, p. 53.

of 30d'.[61] This explicit statement as to how the payment was collected on this manor, enables us to use it an an indicator of the direction of change in peasant prosperity. Subsequent entries make it plain that it was assessed at the rate of $\frac{1}{2}$d per person[62] and by converting the sums paid in different years into persons, changes in the number of poor tenants can be plotted. The number of persons who had an animal to the value of 30d (at current prices about 2 sheep, or 1 pig, or a heifer) rose during the early thirteenth century from 86 persons in 1211 to 137 in 1245, but then fell steadily reaching 102 persons in 1266 and 59 by 1297; it rose momentarily to 3s 4d (80 persons) in 1307 and was frozen thereafter at that sum, presumably because the manorial administration feared its renewed decline.

Another piece of fortuitous information which sheds some light on the problem of poverty arises in connection with the distribution of alms on the Hampshire manors of the bishop of Winchester, in 1258.[63] On this occasion the distribution was clearly in the nature of poor relief since it took the form of giving a farthing-worth of bread for some 90 days, from April 10th to July 8th, to the bishop's poor tenants. At Waltham, for which we have a custumal of almost the very same date (1259–1260), 60 poor tenants (*pauperes tenentes*) received this allowance. Since the total number of tenants at the time was 376 the paupers among them would amount to 16 per cent of the total, but if we assume that they were far more likely to have been smallholders than substantial tenants, and calculate the percentage against the total number of smallholders (10 acres or less), the figure rises to some 27 per cent. This is quite a considerable proportion but we must not forget that the number of smallholders at Waltham increased over the latter part of the thirteenth century and that there are reasons to believe that their position was much worse towards the end of the century, and in the early fourteenth century, than it had been in 1259.

It could be argued that such examples prove nothing, except perhaps, a certain measure of deterioration in a few specific cases; but it must be remembered that it would be utterly wrong to assume that lack of evidence for other places indicates that poverty was absent from them, and it seems significant that when we come across a piece of information which can be used to gauge change in rural prosperity at large, the indications are invariably of growing impoverishment rather than greater prosperity.

[61] Hampshire Record Office, MS. Eccl. Comm. 2/159297: 'quia multi pauperes qui non habent viva animalia ad valenciam 30d.'

[62] This seems to be the reason why the payment is called 'the residue' of Peter's pence, the other $\frac{1}{2}$d. being, presumably, forwarded to the appropriate ecclesiastical authorities.

[63] Hampshire Record Office, MS. Eccl. Comm. 2/159293.

Sale Price of Wheat (in shillings and pence per quarter) on the Bishop of Winchester's Hampshire Manors of Mardon and Ecchinswell.

Year	Minimum–Maximum	Average[1]	Year	Minimum–Maximum	Average[1]
1209		2s 8d	1238		——
1210		——	1239		——
1211		3s 7d	1240		——
1212		2s 8d	1241		——
1213		——	1242		——
1214		2s 2½d	1243		——
1215		——	1244		——
1216		2s 7d	1245		2s 8d
1217		——	1246	3s 6d–4s 6d	3s 11d
1218		4s 9¼d	1247	5s 0d–9s 6d	6s 10d
1219		5s 1¾d	1248	3s 7½d–8s 0d[3]	5s 8d
1220		3s 5½d	1249	3s 0d–4s 0d	3s 6½d
1221		5s 1¾d	1250		——
1222		——	1251		
1223		——	1252	3s 0d–4s 0d	3s 7d
1224		2s 9½d	1253	4s 8d–6s 8d	5s 7d
1225		5s 6½d	1254	2s 10d–3s 8d	3s 3d
1226		5s 1d	1255	2s 4d–3s 8d	3s 1½d
1227		5s 3¾d	1256		——
1228		——	1257	6s 8d–8s 0d	7s 3½d
1229		——	1258	7s 0d–10s 0d	8s 3½d
1230		——	1259	(4s 2d–4s 7½d)	(4s 5d)[4]
1231		——	1260		——
1232	3s 10½d–5s ½d	c.4s 2d[2]	1261		——
1233	3s 4¾d–3s 10½d	3s 7½d	1262		——
1234		——	1263	4s 0d–5s 0d	4s 6d
1235		——	1264		——
1236		3s 8d	1265	4s 8d–6s 0d	5s 3½d
1237		4s 4d	1266	3s 4d–5s 6d	4s 5¾d

[1] The average price when only one entry is given for all sales over the year; average of all individual prices when grain was sold in lots at a specified price.
[2] Clere price used instead of Ecchinswell's.
[3] These are given in descending order in the MS.
[4] Prices in brackets are taken from other Hampshire manors.

Year	Minimum-Maximum	Average	Year	Minimum-Maximum	Average
1267		——	1303	4s 0d–5s 6d	4s 11½d
1268	4s 0d–5s 0d	4s 5d	1304		(3s 7¾d*)
1269	4s 0d–7s 0d	5s 5d	1305	(5s 4d–8s 0d)	(6s 5d)[4]
1270	(5s 0d–6s 0d)	(5s 6d)	1306	5s 8d–6s 8d	6s 1¼d
1271	6s 0d–11s 0d	7s 8d[1]	1307	5s 0d–5s 4d	5s 2d
1272	9s 0d–10s 0d	9s 6d	1308	6s 0d–8s 0d	7s 0d
1273	5s 0d–6s 8d	5s 9d	1309	6s 8d–8s 0d	7s 4d
1274	6s 8d–8s 8d	7s 8d	1310	6s 8d–8s 8d	7s 8½d
1275	7s 6d–10s 0d	8s 8¾d	1311	8s 0d–10s 0d	9s 0d
1276		(5s 8d*)[2]	1312	5s 2d–6s 0d	5s 6½d
1277	5s 0d–9s 4d	7s 4d	1313	5s 0d–6s 0d	5s 5¼d
1278	4s 4d–6s 0d	5s 5d	1314	5s 4d–6s 8d	6s 0d
1279		(4s 2¼d*)	1315	6s 8d–8s 0d	7s 4d
1280		(5s 3¾d*)	1316	10s 0d–24s 0d	15s 5½d
1281		(5s 1d*)	1317	16s 0d–18s 0d	17s 0d
1282		(6s 3¼d*)	1318	8s 8d–10s 0d[3]	9s 4d
1283	6s 8d–9s 6d	8s 2¾d	1319	4s 8d–5s 6d	5s 1½d
1284	6s 0d–8s 0d[3]	7s 1d	1320		(4s 5d*)
1285	4s 0d–6s 0d	4s 11d	1321	6s 0d–7s 4d	6s 9d
1286	4s 4d–4s 8d	4s 6d[1]	1322		(13s 3d*)
1287	4s 8d–5s 0d	4s 10d	1323		(8s 7d*)
1288	2s 6d–3s 6d	3s 1d	1324		6s 8d[5]
1289	3s 0d–4s 0d	3s 6d	1325		9s 3d
1290	5s 0d–6s 0d	5s 6d	1326	5s 0d–6s 8d	5s 9d
1291	6s 0d–8s 0d[3]	7s 0d	1327		5s 4d
1292	5s 6d–6s 8d	6s 0¾d	1328	5s 4d–6s 8d	5s 11d
1293	5s 6d–8s 0d	6s 7½d	1329	6s 0d–8s 0d	7s 3d
1294		(7s 7¼d*)	1330	7s 4d–8s 0d	7s 8d
1295		(8s 2½d*)	1331	8s 0d–10s 0d	9s 0d
1296		(9s 2¾d*)	1332	6s 0d–9s 4d	8s 1d
1297	5s 0d–7s 0d	5s 10d	1333	6s 0d–6s 8d	6s 4d
1298	4s 9d–8s 0d	5s 11d	1334		——
1299	5s 0d–6s 8d	5s 7½d	1335	5s 0d–6s 8d	5s 9d
1300	3s 4d–6s 8d	4s 11¾d	1336	5s 0d–6s 8d	5s 10d
1301	6s 0d–6s 8d	6s 4d	1337	4s 0d–5s 4d	4s 9d
1302	5s 4d–6s 8d	5s 10½d	1338	4s 4d–5s 0d	4s 8d

[1] Mardon only.
[2] Prices marked with an asterisk are taken from D. L. Farmer, 'Some Grain Price Movements in Thirteenth-Century England', *Economic History Review*, X, 1957, p. 212.
[3] These are given in a descending order in the MS.
[4] This figure if from Downton, Wiltshire.
[5] Ecchinswell only.

Year	Minimum–Maximum	Average	Year	Minimum–Maximum	Average
1339	3s 0d–5s 0d	3s 9¼d	1345	4s 0d–5s 0d	4s 6½d
1340	5s 0d–8s 0d	6s 6½d	1346	2s 0d–6s 0d	4s 1d
1341	4s 0d–5s 4d	4s 9d	1347	6s 8d–10s 0d	8s 4d
1342	4s 0d–6s 8d	5s 6d	1348	5s 4d–8s 8d	7s 1d
1343	4s 0d–5s 4d	4s 9d	1349	3s 4d–6s 0d	4s 7d
1344	4s 8d–8s 0d	6s 9½d	1350	8s 0d–9s 0d	8s 6d

Price of Wheat, Oxen and Wool[1]

Year	Wheat	Oxen	Wool	Year	Wheat	Oxen	Wool
1163	—	32·1	—	1180	49·7	32·1	—
1164	—	—	—	1181	—	32·1	—
1165	—	—	—	1182	—	32·1	—
1166	39·6	35·5	—	1183	—	53·6	—
1167	39·6	31·3	—	1184	—	43·5	—
1168	37·3	32·1	—	1185	62·6	44·4	—
1169	58·9	32·1	—	1186	—	46·9	—
1170	32·7	32·1	—	1187	—	48·2	—
1171	33·1	35·0	—	1188	—	41·5	—
1172	35·0	32·1	—	1189	—	42·9	—
1173	44·2	32·1	—	1190	41·0	—	—
1174	51·1	—	—	1191	35·9	—	—
1175	44·2	—	—	1192	33·1	—	—
1176	88·4	—	—	1193	33·1	32·1	—
1177	26·7	—	—	1194	—	32·1	—
1178	27·2	—	—	1195	—	41·1	—
1179	47·9	32·1	—	1196	—	41·7	—

[1] Wheat: sale price at Mardon and Ecchinswell; 1245–49 = 100 (4s 6·3d per quarter).

Oxen: purchase price on the five manors of the Clere Group; 1245–49 = 100 (9s 4d).

Wool: sale price on the five manors of the Clere Group; 1245–49 = 100 (84s 4d per sack of 364 lb.).

Because of the crucial importance of price movements over the late twelfth, and early thirteenth century, to the understanding of the economy of the great estates over the same period, I have extended my own series of Winchester prices back as far as possible by converting figures published by Dr Farmer into index numbers on the same basis as my own series above. All figures up to 1208 (inclusive) are taken from that source, but I have entered them under the calendar date of the closing Michaelmas of each year of account.

Over the period 1209–1350 figures in brackets are taken from neighbouring Winchester manors with the same level of prices; occasionally, I have filled in a gap by using figures from Farmer and these are marked 'F'. Wool prices marked 'P' are taken from an unpublished study of five manors of the Priory of St Swithun, Winchester, deposited at the Institute of Historical Research by Mr Drew; prices on the manors of the Priory were very much the same as those on the manors of the Bishopric used above.

Year	Wheat	Oxen	Wool	Year	Wheat	Oxen	Wool
1197	—	34·8	—	1241	—	—	—
1198	—	41·1	—	1242	—	—	—
1199	—	32·1	—	1243	—	—	—
1200	88·4	—	—	1244	—	—	—
1201	—	63·4	—	1245	58·9	93·8	94·9
1202	140·0	67·9	—	1246	86·6	101·8	110·7
1203	170·8	69·6	—	1247	151·0	101·8	113·7
1204	167·6	68·3	—	1248	125·2	111·6	90·9
1205	—	96·4	—	1249	78·3	92·0	90·9
1206	—	80·4	—	1250	—	—	—
1207	87·0	55·6	—	1251	—	—	—
1208	87·0	62·5	—	1252	79·2	98·2	102·8
1209	58·9	75·0	64·6	1253	123·4	94·4	73·2
1210	—	—	—	1254	71·8	96·4	87·0
1211	79·2	62·9	56·9	1255	69·1	97·3	87·0
1212	58·9	62·7	48·2	1256	—	—	—
1213	—	—	—	1257	161·1	103·1	94·9
1214	48·8	75·4	66·4	1258	183·2	(98·2)	102·8
1215	—	—	—	1259	(97·6)	—	102·8
1216	57·1	61·6	(70·6)	1260	—	—	—
1217	—	—	—	1261	—	—	—
1218	105·4	69·0	(58·1)	1262	—	—	—
1219	113·7	70·1	71·1	1263	99·4	89·7	98·8
1220	76·4	91·5	63·2	1264	—	—	—
1221	113·7	91·7	63·2	1265	116·9	102·9	—
1222	—	—	—	1266	99·0	108·7	94·9
1223	—	—	—	1267	—	—	(87·0P)
1224	61·7	79·2	71·1	1268	97·6	103·8	102·8
1225	122·5	81·0	74·0	1269	119·7	(96·4)	126·5
1226	112·3	87·5	68·8	1270	(121·5)	(99·1)	(110·7)
1227	117·4	85·3	63·2	1271	169·4	128·1	98·8
1228	—	—	—	1272	209·9	(87·5)	(102·8)
1229	—	—	—	1273	127·1	131·0	110·7
1230	—	—	—	1274	169·4	128·6	110·7
1231	—	—	—	1275	192·9	107·1	118·6
1232	92·1	97·3	90·1	1276	(125·2F)	—	(94·9P)
1233	80·1	90·6	98·4	1277	162·1	139·5	134·4
1234	—	—	—	1278	119·7	128·8	126·5
1235	—	—	—	1279	(92·5F)	—	—
1236	81·0	99·1	94·9	1280	(117·4F)	—	(142·3P)
1237	95·8	98·7	97·4	1281	(112·3F)	—	—
1238	—	—	—	1282	(139·5F)	—	(134·4P)
1239	—	—	—	1283	181·9	101·8	(118·6P)
1240	—	—	—	1284	156·5	113·2	—

Year	Wheat	Oxen	Wool	Year	Wheat	Oxen	Wool
1285	108·7	118·8	—	1318	206·3	150·9	150·2
1286	99·4	(107·1)	(126·5)	1319	113·3	142·2	173·9
1287	106·8	101·8	126·5	1320	(97·6F)	174·6	—
1288	68·1	109·8	142·3	1321	149·2	171·7	201·6
1289	77·3	92·2	142·3	1322	(292·8F)	—	(142·3P)
1290	121·5	113·6	142·3	1323	(189·7F)	—	(158·1)
1291	154·7	109·2	(142·3)	1324	147·3	162·5	(165·6)
1292	134·0	128·6	126·5	1325	204·4	151·3	(150·2P)
1293	146·4	107·1	142·3	1326	127·1	129·9	(150·2P)
1294	(168·0F)	—	—	1327	117·9	129·5	158·1
1295	(181·4F)	—	—	1328	130·8	143·8	(142·3P)
1296	(204·0F)	—	—	1329	160·2	123·9	(146·2P)
1297	128·9	112·5	—	1330	169·4	(153·1)	(138·3P)
1298	130·8	125·9	126·5	1331	198·9	118·3	(138·3P)
1299	124·3	175·9	(126·5P)	1332	178·6	(143·8)	146·2
1300	110·0	125·9	—	1333	140·0	129·5	102·8
1301	140·0	117·9	(126·5)	1334	—	—	(94·9P)
1302	129·8	108·9	(118·6)	1335	127·1	119·6	94·9
1303	109·6	109·6	118·6	1336	128·9	136·6	114·6
1304	(80·6F)	—	—	1337	105·0	100·2	—
1305	(141·8)	91·1	—	1338	103·1	(88·4)	(90·9P)
1306	134·9	97·3	145·7	1339	83·3	104·5	(102·8P)
1307	114·2	142·9	173·9	1340	144·6	85·7	—
1308	154·7	158·3	169·2	1341	105·0	98·2	—
1309	162·1	184·8	173·9	1342	121·5	100·9	—
1310	170·3	171·4	158·1	1343	105·0	111·6	—
1311	198·9	(177·9)	142·3	1344	150·1	124·6	(102·8P)
1312	122·5	174·1	(128·9)	1345	100·4	(133·5)	(102·8P)
1313	120·2	168·8	130·4	1346	90·2	126·8	(126·5)
1314	132·6	155·4	158·1	1347	184·2	115·8	(123·3P)
1315	162·1	150·0	158·1	1348	156·5	123·7	(123·3P)
1316	341·6	168·8	142·3	1349	101·3	—	—
1317	375·7	168·8	158·1				

DOCUMENTS

DOCUMENTS

NOTE ON DOCUMENTS

All documents reproduced from manuscript sources are in my own transcription and translation. All documents reproduced from printed sources are in my own translation, with the exception of Documents 8, 10 and 20. My primary consideration when translating was to reproduce the original text as closely as possible, and, since some of the documents were written in a sort of telegraphese, the English version is not always as fluid as it would have been had fluidity of expression been given the top priority. Occasionally, to make the meaning clearer, I have introduced words or phrases which are not to be found in the originals; such words, or phrases, are always given in square brackets.

I have standardized all spellings (within each document) and the use of capital letters, retaining the latter only for personal and place names and for the opening words of sentences, but I have made no attempt to modernize the spelling of all place names mentioned in these documents. I have also provided my own punctuation marks since the originals do not have them. I have used Arabic numerals throughout, instead of the Roman ones used by the originals, and I have written out all money sums in modern form. I have rendered halfpennies and farthings as fractions of a penny, and any other fractional quantity as a fraction of the appropriate unit, instead of writing it out in full as the originals do.

Whenever alternative rendering of some technical term was possible, or whenever I felt uncertain as to the correctness of a particular technical term, I have given the original Latin term in brackets immediately after the word in question, or in footnotes when a lengthier explanation was necessary, but I have tried to keep the latter to the minimum. I have also incorporated in the text all contemporary corrections made in the original document without, as a rule, footnoting such corrections unless there was some special reason for doing so.

FROM [The Account Roll of the Manors of the Bishopric of Winchester for the Fourth Year of the Episcopate of Peter des Roches . 29 September 1208—28 September 1209].[1] Hampshire Record Office. MS. Eccl. Comm. 2/159270A.

DOWNTON [Wilts.]

W. son of Gilbert and Gocelinus the reeve, and Ailwardus the granger (*berebretus*) render account for £7 12s. 11d. of the arrears of the preceding year. They have paid up and are quit. And for £35 2s. 2d. of the rents of assize.[2] And for 12d. of the increment of rent for 1 enclosure which William of Widinton held for nothing. And for 2s. 6d. of the increment of rent for a half-virgate of land which Jacobus Oisel held without services. And for 19s. for 19 plots assized in the New Market. And for 10s. of the increment of rent for 10 plots newly assized[3] this year in the market. Total of all rents: £36 14s. 8d. In acquittance of 1 reeve 5s. In acquittance for re-making the bridge 5s., of 1 forester 4s., of 2 haywards from Downton and Wick 4s., of 1 hayward from Widinton 20d., of 14 ploughmen from Downton, Wick and Nunton for the year 28s., of 2 ploughmen from Widinton for the year 3s. 4d., of 2 ploughmen for half a year 2s., of 1 swineherd, 1 oxherd, 1 cowherd for the year 6s., of 3 shepherds from Wick, Bereford and Nunton for the year 6s., of 1 shepherd from Widinton for the year 20d., of 4 labourers (*operarii*) for the year 8s. Total of acquittances: 74s. 8d. Total remaining: £33 0s. 0d. Likewise, they render account for 13s. 4d. from pannage. And for 21s. 3d. from herbage. And for 13d. from the men who give churchscot. And for 5s. 1½d. from the residue of Peterpence. And for 74s. from 12 oxen sold live. And for 38s. 4d. from 46 ewes sold live.

[1] The title is mine; the roll is headed merely: 'The Fourth Year'.
[2] *Gabulum* here and in other early rolls; *redditus assisus* in later rolls.
[3] i.e. rented.

And for 47s. 8d. from 27 wethers (*multones*), 10 rams sold live. And for 38s. 9½d. from hides sold of 21 dead oxen, 3 cows, 1 bullock (*annalis*). And for 8s. from skins (*pelles*) sold of 32 dead ewes, 14 wethers, 22 hoggs[1] (*hogetti*). And for 7s. from 105 skins of dead lambs sold.

And for 33s. for 1½ barrels (*tonelli*) of wine at scot-ale. And for 22s. from 2 weys (*pondera*) of lard from 195 pigs killed for the larder. And for £16 13s. 4d. from 11 weys of sheep's wool (*lana grossa*), 1½ weys of lambswool, sold. And for £6 6s. 0d. from 18 weys (*capita*) of cheese sold. Total: £38 8s. 11½d. Likewise, they render account for £15 16s. 7d. from 110 quarters, 1 two-bushel measure (*estrica*) of wheat sold. And for 77s. from 38½ quarters of second-grade wheat (*curallum*) sold. And for 53s. 8d. from 27 quarters of mancorn sold. And for £9 12s. 11d. from 91½ quarters of barley sold. And for 12s. from 12 quarters of oats sold. And for 12s. from 6 quarters of beans sold. And for 4s. from 2½ quarters, 1 two-bushel measure of peas sold. Total: £33 8s. 9d.

Issues of the Mill Likewise, they render account for 27s. 5d. from 8½ quarters, 1 two-bushel measure of wheat sold. And for £5 4s. 9d. from 46½ quarters, 1 two-bushel measure of mancorn sold. And for 51s. 4d. from 26½ quarters of malt sold. And for 8s. 9d. from 4 quarters, 1½ two-bushel measures of groats (*gruellum*) sold. Total: £9 12s. 3d.

Profits of Court[2] Likewise, they render account for 12d. from Ernaldus the earl's son (*filius Comitis*) for having his father's land. And for 12d. from Richard May for relaxing the law.[3] And for 12d. from Osbertus Peche for the same. And for 4s. from the widow of Anketil for an entry fine. And for 6s. 8d. from William son of Selida for having the land of Emma. And for 5s. for the marriage of the step-daughter of Bren. And for 5s. from Ralph son of Edith for having the land of James. And for 12d. from Adam *de Roxi* in payment for the recovery of his animals.[4] And for 12d. from Ailet for relaxing the law.[3] And for 10s. from Walter for marrying his daughter. And for 4s. for the heriot[5] of Ivonet. And for 6s. 8d. for the heriot of Siwald. And for 2s. from Ingelram of Wick for a trans-

---

[1] One-year-old sheep.
[2] *Purchasia* here and in other early rolls; *Perquisita* in later rolls.
[3] *Pro lege relaxata.*
[4] *Pro forfengio animalium suorum.*
[5] *Testamentum* here and in other early rolls; *herietum* in later rolls.

gression (*forisfactum*) of pasture. And for 12d. from Roger Belfiz for the same.

And for 12d. from Elyas of Wick for the same. And for 6d. from Ralph Trapel for the same. And for 12d. from Richard Hauer for the same. And for 4s. from Robert Radulphus[1] for the same. And for 2s. from William Dal for the same. And for 18d. from Bernard Caue for the same. And for 18d. from Edward Biliz for the failure to sow one acre.[2] And for 6s. 8d. from Richard Herebert for the wood.[3] And for 2s. from Richard Glide for pasture. And for 12d. from Robert *de Lane* for a default.[4] And for 12d. from Adam Scalc for the same. And for 12d. from Walter the miller for the same. And for 6d. from Stephen Capra for twigs. And for 18d. from William Brictmar for corn, And for 2s. from Geoffrey the shepherd for the wood.[3] And for 12d. from Jordanus son of Norman for an affray.[5] And for 6d. from Norman for a security.[6] And for 12d. from Gilbert Pig for the same. And for 12d. from Richard Parmantarius for a default.[4]. And for 12d. from William Alan for the wood.[3] And for 12d. from William Ruffus of Stanlinche for the wood.[3] And for 12d. from Wluricus Hauer for pasture. And for 2s. from Nicholas Albus for the same. And for 12d. from Roger Wlgar for the same. And for 2s. from Richard Sprot for the same. And for 20s. from Simon Baus for mercy. And for 2s. from William *de Cruce* for pasture. And for 6d. from Ernaldus Crun' for the same. And for 6d. from Richard Grime for the same. And for 2s. from Richard Brun for the same. And for 6d. from Walter Burel for the wood.[3] And for 12d. from Robert Grant for corn. And for 6s. 8d. from Geoffrey Frawine for the same. And for 12d. from William Piscat(or) for pasture. And for 6d. from Ernaldus Breu for an affray.[5] and for 6d. from Ernaldus the ploughman for a default.[4] And for 6d. from Roger Tesse for the same. And for 6s. 8d. from the tithing of Charlton. And for 3s. from the tithing of Downton, And for 5s. [from] the tithing of Wick. And for 4s. from the tithing of Boterham. And for 18d. from the tithing of Widinton. And for 6s. 8d. from the tithing of the

---

[1] *De Roberto Rad'*; should, perhaps, be extended as genitive.
[2] *Pro 1 acra non seminata.*
[3] *Pro Bosco;* i.e., for damage to the wood.
[4] *Pro sursisa.*
[5] *Pro mell'*; almost certainly *pro mellea* (affray) and not *pro melle* (honey).
[6] *Pro plevina.*

church. And for 2s. from Ralph of Wick for marrying his daughter. And for 10s. from Elyas of Wick for the same. And for 4s. from William son of Osgod for having the land of Walter Cumicham. And for 2s. from Walkelinus of Nunton for the relaxation of autumn services. And for 12d. from Roger Tesse for the same. And for 2s. from Walter Hale for the same. And for 12d. from Ailwardus of Nunton for the same. And for 12d. from William the shepherd for the same. And for 12d. from Bernard Dugel for the same. And for 18d. from Norman for the same. And for 12d. from widow Pep for the same. And for 12d. from Godwin Peche for the same. And for 6d. from Richard *de Fraxino* for the same. And for 5s. from Seman Pute for an affray.[1] And for 4s. from Odo for a false alarm.[2] And for 12d. from Elyas Fis for relaxing the law.[3] And for 2s. from Roger Mabon for having his father's land. And for 2s. from Robert Coppe for his land. And for 20s. from the men of the vill for the relaxation of the purchase of a stack of corn.[4] Total: £10 11s. 6d. From tallage £40. Sum total with tallage: £165 17½d.

Cash
Delivery

Paid over to J. the Dean from the Christmas rents £7 10s., by 1 tally. To the same from the Easter rents £8, by 1 tally. To the same from the rents [due on the feast] of St. John the Baptist £8, by 1 tally. To the same from the Michaelmas rents £8 10s., by 1 tally. To the same from grain sold £26, by 2 tallies. To the same from grain, court fines and cheese £20 16s. 10d. To the same from wool £16 13s. 4d. by 1 tally. To the same from tallage £39, by 1 tally. Total: £134 10s. 2d.

Expenses

In the iron-work of 8 ploughs for the year and 1 plough for half a year 32s. 10d. In shoeing of 2 horses for the year 2s. 8d. In wheels for the ploughs 2s. 9d. In 6 ploughs made anew 12d., before the arrival of the carpenter. In wages of the smith for the year 8s. 6. In 1 new, iron-bound cart (*biga*) purchased 5s. 7d. In wheels purchased for 1 cart (*caretta*) for carting manure 12d. In swingle-trees, poles, clouts, halters[5] 14d. In 2 ropes purchased 3d. In 2 sacks purchased

---

[1] *Pro Mell(ea).*

[2] *Pro falso clamore.*

[3] *Pro lege relaxata.*

[4] *Pro relaxa emptionis medie bladi.* Since this payment is in later rolls entered as 'pro tasso refutato', 'medie' must be = 'meie'.

[5] *In paronis, paronellis, bacis, clutis, capistris.*

8d. In 5 locks purchased for the barn 11d. In furnishing
(*parandis*) 2 gates for the sheepfold 2s. In 1 gate for the farm
(*bertona*) 12d. In steel [and] tallow purchased and spindles
repaired, in the mill, for the year, 6s. 10d. In 1 millstone
bought for the mill 33s. In furnishing 1 gate next to the mill
12d. In preparing meat for the larder 3s. In ale bought for
pickling 2s. 1d. In trenching 158 perches around the pasture
in the marsh 32s. 11d., for each perch 2½d. In making a
new dovecote 22s. 11½d. In sawing 100 boards for planking
above the pantry and buttery 6s. 3d. In nails purchased for
boarding above the cellar 16d. In fencing round the garden
with two gates furnished 6s. 7½d. In digging in the gardens
7s. 5d. In winter boon-works of 55 ploughs 9s. 2d. In Lenten
boon-works of 49 ploughs 8s. 6d. In spreading manure over
6 acres 6d. In threshing 24 quarters of wheat in Mardon
for sowing 5s. In winnowing the same 7d. In winnowing
36 quarters of wheat for sowing 3s. 9d. In threshing 192
quarters of wheat 32s., for each quarter 2d. In threshing
20 quarters of mancorn 2s. 6d. In threshing 42 quarters of
barley 3s. 6d. In threshing 53 quarters of oats 2s. 2½d. In
hauling gravel to the bridge and causeway 14d. In expenses
of the dairy, namely, salt, 3 tubs, pans and pots 6s. 10d. In
17 oxen purchased £5 13s. 0d. In weeding 140 acres 5s. 10d.
In stipends (*stipendia*) of 2 carters, 1 oxherd for the year
9s. In stipend of 1 carpenter for the year 6s. 8d. In stipend
of the dairy-maid 2s. 6d. In customary payment to the men
mowing the meadow of Nunton 6d. In 8 ewes purchased 8s.
In stipend of 1 oxherd of Nunton 12d. In carrying 2 casks
(*tonelli*) of wine by Walter Locard in the term of St. Martin
8s. 2d. In carrying 2 casks of wine from Southampton to
Downton by the steward 3s. 6d., on the feast of St. Laurence.
In trenching 22 perches in front of the farm (*bertona*) 6s.5d.,
for each perch 3½d. In the corrody (*corredium*) of Robert
of Lurdon who was sick for 21 days, with his man, 5s. 3d. In
the corrody of Sewalus who guarded 2 horses of the Lord
Bishop for 3 weeks 21d. In the corrody of R. Wacel (inus)
on two occasions, when he was making excuses for non-
attendance[1] to the Lord King at Clarendon 4s. 9d. by
2 tallies. In the corrody of *Magister* R. Bass(et) for 3 journeys
9s. 3½d. In payment to W. son of Gilbert 60s. 10d.[2] In 30

---

[1] *Quando fecit exonia Domino Regi.*

[2] He was the bailiff of the manor and, at this time, 60s. 10d. a year was the usual
salary of a bailiff on the Winchester estates.

ells of canvas bought to put wool in, and for making 2 sacks for the house (*curia*) 5s. In 8 ewes bought with [their] lambs 8s. Total: £25 23d. Total of cash deliveries as well as expenses £159 12s. 1d. And £5 9s. 4½d. are outstanding.

Issues of the Grange

Likewise they render account for 221½ quarters, 1 two-bushel measure (*estrica*), of the total issue of wheat. And for 24 quarters brought from Mardon. Total: 245½ quarters, 1 two-bushel measure. Sown over 351 acres[1] 117 quarters. In Lord Biship's bread 18½ quarters, delivered to John the Dispenser by 3 tallies. Sold, as noted above, 110 quarters, 1 two-bushel measure. Likewise, they render account for 38½ quarters of the total issue of second-grade wheat (*currallum*). Sold, as noted above, all. Likewise they render account for 29[2] quarters 1 two-bushel measure of the total issue of mancorn. Sown over 156 acres 53 quarters, 1 two-bushel measure. In bread for 3 autumn boon-works 9 quarters. Sold, as noted above, 27 quarters. Likewise they render account for 178½ quarters of the total issue of barley. Sown over 102½ acres 49½ quarters. In customary payment to the ploughmen 1 quarter. In customary payment at the carting-away of manure, 2 quarters. In the corrody of 2 carters, 1 carpenter, 1 oxherd, 1 dairy-maid, for the year, 32½ quarters. Fed to the pigs in winter 2 quarters. Sold, as noted above, 91½ quarters. He is quit.

Likewise they render account for 311 quarters 2 bushels of the total issue of oats. Sown over 221½ acres, 110½ quarters. In provender for the Lord Bishop and the Lord King, on many occasions, 131½ quarters 2 bushels, by 5 tallies. In provender for Roger Wacel(inus) 2½ quarters, 3 bushels. In provender for *Magister* Robert Bass(et) 3½ quarters, 1 bushel. In provender for two horses of the Lord Bishop and for the horse of Richard *de Marisco* for 5 weeks, 5½ quarters, 2 bushels. In provender for 2 horses of the Lord Bishop, which stayed at Downton for 16 nights, 4 quarters. Sent to Knoyle 18 quarters. In provender for the horse of Robert of Lurdun' for 3 weeks, 1½ quarters. In provender for 2 cart-horses 7 quarters 2 bushels. Sold, as noted above, 12 quarters. And 14 quarters, 1 two-bushel measure, remain. Likewise they render account for 6½ quarters of the total issue of beans. Planted in the garden half a quarter. Sold, as noted above,

[1] Acreages on this manor do not need converting into measured acres to be comparable to figures obtained from later account rolls.

[2] *Sic* in MS. Should be 89 quarters.

6 quarters. He is quit. Likewise they render account for 4 quarters, 1 two-bushel measure of the total issue of peas. Sown over 6 acres 1½ quarters. Sold, as noted above, 2½ quarters, 1 two-bushel measure. He is quit. Likewise they render account for 4 quarters of the total issue of vetches. Fed to the pigs in winter, all. He is quit.

Livestock   Likewise they render account for 104 oxen remaining from the preceding year. And for 2 added from the idle animals.[1] And for 1 as the heriot of Robert Coppe. And for 17 bought. Total: 124. Sold alive 12. Died 21. Total: 33. And remain 91 oxen. Likewise they render account for 2 plough-horses (*auri*) remaining from the preceding year. All remain. Likewise they render account for 19 cows remaining from the preceding year. And for 7 added from the idle animals.[1] And for 1 found. Total: 27. Died 1. Killed for the use of the Lord Bishop and sent to Cranebourne 2. Total: 3. And remain 24 cows. Likewise they render account for 7 heifers (*genicule*), 2 bullocks (*juvenci*) remaining from the preceding year. Added to the cows 7 heifers. Added to the oxen 2 bullocks. Total: 9. Likewise they render account for 12 one-year-olds (*annales*) remaining from the preceding year. Died 1. And remain 11 of which 5 are heifers, 6 bullocks. Likewise they render account for 13 calves produced this year by the cows, for the others were sterile. In tithe 1. And remain 12. Likewise they render account for 858 ewes remaining from the preceding year. And for 46 ewes [received] as customary payment for herbage,[2] after separation and before shearing. And for 137 ewes (*gercie*) added from the one-year-olds (*hogetti*). Total: 1050. Sold alive in the term of St. Martin 46. Died before separation 20. Died after separation and before shearing 12. Total: 78. And remain 972 ewes. Likewise they render account for 584 wethers (*multones*) remaining from the preceding year. And for 163 males added from the one-year-olds. And for 16 rams of Lindsey, which arrived through brother Walter, before shearing. Total: 763. Sold alive in the term of St. Martin 27 wethers, 10 rams. Delivered to the men of Eblesbourne before shearing 20, by letter of the steward. Died before shearing 14. Total: 71. And remain 692 wethers. Likewise they render account for 322 one-year-olds (*hogetti*) remaining from the lambs of the preceding year. Died before shearing

[1] In MS: 'from the animals killed (*occisis*)', clearly an error for 'idle (*otiosis*)'.
[2] *De consuetudine herbagii.*

22. And remain 300 of which 137 are females (*gercie*) added to the ewes, and 63 males added to the wethers. Likewise they render account for 750 lambs produced by the ewes this year, for 20 were sterile and 30 aborted. In customary payment to the smith [and] 2 shepherds, 3. In tithe 73. Died before shearing 105. Total: 181. And remain 569 lambs. Likewise they render account for 1664 fleeces of sheep (*vellera grossa*) of which 16 were from the rams of Lindsey. In tithe 164. In customary payment to 3 shepherds, 3. Sold, as noted above, 1497 with 16 fleeces of Lindsey which made 11 weys (*pondera*). Likewise they render account for 569 fleeces of lambs. Sold, as noted above, all, which made $1\frac{1}{2}$ weys (*pondus*). Likewise they render account for 138 cheeses from the arrears of the preceding year. And for 19 small cheeses, and for 5 larger ones, from the arrears of the preceding year. And for 273 cheeses which began to be made on 6 April[1] and ceased on the feast of St. Michael, both dates included. And for 96 days they made two cheeses daily, namely, from 27th April[2] until the eve of St. Peter in the Chains, both dates included. Total: 435 cheeses. In tithe 27. In customary payment to the shepherd, [and] the mowers of the meadow of Nunton 2. In customary payment to the ploughmen 3. In the autumn boon-works 10. In expenses of the Lord Bishop in the kitchen 2, by 1 tally. Sold, as noted above, 138 cheeses of the arrears of the preceding year, which made 10 weys (*capita*). Sold, as noted above, 177 cheeses of this year, which made 18 weys (*capita*). In expenses of the Lord King and Lord Bishop on the feast of St. Leonard and St. Martin 19 of the small cheeses [and] 5 of the larger ones, of the arrears of the preceding year. And remain 52 small cheeses which make 1 wey (*caput*). Likewise they render account for 124 pigs remaining from the preceding year. And for 29 produced by the sows. Total: 153 pigs. In tithe 2. Died 9. Killed for the larder 84. Total: 95 pigs. And remain 58 pigs, also 19 piglets. Sum total: 77 pigs. Likewise they render account for 48 hens of the arrears of the preceding year. And for 258 hens from churchscot. Total: 306. In expenses of the Lord Bishop on the feast of St. Martin 36, by 1 tally. In expenses of the same on the feast of St. Leonard 106, by 1 tally. In expenses of the Lord King and Lord Bishop on the feast of the Apostles Peter

[1] *8 Id. Aprilis.*
[2] *A quinto Kal. Maii.*

H

and Paul 131 hens, by 2 tallies. In the corrody of Roger Wacel(inus) 8. In the corrody of *Magister* R. Bass(et) 4. Died 21. Total 306 hens. He is quit.

The
Larder

Likewise they render account for 273 hens, 27 sticks of eels, 4 piglets delivered for the expenses of the Lord King and Bishop. Likewise they have delivered for the expenses of the Lord Bishop the meat of 2 cows brought to Cranbourne. Likewise they render account for 13 carcasses of pigs (*bacones*) of the arrears of the preceding year. And for 5 oxen, 1 quarter-carcass of the old beef, of the arrears of the preceding year. And for 84 pigs from Downton. And for 71 pigs from Mardon. And for 10 pigs from Overton. And for 9 pigs from Clere. And for 14 pigs from Harwell. And for 7 pigs from Knoyle. Total: 208 pigs, and meat of 5 oxen and 1 quarter-carcass. In expenses of the Lord Bishop on the feast of St. Martin 8 carcasses of pigs (*bacones*). In expenses of the same on the feast of St. Leonard 17 carcasses of pigs and the meat of 5 oxen and 1 quarter. In expenses of the same on the morrow of the Holy Cross, delivered to Nicholas the cook, 27 carcasses of pigs. In expenses of the Lord Bishop delivered to the said cook at Knoyle on Saturday before the feast of St. Michael 15 carcasses of pigs. In expenses of the same and the Lord King on the feast of the Apostles Peter and Paul 50 carcasses of pigs. In the corrody of *Magister* R. Bass(et) on the feast of All Saints half a pig's carcass. In the corrody of the same on Wednesday and Thursday before Pentecost 1 pig's carcass. Sent to Knoyle for the autumn boon-works 6 carcasses of pigs. In 3 autumn boon-works at Downton 9½ carcasses of pigs. Total: 134 carcasses of pigs. And remain 74 carcasses of pigs. Likewise they render account for the chines, sausages (?) and pickles (?) of the said pigs.[1] In expenses of the Lord King and Lord Bishop on the feast of St. Leonard all. None remain.

[1] *Pro schinis salcigis et sulcitis.*

FROM The Account Roll of the Manors of the Bishopric of Winchester for the Second Year of the Consecration of John of Stratford [29 September 1324—28 September 1325]. Hampshire Record Office, MS. Eccl. Comm. 2/159337.

DOWNTON [Wilts.]

Arrears

John Ferner the reeve and William Cabbel the granger (*granatarius*) render account for £17 2½d. of the arrears of Hugh Saleman the reeve, in his account of the preceding year. And he is quit.

Rents of Assize

RENTS of ASSIZE. And for £10 11s. 8d.[1] of the total rents of assize at Christmas from the manor of Downton. And for £11 11s. 0d. at Easter. And for £10 11s. 8d. at the Nativity of St. John the Baptist. And for £28 10s. 7½d. at Michaelmas. And for 10s. of the rent of Ralph Druet and William le Chauntour for the land which belonged to John de Gymynges, at the same term-day. Total: £61 14s. 11½d.

Increment of Rent

INCREMENT OF RENT. And for 10s. from William le Chapman of Downton for 6 acres of land, lying in the field of Wick between the land of the lord and of Walter le Aumblour consigned to him this, the first, year, to wit, 20d. per acre. And for 3s. 4d. from Geoffrey le Smyth for 2 acres lying in the field of Wick near the land of the lord, and it lies in length between the land of the said William and the land of Hugh atte Bolehalle, 20d. per acre. And for 3s. 4d. from Thomas Coppe for 1 plot of land containing half an acre of land in Witheton from the lord's demesne. And for 3s. from Thomas Trapul junior for half an acre of land in Witheton from the lord's demesne. And for 4s. from John le Coupere for 4 acres of land near la Bury in Witheton from the lord's demesne. And for 4s. from Thomas Trapul for 4 acres of land from the lord's demesne in Witheton. And for 12d. from Ralph le Taillor for 1 acre of land from the

[1] 10d. crossed out, 8d. substituted.

lord's demesne in Witheton. And for 12d. from John Paskes for 1 acre of land from the lord's demesne in Witheton. And for 12d. from William le Eir for 1 acre of land from the lord's demesne in Witheton. And for 12d. from John le Hore for 1 acre of land from the lord's demesne in Witheton. And for 2s. from Isabella daughter of Adam le Fishare for 2 acres of land from the lord's demesne in Witheton. And for 2s. from Robert Hughes for 2 acres of land from the lord's demesne in Witheton. And for 12d. from Walter le White for 1 acre of land from the lord's demesne in Witheton. And for 4s. from John le Coupere for 4 acres of land from the lord's demesne in Witheton. And for 12d. from Thomas Coppe for 1 acre of land from the lord's demesne in Witheton. And for 7s. from Alexander le Kyng for 12 acres of land in Tymberhulle consigned to him this, the first, year. And for 18d. from John son of Ralph Coppe for having 1 rood of land in Witheton. And for 12d. from Margery who was the wife of William Gale for 1 rood of land from the lord's demesne in Witheton and 1 islet (*insula*) in the lord's river, consigned to her this year. Total: 50s. 2d. Total rent with increment: £64 5s. 1½d. ACQUITTANCES. In acquittance of 1 reeve for the year 5s. In acquittance of 1 forester for the year 4s. In acquittance of 2 haywards from Downton and Wick for the year 4s. In acquittance of 1 hayward from Witheton, who guards Pryfet, for the year 20d. In acquittance of 8 ploughmen for the year 16s., to wit, each of them 2s. In acquittance of 1 ploughman from Witheton for the year 20d. In acquittance of 2 oxherds for the year 4s. In acquittance of 2 shepherds from Nounton and Wick for the year 4s. In acquittance of 1 shepherd from Witheton for half a year 10d. In acquittance of 1 virgate of land for the repairing of the bridge, as long as it pleases the lord, 5s. In acquittance of 1 swineherd for the year 2s. Total: 48s. 2d. LAPSED RENTS.[1] In lapsed rent of 2 fardels of land drawn into the town 6s. annually. In lapsed rent of 3 fardels of land handed over (*liberate*) to Fulc of Waleton 2s. annually. In lapsed rent of 32½ acres of land which is called *Cosettelond* 27s. 1d., to wit, each acre 10d., by [the authority of] John Gervays the Lord Bishop, which acres Simon of Stopeham held and he renders each year 18s. 11½d. which are included in the rent above, to wit, for each acre 7d. In lapsed rent of the

Acquit-
tances

Lapsed
Rents

---

[1] *Defectus* (*Redditus*).

fulling mill 10s. annually, for there is no one who seems to
want to hold it for the old rent. In lapsed rent of the land
which is called *le Hangres* which formerly belonged to Elyas
le Drapyr which Roger of Stopeham did not wish to hold any
longer, nor is there anything there on which distraint can be
made, 10s. 6d. Total: 55s. 7d. Total of acquittances and lapsed
Cumin   rents: 103s. 9d. Total net rents: £59 16½d. CUMIN. And
for 6d. for 1 pair of gilded spurs for the rent of Ralph of
Bereford. And for 1d. for 1 pound of cumin, or 1d., at the
choice of the tenant, from William le Chapman for the garden
formerly of Roger of Wick. Total: 7d. ISSUES OF THE
Issues   MANOR. And for 24s. 4d. from pigs' pannage at the feast
of the   or St. Martin, to wit, for a pig over one year 1d., and if it
Manor   is under one year ½d. From foreign pannage nothing this
year for there was no mast. And for 8s. 3d. from the grazing
(*herbagium*) of oxen and ewes at Hockday[1] from the men of
Nounton, to wit, for a fully-grown ox 4d., for 5 ewes 1d.
And for 7s. 9d. from the men of Witheton for the same. And
for 4s. 9d. from the men of Wick and Waleton for the same,
to wit, for a fully-grown ox 1½d. because they do not give
silver for ewes but [give] a wether (*multo*) for herbage. And
for 13s. 4d. received for winter pasture sold in the park, this
year. And for 2s. from winter pasture sold in *Milkhulle*
this year. And for 3s. 4d. from winter pasture sold this year
in *Tymberhulle*. And for 10s. from the sheep pastured in the
field of Witheton in winter and lying in the lord's fold. And
for 5s. 10d. from 160 hoggs[2] pastured in the field of Wick.
And for 5s.4d. from the pasture in *la Grotene* in the field of
Wick. And for 2s. for the ditch next to [the land of] Roger
Alayn this year. And for 10s. from winter pasture of Cowick
sold this year. From *Poresmere* nothing this year because of
the lord's beasts. And for 6s. from 144 'convalescing'[3]
[animals] pastured on the fallow in the field of Wick, to wit,
per head ½d. And for 4s. 6d. from 3 roods of underwood
sold this year in *Thorndon*. And for 32s. 1d. from 7 acres
and two parts of 1 acre of underwood sold in . . .[4] *ferthynges-
lyghe* this year. And for 9s. from peat (*turbaria*) sold in
winter and Lent this year. And for 4s. 4d. from the heath

[1] Second Tuesday after Easter.
[2] *Hogetti*, i.e. one-year-old sheep.
[3] *De 144 cubbatis*. The term *cubbatus* seems to indicate any animal in poor condition
(possibly recovering from an illness) put out to graze to improve its condition.
[4] A small piece is torn out of the margin at this point.

(*bruera*)[1] sold this year in winter. And for 18d. from a certain old hedge in *le Shepecrofte* sold this year. And for 12d. from 1 old hedge sold in the same place. And for 20s. from summer pasture in the park sold this year. And for 4s. from summer pasture in *Milkhulle* sold this year. And for 8s. from summer pasture in *Tymberhulle* sold this year. And for 5s. from summer pasture in Cowick sold this year. And for 3s. from summer pasture in *Grendene* sold this year. And for 15s. 5½d. from beasts pastured [with the beasts][2] of the lord in *Suthmede* this year in the summer. And for 4s. 6d. from the pasturing of beasts in *la Grene* this summer. And for 12d. from the pasture in *la Mote* sold this year in summer. And for 18d. from old tree-roots sold this year for making charcoal. And for 3s. 8d. from peat sold this year in summer. And for 8s. from the heath[1] sold this year in summer. And for 36s. 8d. from the grazing of the meadow of Nounton sold this year in summer. And for 13s. 4d. from the grazing of the pasture of the oxen[3] sold in the same place in summer. And for 10s. from the grazing of the meadow which is called *la Nywemede* in Witheton sold in summer. And for 10s. from the grazing [of the pasture] of the oxen[3] which is called *la Hulle* in the same place. And for 10s. 2d. from the grazing of *Editheham* sold in the same place. And for 8s. from the grazing of 1 *Daywyne* sold in the same place. And for 6s. 8d. from the grazing in *la Grene* sold this year. And for 20s. from the meadow in Nounton sold after the mowing. And for 13s. 4d. from *Estmede* sold after the mowing. And for 16s. from the pasture in *Suthmede* sold after the mowing. And for 22s. 6d. from the new hay sold this year. From the pasture in *Rodemede* nothing this year because of the lord's beasts. And for 6s. 8d. from the pasturing of animals on the heath sold this year. And for 18d. from the marl (*marlera*) sold. And for 4s. from the pasture on *Marrigge* sold. From the loppings (*ramili*) in Cowick, or furze, (*jenectum*) nothing this year. From the underwood in *Prifet* nothing this year. And for 41s. from 36 trees (*roffri*)[4] sold in *Burghenemore*. And for 39s. 8d. from 18 old trees (*roffri*) in the same place sold by the steward. And for 110s. 6d. from 37 trees (*roffri*) sold

---

[1] i.e. The right to pasture animals on the heath.
[2] A small piece is torn out of the margin at this point.
[3] i.e. A separate pasture reserved for oxen.
[4] This word is usually used to denote a tree not fit to be used as timber.

this year in *Burghenemore*, the price of each 3d.[1] less 6d. in all. And for 15s. 2d. from 6 old trees (*roffri*) sold in the same place. And for 4s. from the residue of Peterpence. And for 13d. from churchscot in Bereford. And for 12d. from 1 hide of a dead[2] horse sold. And for 2s. from the hide of a dead cow sold. And for 2s. from 4 fleeces[3] of wethers (*multones*). And for 4s. from 12 ewes which died before shearing.[4] And for 4d. from 1 carcass of 1 dead ewe sold. And for 16d. from skins of 2 wethers [and] 6 ewes which died after shearing. And for 3s. 1½d. from 25 fleeces sold of lambs which died before separation, the price per fleece 1½d. And for 18s. from the ploughing of 37 acres[5] sold this year in winter. And for 7s. from the ploughing of 14 acres sold in Lent.[5] And for 114s. 2¼d. from 2740½ winter day-works (*opera*) sold, the price per day-work ½d. And for 77s. 7d. from 1862 summer day-works sold, the price per day-work ½d. And for 56s. from the autumn day-works of 3 virgates, 8 half-virgates, 2 fardels sold this year. And for 37s. 7½d. from 903 day-works sold after the autumn, the price per day-work ½d. And for £4 6s. 1½d. from 6 weys (*pondera*), 4 cloves (*clavi*) and 6 pounds of summer cheese sold this year, the price per wey 14s. And for 8s. 2d. from 14 cloves of butter sold this year, the price per clove 7d. And for 8d. from 200 hen eggs sold. And for 13s. 8d. from 1 cask (*pipa*) and 68 gallons of cider sold. And for 20s. *de tasso refutato*[6]. And for 3s. from John Speie for fishing in the river.[7] And for 3s. 4d. from Ralph Potul for the same. And for 3s. from William Withe for the same. And for 18d. from John le Portere for the same. And for 2s. from Henry Bolle for the same, sold this year. And for 7s. 4d. from 6 cloves and 2 pounds of broken wool sold. And for 38s. 6d. from 308 hens, received as churchscot, sold, the price of each 1½d. Total: £56 11s. 9½d.

Sale of SALE OF LIVESTOCK. And for 3s. from 1 feeble (*debilis*)
Livestock mare sold. And for 49s. from 3 oxen sold towards the feast

---

[1] *sic* in MS., should be 3s.

[2] Throughout this section the phrase *mortus de morina* is used. In this period this seems to denote accidental death rather than death from murrain.

[3] *Pelles* in MS., but since the skin was with the wool on, I have rendered it as 'fleece'.

[4] *sic* in MS., clearly fells, not carcasses, are meant.

[5] i.e. Customary services of ploughing so many acres.

[6] This seems to be a payment for relaxing the customary obligation of purchasing a quantity of the lord's corn.

[7] *Pro piscaria et* (!) *ripario; et* is clearly an error for *in*.

of St. Martin, whereof the price of 1 16s., and 2 the price per head 16s. 6d. And for 14s. from 1 'convalesced' (*cubbatus*) ox sold. And for 10s. 6d. from 1 ox sold because [it was] infirm. And for 2s. from 1 calf sold because [it was] feeble. And for 33s. 4d. from 20 'convalesced' wethers (*multones cubbati*) sold, the price per head 20d. And for 18d. from 1 'convalesced' ram sold. And for 32s. from 24 'convalesced' ewes sold, the price per head 16d. And for 24s. from 24 lambs sold because [they were] feeble. And for 7s. received from 2 pigs sold, the price per head 3s. 6d. Total: £8 16s. 4d.

Annual
Recognition

ANNUAL RECOGNITION.[1] And for 6d. from Thomas of Bottenham for the annual recognition. And for 6d. from Roger Almer for the same. From John son of William *de Cruce* nothing because [he is] dead. And for 6d. from Geoffrey Whitemay for the same. And for 3d. from Alexander Redde for the same. And for 3d. from John Radde for the same. From John Corel nothing because [he is] dead. From John Sprot nothing because [he is] dead. From John Vecke nothing because [he is] dead. From Gilbert Clement nothing because [he is] dead. And for 6d. from Thomas Alwyne so that he could remain and serve outside the liberty, as long as it pleases the lord, provided he came to 1 lawday a year. And for 4d. from William Whitemay so that he could remain and serve outside the liberty, as long as it pleases the lord, provided he came to 2 lawdays a year. And for 3d. from William le Bols for the same. And for 6d. from John son of William Alwyne for the same. And for 6d. from Roger[2] Portman for the same. And for 6d. from William Portman of Wick for the same. And for 6d. from John Bocke of Waleton for the same. And for 2d. from John Kikayn for the same. And for 3d. from Elyas Kikayn for the same. And for 3d. from John Ingram for the same. And for 3d. from William Hughe of Witheton for the same. And for 2d. from John Hogge for the same. And for 3d. from Clement Richard for the same. And for 3d. from Richard le Couk for the same. And for 3d. from John son of John atte Watere for the same. And for 2d. from Vincent Leuesteman for the same. And for 3d. from Adam atte Mulle for the same. And for 2d from William Odom for the same. And for 3d. from John Ingram for the same. And for 2d. from John Coure for the

---

[1] The Winchester documents consistently use this term for what elsewhere is called *chevagium*.

[2] John is crossed out and Roger substituted.

same. And for 2d. from John atte Styghele for the same. And for 6d. from William Richard so that he could remain, and serve outside, as long as it pleases the lord, provided he came to 2 lawdays a year and remained a villein as previously, pledge Ralph Richard. And for 3d. from John son of John le Shephurde for the same, pledge John Ferner.

Sale of Grain

Total: 8s. 7d. SALE OF GRAIN. And for £29 16s. 2¼d. from 76½ quarters of wheat sold, whereof 2 quarters the price per quarter 6s. 4d., 44 quarters 4½ bushels the price per quarter 6s. 8d., 3 quarters the price per quarter 8s., 6 quarters 7½ bushels the price per quarter 9s., 20 quarters the price per quarter 10s. And for 40s. from 8½ quarters of second-grade wheat (*curallum*) sold, whereof 8 quarters the price per quarter 4s. 8d., half a quarter the price 2s. 8d. And for £24 2s. 4½d. from 100 quarters 5 bushels 1 peck of barley sold, whereof 72 quarters the price per quarter 4s., 10 quarters the price per quarter 7s., 18 quarters 5 bushels 1 peck the price per quarter 6s. 8d. And for 73s. 7½d. from 20 quarters 7 bushels of oats sold, whereof 1 quarter the price 2s. 4d., 4 quarters the price per quarter 2s. 8d., 2 quarters 7 bushels the price per quarter 3s., 13 quarters the price per quarter 4s. And for 41s. 8d. from 7 quarters 7½ bushels of peas sold, whereof the price of 1 quarter 4s. 8d., 6 quarters 7½ bushels the price per quarter 5s. 4d. And for 24s. 5d. from 5 quarters 3 bushels of vetches sold, whereof 2 quarters the price per quarter 4s. 4d., 3 quarters 3 bushels the price per quarter 4s. 8d. Total: £62 18s. 3¼d. ISSUES OF

Issues of the Mill

THE MILL. And for 63s. 4¾d. from 9½ quarters of wheat, whereof 4 quarters 1 bushel the price per quarter 6s. 4d., the price of 1 quarter 6s. 8d., 1½ quarters the price per quarter 8s., 1 quarter ½ bushel the price per quarter 8s. 8d., the price of 1 quarter 5s. 4d., 6½ bushels the price per bushel

Barley

7½d. Total as shown. BARLEY. And for £11 12s. 6d. from 47 quarters 1 bushel of barley, whereof 12 quarters 6 bushels the price per quarter 4s., 10½ quarters the price per quarter 4s. 8d., 13 quarters 7 bushels the price per quarter 6s. 8d., 10 quarters the price per quarter 4s. Total: £11 12s. 6d.

First-grade Malt

FIRST-GRADE MALT (*Brasium capitale*). And for 78s. 10d. from 11 quarters 1 bushel of first-grade malt sold, whereof 6 bushels the price per bushel 10d., 2 quarters 6 bushels the price per quarter 6s. 8d., 3 quarters 3 bushels the price per quarter 8s., 1 quarter 1 bushel the price per quarter 8s. 8d., and 3 quarters 1 bushel the price per quarter

Second-
Grade Malt

Oat
Flour
Powder

Fishery

Entry and
Marriage
Fines

6s. Total as shown. SECOND-GRADE MALT (*Brasium cursale*). And for £11 4s. 2d. from 43 quarters 2 bushels of second-grade malt of the issues of the mill sold, whereof 2 quarters the price per quarter 4s., 10½ quarters the price per quarter 4s., 1 quarter the price per quarter 4s. 4d., 6 quarters 3 bushels the price per quarter 4s. 8d., 15 quarters 3 bushels the price per quarter 6s. 8d., 8 quarters the price per quarter 4s. 8d. Total as shown. OAT FLOUR[1]. And for 15d. from 1 bushel of oat flour of the issues of the mill sold. Total as shown. POWDER.[2] And for 20d. from 6 bushels of the mill's powder sold, whereof 4 bushels the price per bushel 3d., 2 bushels the price per bushel 4d. Total as shown. FISHERY. And for 26s. 8d. from the eel-fishery[3] sold.

ENTRY AND MARRIAGE FINES.[4] And for 5s. from the tithing of Bottenham at the Hundred [Court] of St. Martin. And for 6s. 8d. from Charleton for the same. And for 2s. for the tithingpenny of Witheton for the same. And for 6s. 8d. for the tithingpenny of the church[5] for the same. And for 5s. for the tithingpenny of Downton for the same. And for 5s. for the tithingpenny of Wick for the same. And for 30s. 4d. from those same tithingmen at the Hundred [Court] of Hockday for the same. And for 20s. from William Ailward to have Lucia Syring with her land, to wit, 1 messuage and 5 acres of her land in Nounton. And for 3s 4d. from John Arnays to have 1 messuage and 2 acres of land in Downton which belonged to John Arnays his father. And for 2s. from Thomas Coppe to have half an acre of land from the lord's demesne in Witheton. And for 2s. from Thomas Trapul junior, to have half an acre of land from the lord's demesne in Witheton. And for 18d. from John Coppe to have 1 rood of land from the lord's demesne in Witheton. And for 8s. from John le Coupere to have 4 acres of land from the lord's demesne in Witheton. And for 8s. from Thomas Trapul to have 4 acres of land from the lord's demesne in Witheton. And for 2s. from Ralph le Taillour to have 1 acre of land from the lord's demesne in Witheton. And for 2s. from John Paskes to have 1 acre of land from the

[1] *Farina avene.*
[2] *Pulvis molendini*, probably flour swept off the stones.
[3] *Piscaria anquillarum;* right to fish sold, or the eels themselves sold.
[4] *Fines et Maritagia.*
[5] *De thutyngpeny de La Churche;* i.e. from the tithing of the church.

lord's demesne in Witheton. And for 2s. from William le Eyer to have 1 acre of land from the lord's demesne in Witheton. And for 2s. from John le Hore to have 1 acre of land from the lord's demesne in Witheton. And for 4s. from Isabella daughter of Adam le Fyschare to have 2 acres of land from the lord's demesne in Witheton. And for 4s. from Robert Hughes to have 2 acres of land from the lord's demesne in Witheton. And for 2s. from Walter le Whyte to have 1 acre of land from the lord's demesne in Witheton. And for 8s. from John le Coupere to have 4 acres of land from the lord's demesne in Witheton. And for 2s. from Thomas le Coupere to have 1 acre of land from the lord's demesne in Witheton. And for 30s. from Isabella, who was Roger's le Muleward wife, to retain 1 messuage and half-virgate of land in Downton which belonged to the said Roger her husband. And for 3s. 4d. from Richard Whithorn to have Alice Pynnok with her land, to wit, 1 cottage and 1 toft in Waleton. And for 53s. 4d. from Matilda who was Clement's *in La Lane* wife, to retain 1 messuage and 1 virgate of land in Charleton which belonged to the said Clement her husband. And for 30s. from Walter Piperwhyt for Isabella who was Roger's le Muleward wife with her land, to wit, 1 messuage and half-virgate of land in Downton which belonged to the said Roger her husband to retain them.[1] And for 2s from Agnes who was John Wythorn's wife to retain 4 acres of land from the lord's demesne in Wick, which belonged to the said John her husband. And for 20s. from Cecilia who was Robert Aylward's wife to retain 1 messuage and 1 virgate of land in Bottenham which belonged to the said Robert her husband. And for 3s. 4d. from Nicholas *de Lyndwode* for Lucia who was the wife of Richard le Monekes with her land, to wit, 1 cottage 1½ acre of land in Downton, which belonged to the said Richard her husband, to retain them.[1] And for 3s. 4d. from Stephen Regate to have 1 acre of land from the lord's demesne by the surrender of William le Fior. And for 13s. 4d. from William Ailwyne to have Isabella Cuppyng with her land, to wit, 1 messuage and 8 acres of land which belonged to John Cuppyng her husband, and 8 acres of land from the lord's demesne in Wick. And for 12d. from Edith Cuppyng

---

[1] *sic* in MS. The clerk has clearly got the standard phrase, summarising an entry fine from a widow for her husband's holding, mixed up with the phrase summarising a fine from a man for a widow with her land.

to have 2 acres of land from the lord's demesne in Wick by
the surrender of Isabella Cuppyng. And for 3s. 4d. from
William Hogge to have 1 messuage and 1 curtilage and
2 acres of land in Nounton which belonged to Juliana le
Hynges and which came into the lord's hands as an escheat
because the said Juliana died without an heir. And for 12d.
from Edith Cuppyng to have 2 acres of land from the lord's
demesne in Wick by the surrender of Isabella Cuppyng her
mother. And for 20s. from William le Chapman to have
6 acres of land from the lord's demesne in the field of Wick.
And for 3s. 4d. from Geoffrey le Smith to have 2 acres
of land from the lord's demesne in the field of Wick. And
for 12s. from Alexander le Kyng to have 12 acres of land
from the lord's demesne in Tymberhulle. And for 12d. from
John Goruille for marrying his daughter Matilda within
[the liberty]. And for 2s. from Walter atte Mulle for marrying
his daughter Margery within [the liberty]. And for 2s. from
Roger Cole for marrying his daughter Joan outside [the
liberty]. And for 2s. from William Deynge for marrying his
daughter Christiana within [the liberty]. And for 12d. from
William le Eir for marrying his daughter Margery outside
[the liberty]. And for 5s. from Margery who was the wife
of William le Gale to have 1 rood of land in Bottenham and
1 small islet (*insula*) in the lord's river. Total: £17 2s. 6d.

Pleas and Perquisites PLEAS AND PERQUISITES. And for 73s. 1d. from 2
tourns held by the steward. And for £8 4s. 2d. from 9 courts
held by the Bailiff. And for 63s. 7d. from the fine of the
lord's tenants to retain demesne lands. Total: £15 10d.

Sales *super Compotum* SALES *SUPER COMPOTUM*.[1] And for £4 11s. 7½d. for
things sold *super compotum*. Total: as shown. TOTAL OF
Cost of Ploughs ALL THE RECEIPTS: £256 4½d. COST OF PLOUGHS.
In the iron-work (*ferramenta*) of 3 ox-ploughs and 2 horse-
ploughs according to a certain agreement, together with
manufacturing plough-shares, coulters and other iron parts
(*ferramenta*) pertaining to ploughs, 30s., so however that the
smith will find new shares and coulters this year. In shoeing
12 horses, for the year 8s. In 5 pairs of wheels bought anew
17½d., the price per pair 3½d. In 2 yokes bought anew 2d.

---

[1] *Venditio super compotum*. Losses and discrepancies discovered at the time of the
audit, increases charged against the accounting officials if the auditors thought that
some produce was sold at a lower price than should have been the case, but also at
times genuine sales concluded after the account had been closed, were all entered
in this section as 'sales'.

In boon-works of 29 ploughs which ploughed 58 acres in winter, to wit, each plough 2 acres, 9s. 8d., for each plough 2d. In boon-works of 24 ploughs which ploughed 24 acres in Lent 4s., for each plough 2d. In mending and sharpening the iron teeth of 2 harrows together with 2 teeth bought for them anew 10d. In shoeing 4 oxen 6d. *In fimis levandis de fossa*[1] 4d. In 1 seed-basket bought 2½d. In stipend of 1 stot-herd (*stothurde*)[2] for the year 4s. Total: 59s. 2d.

Cost of the Cart

COST OF THE CART. In 1 pair of iron-bound wheels bought anew 13s. 4d. In 1 pair of wheels made anew from the lord's timber 18d. In 2 hubs (*naves*) bought for them 6d. In mending 1 old rim (*ligatura*) together with large nails bought for the wheels of 1 cart, and affixing it to the said wheels, 2s. 11d. In 2 axles bought anew, and [in] fitting the cart with axles, 8d. In 12 clouts with nails bought for the cart 12d. In 2 pounds of grease bought 4d. In 2 collars bought anew 14d. In 2 pairs of traces bought anew 5d. In 2 cart-ropes (*corda carecte*) bought 12d. In 4 nave-boards (*navebordes*) bought anew 2d. In making 9 halters anew 2d. In 1 wheel bought for the barrow 2d. In stipend of 1 carter for the year 4s. In stipend of 1 carter for half a year 2s. Total: 29s. 4d.

Purchase of Livestock

PURCHASE OF LIVESTOCK. In 1 cow with [its] calf bought 12s. 7d. In 14 hoggs (*hoggastri*)[3] bought 18s. 8d., the price per head 16d. In 24 hoggs (*hoggastri*)[3] bought 34s. 7d., the price per head 17d. In 6 lambs bought 5s. In 6 lambs bought 6s. In 4 pigs bought 10s., the price per head 2s. 6d. In 1 cock and 5 hens bought 9d. And in 2 cows bought from the reeve of Founthill 18s. In 2 cows bought from the reeve of Bishopstone 18s. And in 50 ewes bought 66s. 8d. Total: £9 10s. 3d.

Cost of Buildings

COST OF BUILDINGS. In [payment to] 1 roofer (*coopertor*) roofing over the bailiff's room (*camera*) and granary for 2 days 12d. In 7 hinges bought for the doors of one of the manorial buildings,[4] together with the nails bought for affixing the same, and for making whatever else is necessary, 10d. In mending the east

---

[1] Either 'for moving the manure out of the ditch' (surrounding the manorial complex of buildings) in which animals were grazed, or 'for moving clay out of the moat' (i.e. dredging it) if there was a moat, rather than a ditch, around the manorial buildings. The former seems much more likely.

[2] The man looking after 'stots', i.e. plough-horses.

[3] Young sheep are meant here, though the same word is used of young pigs also.

[4] *Pro ostio domus in Curia*. The word *Curia* is frequently used in the sense of the whole compact complex of manorial buildings centred on the manor house, and the yard.

gate next to the mill 6d. In castrating 18 piglets 6d. In sawing 106 feet of boards for the west bridge within the manorial compound (*in Curia*) 9d. In 125 board-nails bought **Cost of** for it 5d. Total: 4s. COST OF THE DAIRY. In 6 bushels **the Dairy** of salt bought for the dairy 22d., whereof, 4 bushels the price per bushel 4d., and 2 bushels the price per bushel 3d. In [one] press bought 6d. In earthenware pots and pans bought 2d. In linen and woollen cloth bought for the dairy 6d. In 1 cheese-mould bought 3d. In 1 small vat (*cuvinella*) bought 6d. In stipend of the dairy-maid 2s. 6d. **Cost of** Total: 6s. 3d. COST OF THE SHEEP-HOUSE. In 6 **the Sheep-** gallons of tar bought 3s., the price per gallon 6d. In 7½ **house.** gallons of tallow bought 9s. 5d., whereof, 4 gallons the price of each 16d., and 3½ gallons the price of each 14d. In [payment to] 3 carpenters mending the structure of the ewe-house[1] for 4 days 2s. 6d., each of them received per day 2½d. In 3 ells of canvas bought to pack lamb's wool in, 12d. Total: **Threshing** 15s. 11d. THRESHING AND WINNOWING. In thresh-**and** ing 120 quarters 6 bushels 1 peck of wheat, 8½ quarters of **Winnowing** second-grade wheat (*curallum*), 10 quarters 4½ bushels of peas, 10½ quarters of vetches, on piece-work basis (*ad tascham*), 25s. ½d., to wit, per razed quarter 2d. In winnowing the same 2s. 6d., to wit, for 5 quarters 1d. In threshing 180 quarters 2 bushels of barley, on piece-work basis, 18s. ¼d., to wit, per quarter of 10 bushels[2] 1½d. In winnowing the same 2s., to wit, for 7½ quarters of 8 razed bushels 1d. In threshing 62 quarters of oats, on piece-work basis, 2s. 7d., to wit, for a quarter of 8 bushels ½d. In winnowing the same 6d., to wit, for 10 quarters 1d. In cleaning wheat for seed **Weeding,** 2s. In 2 sacks bought 8d. Total: 53s. 3¾d. WEEDING, **Mowing and** MOWING, AND THE COST OF THE AUTUMN. In **the Cost of** weeding the corn nothing this year because it was weeded **the Autumn** by the customary tenants. In mowing the meadow [called] *la Mote* 4d. In customary payment [at the mowing] of [the meadow called] *Rodmede*, 6d. In 1 boon-work of 130 men reaping and binding the whole corn of Cowick 7s. 9d., for it is not bound to be reaped, or bound, by the customary **Cost of** tenants. Total: 8s. 7d. COST OF THE MILL. In re-making **the Mill** 2 broken spindles (*fusilla*), together with the iron bought

[1] *Domum bercar. matr.* The correct extension seems to be: *domum bercarie matricium*, though it could also be extended into *domum bercarii matricium*, i.e. 'the house of the shepherd looking after the ewes'.

[2] i.e. the payment is on the basis of 1 heaped quarter equal to 10 razed bushels.

for the same, 14d. In 1 mill-rind (*enka*) made anew 18d. In 2 trundle-wheels (*trundelli*) with iron bands (*ligamina*) made anew 12d. In board-nails bought for them 1d. In 6 pairs of cogs bought 3s., the price per pair 6d. In 9 pairs of rungs (*ronge*) bought 18d., the price per pair 2d. In sharpening bills[1] 3s. 4d. In 1 mill-stone bought for the mill anew 60s. In the carriage of the said mill-stone 10d. In mending 1 punch (?) (*bikketus*) for perforating the aforesaid mill-stone 4d. In tallow and soap bought for greasing the cog-wheels (*cogwegheles*) 3s. 4d., the price per pound 1d. In sawing timber for 1 cogwheel 2d. In sawing timber for the exterior wheel 4d. In sawing 1 beam (*trabs*) for the mill's dam (*stagnum*) 3d. In mending wooden bands (*ligamina*) around the mill-stone 4d. In checkbands (?) (*checkbendes*) and 3 hasps bought 3d. In 150 spike-nails bought 20d. In sawing 480 feet of boards and timber for the walls for the mill 3s. 7d. In hiring (*conducti*) 4 men to stop up the water at the mill 3d. In 2 baskets for carrying grain bought for the mill 3d. In 1 hurdle made for the eel-bed 7d. In stipend of 1 miller, who is the caretaker (*custos*) at the mill, for the year 8s. In tithe of the mill for the year 20s. Total: 111s. 10d. FOREIGN

Foreign Expenses

EXPENSES. In stipend of 1 man who caught 16 moles in the meadow 2d. In 90 perches of hedge made around *Loshangrc*[2] 2s. 6d., to wit, for 3 perches 1d. In stipend of 1 groom (*garcio*) sent to Somerton with 1 letter, 6d. In stipend of 1 groom sent to the Steward at Stratford 12d. Total: 4s. 2d. THE STEWARD'S EXPENSES. In expenses

The Steward's Expenses

of *Magister* Robert of Stratford on his visits, to wit, on Thursday next after the feast of St. Martin, on Friday on the morrow [of the feast of St. Martin], and on Tuesday on the feast of St. Edmund the King next following, 10s. 6½d., on Friday and Saturday next following after the Circumcision of Our Lord 9s. 1d., on Thursday in the week of Pentecost 11s. 5½d., on Friday next after the feast of St. Barnabas the Apostle 9s. 3½d. In wages of 1 groom taking care of 1 horse by the order of the Steward, for 23 days, 2s. 10½d., per day 1½d. In 1 quarter, half a bushel of oats bought 2s. 3¼d., for the provender for the said horse staying [there] for 24 nights, which had each night for 4 nights half a bushel, and for 20 nights each night one-third of a bushel. In 3½ bushels

[1] *In bill. acuend.*, there is no knowing whether the singular or the plural is intended; I assumed the latter.
[2] The original name for Cowick.

of oats bought 12¼d., the price per bushel 3½d., for the provender for 1 hourse staying [there] for 7 nights, which had each night half a bushel. Total: 46s. 6¾d. TOTAL

Cash
Deliveries

OF ALL THE EXPENSES: £26 9s. 4½d. CASH DE-LIVERIES. Handed over to Lord Thomas of Folquardeby, the Treasurer at Wolvesey, by 1 tally, £212 10s. 6d. And

Wheat
responds
three times
itself[1]

thus £17 6d. are outstanding. WHEAT. Likewise they render [account] for 120 quarters, 6 bushels, 1 peck of wheat received of this year's total issue of the grange, by razed measure. Total: as shown. Of which, sown over 105 acres in the field of Wick, 10 acres in the field of Nounton: 35 quarters 7½ bushels, to wit, per acre by the perch, 2½ bushels. Sold: 76½ quarters. Sold *super compotum:* 8 quarters 2 bushels, 3 pecks for 55s. 7½d. Total: as above, and equals.

Second-
grade
wheat
Barley
responds
8 qtr. 6 bsh.
less than
3½ times
itself

SECOND-GRADE WHEAT (*Curallum*). And for 8½ quarters of second-grade wheat of this year's total issue of the grange, by razed measure. And sold: all. BARLEY. And for 180 quarters 2 bushels of barley of this year's total issue, by razed measure. Total: as shown. Of which, sown over 99 acres in the field of Wick, 10 acres in the field of Nounton, 9 acres in the field of Witheton: 59 quarters, to wit, per acre by the perch, 4 bushels. Mixed [with other grain] for the liveries of the manorial servants (*famuli*): 17 quarters 4½ bushels and [1] peck. In extracting manure, by the customary services of the customary tenants: 2 quarters. In boon-works in the autumn: 1 quarter. Sold: 100½ quarters 1 bushel [and 1] peck. Total: as above, and equals.

Oats
responds
twice
itself

OATS. And for 62 quarters of this year's issue of oats. Total: as shown. Of which, sown over 25½ acres in Cowick, 34 acres in the field of Wick, and 3 acres in the field of Witheton: 31 quarters 2 bushels, to wit, per acre by the perch, 4 bushels. In provender for 4 cart-horses, 12 plough-horses (*affri*) at the time of the Lent sowing: 5 quarters 1 bushel. Ground to

Peas
responds
3 bsh. less
than 3½
times
itself

make pottage for the manorial servants[2]: 1 quarter 4 bushels. Sold: 20 quarters 7 bushels. Sold *super compotum:* 3 quarters 2 bushels for 8s. 8d. Total: as above, and equals. PEAS. And for 10 quarters 4½ bushels of this year's total issue of peas, by razed measure. Total, as shown. Of which, sown over 1½ acre in the field of Wick, 3 acres in the field of Nounton:

---

[1] These are marginal calculations of yield calculated as a multiple of the seed sown as recorded in the preceding account roll. In the case of wheat, *curallum* has been included in the total produce.

[2] *In farina pro potagio famulorum faciendo.*

1 quarter 3 bushels, to wit, per acre by the perch, 2½ bushels, less 1 peck in all. Mixed below with barley for the liveries of the manorial servants: 1 quarter. Fed to the pigs: 2 bushels. Sold: 7 quarters 7½ bushels. Total as above, and equals. VETCHES. And for 10½ quarters of this year's total issue of vetches, by razed measure. Total: as shown. Of which, sown over 4½ acres in the field of Nounton, 15 acres in the field of Wick: 4 quarters 7 bushels, to wit, per acre by the perch, 2 bushels. Fed to the pigs: 2 bushels. Sold: 5 quarters 3 bushels. Total: as above, and equals. LIVERIES OF THE MANORIAL SERVANTS. (*Liberatio Famulorum*). And for 17 quarters 4½ bushels and [1] peck of barley, and for 1 quarter of peas received, as above, for the liveries of the manorial servants. Total: 18 quarters 4½ bushels and [1] peck. Of which, in livery of 1 warrener from the fifth day of July until the feast of St. Michael, for 16 weeks and 3 days: 1 quarter 5 bushels; he gets a quarter for 10 weeks. In livery of 1 carter, 1 stot-herd, for the year: 10 quarters 3 bushels, each of whom gets a quarter for 10 weeks. In livery of the other carter from the 14th day of April until the feast of St. Michael, for 24 weeks: 2 quarters 2½ bushels, 1 peck; he gets a quarter for 10 weeks. Given to a certain man following the harrows at the time of each of the two sowings, for 16 weeks: 1 quarter; he gets half a bushel per week. In livery of 1 dairymaid for half a year: 1 quarter. Also to her from the feast of the Annunciation of the Blessed Mary until the feast of St. Michael, for 27 weeks: 1 quarter 6½ bushels; she get a quarter for 12 weeks. Sold *super compotum:* 3½ bushels for 2s. 7½d. ISSUES OF THE MILL. And for 9 quarters 4 bushels of wheat accruing from the issues of the mill this year. And sold: [all. BARLEY.][1] And for 53 quarters 5 bushels of barley accruing from the issues of the mill this year. Total: as shown. Of which, in livery of 1 miller, who is caretaker at the mill, by certain agreement, for the year: 6½ quarters; he gets a quarter for 8 weeks. [Sold: 47 quarters][1] 1 bushel. Total: as above, and equals. FIRST-GRADE MALT. (*Brasium Capitale*) And for 11 quarters 1 bushel of first-grade malt accruing from the issues of the mill. And sold: all. SECOND-GRADE MALT (*Brasium Cursale*). And for 43 quarters 2 bushels of second-grade malt

Vetches responds 4½ bsh. more than 3 times itself

Liveries of the Manorial Servants

Issues of the Mill Barley

First-grade Malt

Second-grade Malt

---

[1] A small patch is torn out of the margin at this point, but the text could not have been anything else.

[accruing from the issues of the mill].[1] And sold: all. OAT

Oat
Flour
Powder
Cart-
horses

FLOUR (*Farina Avene*). And for 1 bushel of oat flour accruing from the issues of the mill. And it is sold. POWDER (*Pulvis*). And for 6 bushels of powder accruing from the issues of the mill. And sold: all. [CART-HORSES. Likewise they render account for][1] 4 cart-horses remaining from the preceding year. And for 1 mare accruing as heriot of Clement *in la Lane*. Total: 5. Of which, added to the plough-

Plough-
horses

horses: 1. And remain 3 horses and 1 mare. PLOUGH-HORSES (*Affri*). [And for 13 plough-horses][1] remaining from the preceding year. And for 1 received from the cart-horses. Total: 14. Of which, sold: 1. Died: 1. Total: 2. And

Oxen

remain 12 plough-horses, of which 7 [are] males. OXEN. And for 32 oxen [remaining from the preceding year][1]. And for 1 accruing as heriot of Robert Ailward of Bottenham. Total: 33. Of which, sold towards the feast of St. Martin: 3. 'Convalesced'[2] and sold: 1. And sold because [it was] feeble

Cows

(*debilis*): 1. Total: 5. And remain [28 oxen].[1] COWS. And for 1 cow remaining from the preceding year. And for 2 cows bought from the reeve of Founthill. And for 1 cow, with its calf, obtained by purchase. And for 1 cow bought from Bishopstone before calving. And for 1 bought after calving. Total: 6. Of which, died: 1. And remain 5 cows.

Calves

CALVES. And for 1 calf with the cow by purchase. And for 2 produced this year, and not more because the two cows received from Founthill were sterile. Total: 3. Of which,

Wethers

sold: 1. And remain 2 calves. WETHERS (*Multones*). And for 234 wethers received from [those] remaining from the preceding year. And for 53 accruing from herbage[3] at Hockday. Total: 287. Of which, died before shearing: 4, and after shearing: 2. In customary payment for mowing the meadow [called] *Rodemede*: 1. 'Convalesced' and sold after

Rams

shearing: 20. Total: 27. And remain 260. RAMS. And for 12 rams remaining from the preceding year. Total: as shown. Of which, 'convalesced' and sold after shearing: 1. And

Ewes

remain 11 rams. EWES. And for 325 ewes remaining from the preceding year. And for 50 obtained from Bishopstone by purchase before lambing. And for 38 added from the one-year-olds (*hogastri*). Total: 413. Of which, died before

---

[1] A small patch is torn out of the margin at this point, but the text could not have been anything else.

[2] *In cubbatis et venditis.*

[3] i.e. a customary payment for grazing rights.

lambing: 4, after lambing and before shearing: 8, and after shearing: 6. 'Convalesced' and sold after shearing: 24. And sold *super compotum:* 1 for 16d. Total: 43. And remain 370 ewes. ONE-YEAR-OLDS (*Hogastri*). And for 38 one-year-olds obtained by purchase after shearing. Total: as shown. And all are added to the ewes above. And none remain.

One-year-olds

Lambs

LAMBS. And for 333 lambs produced by the ewes this year, and not more because 14 aborted, and 23 were sterile, and 4 died in lambing. And for 12 bought. Total: 345. Of which, died before separation: 25. In tithe: 31. In customary payment to 1 reeve, 1 granger, 1 hayward, 1 forester, 1 shepherd, and 1 shepherd looking after the lambs (*custos agnorum*): 6. Died after separation and before shearing: 3. And sold before shearing: 24, because [they were] feeble (*debilis*). And sold *super compotum:* 4 for 3s. 4d. Total: 89. And remain 252 lambs. BOAR. And for 1 boar added [from the one-year-olds]. And remains 1 boar. SOWS. And for 3 sows remaining from the preceding year. And for 1 added [from the one-year-olds]. Total: 4. Of which, died 1, in July. And remain 3 sows. PIGS. And for 33 pigs added from the one-year-olds. And for 4 bought. Total: 37. Of which, added to the sows: 1. And sold: 2. Total: 3. And remain 34 pigs.

Boar
Sows

Pigs

One-year-olds

ONE-YEAR-OLDS (*Hogetti*). And for 27 one-year-olds remaining [from the preceding year]. And for 7 remaining from the piglets of the preceding year. Total: 34. And 33 are added above to the pigs and 1 to the boars. PIGLETS. And for 45 piglets produced this year, to wit, 14 in November, 10 in February, 12 in July, 9 in December. Total: as shown. Of which, in tithe: 4. In customary payment to the reeve, granger (*granatarius*), forester and swineherd: 4. And sold *super compotum:* 2 for 8d. And remain 35 piglets. WOOL (*Lana Grossa*).[1] And for 283 fleeces (*vellera*)[2] of wethers, 12 fleeces of rams, and for 362 fleeces of ewes, obtained at the shearing. Total: 657. Of which, in tithe: 66. In customary payment to 2 shepherds: 2. And sent to Wolvesey[3] 589, which made 5 weys (*pondera*) and 8 cloves. LAMB'S WOOL. And for 240 lamb's fleeces obtained at the shearing. And all [were] sent to Wolvesey, which made 19 cloves. BROKEN

Piglets

Wool

Lamb's
Wool
Broken
Wool

---

[1] i.e. wool of all sheep other than lambs.
[2] i.e. wool-crop of a single animal.
[3] i.e. The Bishop's palace in Winchester: to be sold there, centrally, together with the rest of the wool of the bishopric.

Summer
Cheese[1]

WOOL (*Lana fracta*). And for 6 cloves 2 pounds of broken wool obtained at the shearing. And sold. SUMMER CHEESE. And for 165 cheeses made in summer which began to be made on Wednesday in the week of Easter and ceased on Saturday on the feast of St. Matthew the Apostle, both days included. Of which, in tithe: 16. In customary payment to the reeve, granger (*granatarius*), Hayward, and 1 shepherd: 4. In customary payment at the mowing of the meadow [called] *Rodmede:* 1. In customary payment to the ploughmen: 2. And sold: 142, which made 6 weys (*pondera*)

Butter
Hides

4 cloves and 6 pounds. BUTTER. And for 14 cloves of butter of this year's issue. And sold: all. HIDES. And for 1 hide of 1 plough-horse and for 1 hide of 1 cow, which died.

Fleeces

And they are all sold. FLEECES (*Pelles grosse*). And for 4 fleeces of wethers and 13 of ewes, which died before shearing. Total: 17. Of which, in tithe: 1. And sold: 16

Skins

fleeces. SKINS (*Pelles nude*). And for 2 [skins] of wethers and 6 [skins] of ewes, which died after shearing. And they

Lamb's
Fleeces

are sold. And none remain. LAMB'S FLEECES. And for 28 fleeces of lambs which died before separation. Of which, in tithe: 3. And remain 25 lamb's fleeces. And they are all

Swans

sold. SWANS. And for 12 swans obtained from Wolvesey, sent by Lord Thomas of Folquardeby. Total: as shown. Of which, died: 4. And sold *super compotum:* 2 for 6s. 8d.

Capons

Total: 6. And remain 6 swans. CAPONS. And for 24 capons made and added from the chickens. And remain 24 capons.

Hens
Chickens

HENS. And for 1 cock 5 hens received by purchase. And remain 6. CHICKENS. And for 24 chickens produced by the hens this year. And turned into capons above: all. And

Eggs
Churchscot

none remain. EGGS. And for 200 eggs produced by the hens this year. And all are sold. CHURCHSCOT. And for 368 hens accruing this year from churchscot.[2] Total: as shown. Of which, in default of 3 burgages and 1 fardel of land given (*liberate*) to Fulc of Walton: 16. In default of the mill of Stanlynche: 4. In default of 20 widows, to wit, the widow of William Gilebot, Joan the widow of Stonyng, the widow of Walter Badekok, the widow of John le Denenyshe, the widow of William atte Styghele, the widow of John Robat, the widow of William Ailward, the widow of Robert Crompe,

---

[1] The following calculation of the yield per cow and ewe is entered on the margin: 'cow responds for 5s., ewe for 3d. together with 9 cheeses from the customary tenants estimated at 5s., plus in all 12½d.'

[2] i.e. a customary payment of hens at Easter.

the widow of Trottok, the widow of le Monekes, the widow
of le Denenyshe, the widow of Cotte, the widow of Cuppyng,
the widow of Tarente, the widow of le Bal, the widow of
Dodde, the widow of Cuppyng, the widow of Shorie, the
widow of le Swynes, and John Dodde because he had no
wife: 40 hens. Total: 60. And sold: 308: Total: as above.

Cider
And none remain. CIDER. And for 1 cask (*pipa*) of cider
and for 1 barrel containing 68 gallons. And all are sold. And

Virgater:
none remain. VIRGATERS: WINTER [WORKS]. And

Winter
for 4134 winter works[1] (*opera*) received this year from the

[Works]
lord's 39 customary tenants from the feast of St. Michael
to the feast of the Annunciation of the Blessed Mary, for
106 working-days, who worked daily except Saturdays and
feast-days. Total: as shown. Of which, in acquittance of 1
reeve for the aforesaid time: 106 works. In acquittance of
1 granger (*bertonarius*): 106 works. In acquittance of 1
swan-keeper: 106 works. In carting manure: 180 works.
In roofing the ewe-house: 195 works. In cutting down and
carrying twigs (*virge*) and spikes (*spykes*) for making new
hurdles and mending the walls of the said ewe-house: 40
works. In carrying the roofing material (*coopertura*) to the
said ewe-house: 30 works. In harrowing in winter for the
sowing of wheat: 481 works. In making hurdles for the
sheepfold: 50 works. In harrowing in Lent: 147 works. In
cleaning the mill-pond (*stagnum*): 50 works. In carrying
timber to the mill: 25 works. In carrying thorns (*spine*) and
brambles (*vepres*) for enclosing within the manorial compound (*in curia*): 50 works. In making the said enclosure:
25 works. In gathering spikes for the barn and mill: 40
works. In suit of court at the law-day[2] and at 2 courts: 75
works. In cutting down and carrying thorns and brambles
for the dairy: 25 works. Sold: 2353 works. And sold *super
compotum:* 50 works for 2s. 1d. Total: as above. And none

Winter
remain. WINTER [WORKS]: HALF-VIRGATERS. And

[Works]:
for 1219 winter works received this year from 23 customary

Half-
tenants of the lord holding half-virgates, to wit, for 53

virgaters
working-days, who worked every other day during the aforementioned time. Total: as shown. Whereof, in carting
manure: 115 works. In harrowing for the winter sowing: 337
works. In harrowing *pro Dostloft*[3]: 45 works. In making

---

[1] A day's work is meant throughout.
[2] i.e. the day on which the tourn was held.
[3] A customary harrowing of some sort.

hurdles: 56 works. In carrying thorns and brambles: 23 works. In carrying fire-wood (*busca*) to the manor house (*curia*): 7 works. In gathering spikes: 23 works. In carrying timber to the mill: 23 works. In suit of court at the tourn of Hockday and at 2 courts: 69 works. In hurdles for the eel-bed: 36 works. In gathering twigs for the said hurdles: 20 works. In repairing and making the mill-pond (*stagnum*): 71 works. In carrying earth for the repair of defects around the mill and pond: 40 works. Sold: 354 works. Total: as above. And none remain. SUMMER [WORKS]: VIR-GATERS. And for 2847 works from 39 customary tenants of the lord holding virgates, for 73 working days this year, from the feast of the Annunciation of the Blessed Mary to the 1st of August (*Gula Augusti*), who worked daily except Saturdays and feast-days, and the weeks of Easter and Pentecost. Total: 2847 works. Of which, in acquittance of 1 reeve during the aforementioned time: 73 works. In acquittance of 1 granger (*bertonarius*): 73 works. In acquit-tance of 1 swan-keeper: 73 works. In ploughing for [the sowing of] barley: 33 works. In harrowing for the same: 114 works. In gathering twigs and spikes: 60 works. In weeding the corn: 315 works. In washing and shearing sheep: 107 works. In suit of court at the tourn of Hockday and at 1 court: 72 works. In mowing and lifting 22 acres 3 roods of meadow: 91 works. In carrying hay: 91 works. And sold: 1744 works. Total: as above. And none remain. SUMMER [WORKS]: HALF VIRGATERS. And for 839½ works received from 23 half-virgaters for 36 working-days and a half, who worked every other day during the aforementioned time. Total: as shown. Of which, in acquittance of 1 *dayman* from Sunday next after the feast of Easter to the 1st of August: 32 works. In ploughing for [the sowing of] barley: 44 works. In carrying thorns and brambles for enclosing in the manorial compound (*in curia*): 20 works. In making the said enclosure: 22 works. In carrying fire-wood to the manor-house (*curia*): 24 works. In carrying thorns and brambles for the dairy and in performing other necessary [tasks] in the manorial compound (*curia*): 66 works. In harrowing for [the sowing of] barley: 44 works. In gathering spikes and twigs: 69 works. In weeding the corn: 119½ works. In washing and shearing lambs: 44 works. In suit of court at the tourn of Hockday and at 1 court: 46 works. In mowing and lifting hay: 92 works. In carrying hay: 92 works. In

Summer [Works]: Virgaters

Summer [Works]: Half-virgaters

Autumn
[Works]:
Virgaters
and Half-
virgaters

carrying wool to Wolvesey: 18 works. And sold: 107 works. Total: as shown. And none remain. AUTUMN [WORKS]: VIRGATERS AND HALF-VIRGATERS. And for 1521 works received from 39 virgaters, and for 897 works from 23 half-virgaters, each of whom ought to work every working-day except Saturdays, to wit, for 39 working-days this year, between the 1st of August and the feast of St. Michael. Total: 2418 works. Of which, in acquittance of 1 reeve: 39 works. In acquittance of 1 granger (*bertonarius*): 39 works. In acquittance of 1 swan-keeper: 39 works. In acquittance of 3 haywards, 1 shepherd looking after the wethers in Nounton, 1 *dayman:* 195 works. In reaping, binding and gathering 260½ acres of various kinds of corn: 621 works. In carrying the said corn: 126 works, and not more because of the lord's cart. In gathering stubble: 153 works. In cutting down and carrying thorns and brambles for enclosing the farm-yard (*bertona*) of Witheton: 4 works. In making the said enclosure: 4 works. In gathering spikes and twigs: 12 works. In sale of works of 3 virgates, 8 half-virgates, from the 1st of August to the feast of St. Michael: 273 works. And sold together (*in communi*) after the feast of St. John *ante Portam Latinam:* 903 works. And sold *super compotum:* 110 works for 9s. 2d. Total: as above. And none

Fardel-men:
Winter
[Works]

remain. FARDEL-MEN:[1] WINTER [WORKS]. And for 528 works received from 22 fardel-men for 24 working-days occurring this year between the feast of St. Michael and the Annunciation of the Blessed Mary, who worked 1 day a week except feast-days. Total: as shown. Of which, in acquittance of 1 shepherd looking after the wethers in Witheton, 1 shepherd looking after the ewes, 1 swineherd, 2 oxherds, 9 ploughmen: 336 works. In spreading manure: 40 works. In repairing the mill-pond (*stagnum*): 16 works. In cutting down and gathering spikes and twigs for the sheep-house: 24 works. In roofing the said sheep-house: 24 works. In gathering twigs and spikes for the barn and the mill: 32 works. Sold: 32 works. And sold *super compotum:* 24 works for 12d. Total: as above. And none remain.

Fardel-men:
Summer
[Works]

FARDEL-MEN: SUMMER [WORKS]. And for 352 works received from 22 fardel-men for 17 working-days occurring this year between the feast of the Annunciation of the Blessed Mary and the 1st of August, for 18 weeks,

[1] Tenants holding quarter-virgates.

who worked 1 day a week except feast-days. Total: as shown. Of which, in acquittance of 1 shepherd looking after the wethers, 1 shepherd looking after the ewes, 1 swineherd, 2 oxherds, 9 ploughmen, and 1 shepherd looking after the lambs: 240 works. In making an enclosure around *la Mote:* 54 works. In washing and shearing sheep: 18 works. In washing and shearing lambs: 18 works. Sold: 11 works. And sold *super compotum:* 11 works for 5½d. Total: as

Fardel-men: above. And none remain. FARDEL-MEN: AUTUMN
Autumn [WORKS]. And for 198 works received from 22 fardel-men,
[Works] of whom each ought to perform each week 1 day-work (*opus*), between the 1st of August and the feast of St. Michael. Total: as shown. Of which, in acquittance of 1 shepherd looking after the wethers, 1 shepherd looking after the ewes, 1 swineherd, 2 oxherds, 1 shepherd looking after the lambs, 9 ploughmen, 1 man looking after the 'convalescing' animals (*custos cubbatorum*): 144 works. In reaping, binding, and gathering 13½ acres or various kinds of corn: 54 works. Total: as above. And none remain.

FROM *The Domesday Book or the Great Survey of England of William the Conqueror AD.MLXXXVI; Facsimile of the part relating to Hertfordshire*, Ordnance Survey Office, Southampton, 1863, p. ix.

THE LANDS OF ST. PAUL'S, LONDON [1086]

The same Canons hold Erdelei [Ardleigh] in the Hundred of Odesei. It is assessed at 6 hides. There is land for 10 ploughs. In the demesne are 3 hides, and there are 2 ploughs and [there] could be a third. There 12 villeins (*villani*) have 7 ploughs. There [are] 6 bordars (*bordarii*) and 2 cottars and 4 slaves (*servi*). [There is] meadow for 2 oxen. [There is] pasture [sufficient] for the livestock. [There is] wood for 200 pigs. In all profits it is worth £7. At the time of King Edward [it was worth] £10. This manor belonged and belongs (*jacuit et jacet*) to the church of St. Paul.

FROM *The Domesday of St. Paul's of the Year MCCXXII*, William Hale ed., Camden Society 69, 1858, pp. 21–27.

Inquisition made in the Manor of Ardleigh [Herts.], Theobald the Archdeacon of Essex being the 'Farmer[1]' at the time [1222].

The names of the jurors	This is the verdict of the jurors

Geoffrey Mariot
Simon Cuntreweger
Robert son of Fulk } free men
Angerus son of Osbert
Godfrey son of Alan
William the beadle
Robert son of Jeronimus
Godulfus
Hugh Bruning
Turstanus

Those say that the manor 'defended itself against the King'[2] for 5 hides, apart from the demesne, and is free of all suit of the shire and hundred [courts] and anything else that pertains to the King in chief and to his bailiffs. They also say that [there] are in the demesne

460 and 12 acres, by five times twenty[3], of arable land, and 8 acres of meadow. [There is] no pasture except in the woods. Also [there are] in the park, around the manorial complex of buildings,[4] 60 acres, together with the 8 acres of tenants' land which he had exchanged for as many [acres] from the demesne, and with 8 acres from the demesne. And in the foreign wood[5] not endowed [with saleable produce there are] 40 acres. And in another, enclosed, wood endowed with undergrowth, and withies (*virge*), and larger trees, [there are] 10 acres. Cultivation can be carried out with 3 ploughs of 8 heads together with the customary services of the vill. There can be stocked there 6 cows with one bull, and 200 sheep, and 60 pigs. Also [there is] in demesne [one] wind-mill which can be farmed out for 20s., apart from any annual expenditure it may require, which [mill] Richard of Stapleford

---

[1] *Firmarius*, i.e. a person to whom the manor was leased out.
[2] i.e. it was assessed at 5 hides for the purposes of royal taxation.
[3] i.e. by the short hundred (as opposed to the long hundred of 120).
[4] *circa curiam*.
[5] Not part of the demesne and thus not fully under the landlord's control.

made, and he gave half an acre of demesne land to Ralph son of William in exchange for the site of the said mill. They also say that the manor had been improved by Richard of Stapleford, in lands marled, in the new mill, and in the buildings constructed, to the value of 5 marks,[1] but that the woods had been impoverished to the value of 40s. during his time and in the time of peace; however, during the time of Theobald, the Archdeacon of Essex, the manor has been improved to the value of 6 marks.

These hold from the demesne

Ralph son of William of Crawnie 3 acres for 12d.
Roger son of Ailwinus 6 acres for 2s.
Geoffrey son of John *de cruce* 7 acres for 2s. and 4d.
    Also 8 acres for 32d.
Odo son of William 8 acres for 32d.
William son of Godwin 3 acres for 12d.
Four acres which Richard, the new man, held are in the demesne
    above.
Michael son of Adam 1 acre for 2d., which Nicholas the Canon gave
    to him in augmentation. Also 1 rood for 5d. by[3] Richard of
    Stapleford.
William Abel half an acre for 2d. with the daughter of Blidewinus.
Richard Stokkere 1½ acres for 6d.
Godulfus *de bruera* 12 acres for 4s. by Ralph *de diceto*, the Dean.
    Also 2 acres for 12d. by Richard of Stapleford, and 2 capons.
Hugh, the shepherd, half a virgate for 5s., and 2 hens, and 15 eggs.[2]
Richard *de bruera* 7½ acres for 2s. 6d.
Ralph son of William of Crawnie 5 acres for 2s.
Margery the widow of William the smith 3 roods for 6d.
Serlo son of Robert 1 acre for 6d., formerly of Winemerus, by Richard
    of Stapleford.

These hold for money rent (*ad censum*)

Walter *de mora* with the nephew and heir of Hamo half a hide, for
    which he is bound to acquit the manor of suit of Shire and
    Hundred [courts] whenever the manor should owe it. Also, half
    a virgate for 2s. 6d., which was of Robert Franceis, which his
    predecessors had by *Magister* Albericus. Also, 1 virgate for 3s.

---

[1] A mark was a unit of accounting equal to 13s. 4d.
[2] Hens and 15 eggs, is crossed out.
[3] i.e. by the authority of.

for the outcry concerning the land of Wlpet[1], whereof he has a charter of the Chapter without any witness. Also, 1 acre of villein land for 6d., by Nicholas the Archdeacon of Huntingdonshire. Also, 1½ acres for 3d., by *Magister* Herewicus. He now renders for all those lands and others below, 14s. 11d.

Simon Cultreweg 1½ virgates for 7s. and he ought to plough in each sowing-season 2 acres, as his father swore [to do] but he denies. Also, 1 acre for 2d., by *Magister* Hugh of London. Also, 9 acres of assart for 24d., 8 of which his father had by the toleration of the Archdeacon. He also [holds] 1 acre, by S. *de Clai*, for 4d. And 2 acres for 12d.

Geoffrey Mariot 16 acres for 3s. for all the service[2], by charter of the Chapter. Also, 1 acre and 1 messuage for 12d.

Robert son of Fulk half a virgate for 2s. 6d. for all the service, and 4½ acres of assart for 18d.

Godfrey son of Alan 1 virgate for 5s. And he ought to plough in each sowing-season 2 acres. Also, 3½ acres for 16d.

Geoffrey son of Odo 1 messuage for 6d. and 6 acres of old assart and new for 2s. and 2 acres less 1 rood for 7d. for a quit-claim of a half-virgate which he held for money rent; it is now assigned to another for labour services (*ad operationem*). Also, 1 messuage of new assart, by Richard of Stapleford, for 2d. and 1 capon and in exchange for some land enclosed in the park.

These hold old assarts (*de essarto veteri*)

John, with the nephew of Wlimardus, holds half a virgate for 3s. Also 4 acres and 1 rood of assart for 17d. And he ought to plough 3 acres a year, and to mow and lift hay once, [and] to reap twice in autumn, with [the lord providing] bread and ale. [He shall give] 2 hens at Christmas, 15 eggs at Easter. Also, he holds 1 rood for 3d., by Richard of Stapleford. Also, 3 roods for 3d.

Geoffrey Mariot 6 acres, which be bought from the heir of Ernoldus, for 25d., and he ought to reap twice in autumn, and [to give] 1 hen

---

[1] *Pro 3s. pro clamore de terra de Wlpet.* The meaning of this passage is not entirely clear. It would seem to mean that the virgate was originally held for the obligation to represent the landlord in legal proceedings touching the land of Wlpet (a suit of court in effect), but that this obligation was commuted to a rent of 3s. by charter.

[2] i.e. No other services, except the money rent, are due from him.

and 6 eggs, and to mow and lift hay. Also 3 acres of new assart for 2s., by Richard of Stapleford. Also, a small plot (*parva placia*) for 1 capon.

Mariota 3 acres for 12d., by Nicholas the Archdeacon.

Geoffrey Tropinel 6½ acres for 26d., for the same service. Also, 1 acre and 1 rood for 20d. Also, 3 acres for 12d., by charter of the Chapter.

Hugh the beadel 4½ acres for 18d. and for the same service.

Angerus 11 acres and 1 rood for 3s. and 7d., [acquired] by his father who bought them from the heir of Paganus the carpenter, for the same service.

John son of William 9 acres for 3s., for the same service. Also, half a rood for 2d.

William son of Baldwin 2 acres for 8d., for the same service.

William the beadel 6 acres and 1 rood for 25d., for the same service, formerly of Ralph to whom it no longer belongs,[1] by S. *de Clai*.

John son of Herbert 1 acre for 4d. Also, a small addition (*augmentum*) for 4d.

Robert son of Edmund 1 acre for 4d. Also, a small addition for 1d.

Roger son of Robert 3 acres for 12d.

Godulfus 5 acres for 20d., formerly of Robert.

William Tropinel 5 acres for 20d. and for all the service. Also, half a rood for 2d.

Wiliam son of William 4 acres for 16d.

Kueneva and Edelina daughters of Gilbert 4 acres for 16d.

Robert son of Richard Koterel 8 acres for 32d., and he ought to reap and perform boon-works.

John son of William Stiuur 4 acres for 16d.

Cristina the widow of William son of Edward 7 acres for 28d.

Turstanus son of Semerus 4 acres for 16d.

Walter the carpenter 3 acres and 1 rood for 13d. which he bought from Richard le Cupere.

Gilbert the smith 1 acre and 1 rood for 5d. Also, 2½ acres for 10d.

Isabella the widow of John son of Ranulfus 2 acres and 1 rood for 9d. Also, 2 acres for 8d.

Ralph son of William of Crawnie 1 plot (*placia*) next to the park for 3 capons.

Geoffrey *de fonte* 1½ acres for 6d.

Richard *de ponte* half an acre for 2d.

Robert son of Roger son of (a) merchant 1½ acres for 6d. Also, a small addition for 1d.

---

[1] *cui non attinet.*

Angerus son of Osbert 2 acres for 8d., by the purchase of the pre-
decessor of Geva whose daughter he has.[1] Also, a garden for ½d.

Wimmerus son of Peter 2 acres for 8d. Also, half an acre for 4d.

Robert [son of] Gerelinus with the daughter of Juliana 2 acres for 8d.

Juliana daughter of Ailwinus 2 acres for 8d. and a small addition
(*incrementum*) for 3½d.

Walter *de la more* 3 acres for 12d., formerly of Geoffrey the plumber
to whom it no longer belongs,[2] by Nicholas the Archdeacon.

William son of Godwin 1½ acres for 6d.

Hugh son of Hugh Brunild 1 quarter[3] for 18d. and 8 acres for 32d.
Also 2 acres for 8d. by the Chapter. Also 1 acre and 1½ roods
for 12d., by Richard of Stapleford.

Richard son of Hugh 6½ acres for 3s.

Osbert son of Walter 5 acres for 20d. Also, half an acre for 8d., by
Richard of Stapleford.

Simon Cultreweg 2 acres for 8d., to whom they have reverted. Note:
the jurors should enquire more fully into this and inform the
Chapter.

John with Matilda daughter of Hugh *de la more* 3½ acres for 14d.
Also, 2 acres and 1 rood for 18d.

Walter *de mora* 14 acres for 4s. and 8d., formerly of Elvina to whom
it no longer belongs,[2] of whose entry they are ignorant.[4]

Hildemar son of Theodoric 1 quarter for 18d. and 3½ acres for 14d.
Also, 1 acre for 4d.

Walter *de mora* half a virgate for 2s. 6d., who proved his right to it
(*eam disrationavit*) against Osbert in the county court.

Wimarch 3½ acres for 14d. and 3 roods for 8d., by Richard of Stapleford.

Robert the carpenter 1½ acres for 7d., by the same.

Angerus son of Robert 1 messuage for 2d., by R. and T. the 'farmers'
(*firmarii*).

Ralph Dudde 1 messuage for 2d., by Richard of Stapleford.

Richard the carter 1 messuage for 2d., by the same.

Luke son of the parson 1 curtilage for 6d., by the same.

Geoffrey the presbiter 1 messuage for 2d., by the same.

Alditha Tropinel 1 plot (*placea*) for 2d., by the same.

Godfrey de Tokinton' 2½ acres for 11½d., by J. *de Hospitali*, by charter
of the Chapter. Also, half an acre for 3½d., by Richard of Stapleford. Also, 3½ acres, formerly of Winemerus Casun, for 14d.

---

[1] i.e. He is married to her.
[2] *cui non attinet.*
[3] i.e. A quarter of a virgate.
[4] i.e. They do not know by whose authority he took possession of this holding.

Agnes Writele 1 acre for 4d.
Margaret the weaver 1 acre for 4d.
Wiliam son of Godfrey *de fonte* 1 rood for 1d.
Walter *de mora* half an acre for 2d., by J. *de Hospitali*, and 1 garden for
    1d. Also, half an acre towards the assart of Geoffrey Mariot for 3d.
Robert King 1 rood for 1d.
Geva the widow of William Tikehorn.[1]

These perform labour services (*sunt ad operacionem*)

Geoffrey son of Hamo holds half a virgate and owes 8d. of woodsilver,
and 3d. of maltsilver, and the ploughing of 9 acres a year. And
[he ought] to harrow 3 acres, if it is sown for harrowing in winter,
and at the ploughing-boons he shall plough 1 rood, that is a
fourth part of an acre, without food [from the lord]; and two
roods ploughed in this way count to each whole virgate for 1 day's
work (*opus*). [He ought to give] 15 eggs at Easter and to
perform the service of carrying 9 quarters [of grain][2] to London,
and it counts to him for 1 day's work. And [he owes] 2 day's work
a week, feast-days excepted, and every week in autumn 2 boon-
works.
William Abel with the daughter of Blithewinus half a virgate for the
same service.
Geoffrey son of William *de bruera* for the same service half a virgate.
William the beadel, son of Richard the carpenter, half a virgate for the
same service.
Arnold son of Herbert half a virgate for the same service.
Robert son of Germanus and William *niger* half a virgate for the same
service, and in addition they shall provide 2 men for the boon-
works in autumn besides the aforementioned service.
Four acres of the half-virgate formerly of Robert and Winemerus are
in the demesne, and 10 acres of the same [half-virgate] Hugh
son of Geva has by charter of the Chapter, as he says. Also,
[he has] 5 acres of assart to make up a half-virgate for which
he renders 3s. Also, 2 acres for 8d., by S. *de Clay*. Also, 1½ acres
of wood (*grava*), by J. *de Hospitali* for 6d.
Geva the mother of Hugh 2 acres for 2s., by Richard of Stapleford.
Robert son of Edmund half a virgate for the same service.
Hugh son of John half a virgate for the same service.
Robert *blundus* half a virgate for the same service.
Michael son of Adam half a virgate for the same service.

[1] No holding is entered against her name.
[2] *Et portare summagium 9 summarum.*

Richard son of Turstanus half a virgate for the same service.
Richard *de ponte* and Hugh Brunild half a virgate for the same service.
Serlo son of Robert half a virgate for the same service.
Roger son of Robert half a virgate for the same service.
William the beadle son of Ralph half a virgate for the same service.
Godardus half a virgate for the same service, formerly of Odo.
Gilbert son of Aluredus, the smith, half a virgate for making the iron-
    work of the manor (*curia*), and he ought to plough 3 acres in
    each ploughing-season. Also, he holds 1 quarter for 26d.
Ralph son of William of Crawnie half a virgate, owing the same
    service, for 3s., by Robert the servant of Nicholas the Archdeacon.

These are cottars

Two acres formerly of Ailwinus are in the demesne and Geva has one
    [of them].
William son of Baldwin 3 acres.
Two acres formerly of William are in the hands of Simon Cultreweg,
    by N. the 'farmer', and one is included in the park.
Adam the shepherd 3 acres, formerly of Aldiva.
Those owe every Monday 1 day's work (*operacio*), and [they ought]
    to carry, and drive pigs, to London. Each of them owes one hen
    and 3 eggs for 3 acres, and each cottage (*coteria*) ought to reap
    half an acre for 1 day's work.

5

FROM *Historia et Cartularium Monasterii Sancti Petri Gloucestriae,* William Hart ed., London 1867, III, 35–41.[1]

The extent of the manor of Littleton [Hants.] as to what, and how much, the same manor is worth in all the issues per year, made in the presence of Lords (*domini*) R. of Sondhurste, the Cellarer, and Thomas of Tyringhame, on oath of the senior and more discreet men of the same manor, in the fiftieth year[2] [1265/66].

Who say on their oath that in the field of Middelforlong, and Orcherdforlong, and Medforlong [there] are 84 arable acres.
And in Thursbrakedenelonde, and in Six Acres, and in Schepeslande [there] are 24 arable acres.
And in Fenfurlonge [there] are 26 arable acres.
And in Waterdelle [there] are 17 arable acres.
And [in] Oppethebutten [there] are 6 arable acres.
And in Langelonde, and in Pikedelonde next to *Douna* [there] are 9 arable acres.
And in Wodeforlonge [there] are 8 arable acres.
All the said parcels (*particule*) are looked upon as constituting one field.[3]
Total: 174 arable acres, the price per acre 6d.
And the total is 111s. 6d.[4]
Also, in the aforesaid field, in a certain *cultura*[5] which is called Foxenhulle, [there] are 66 arable acres, the price per acre 3d.

[1] The editor has written out in full all sums, whether acres or money, but I have reverted to the use of figures which I take to have been the practice followed in the original document. Most of the footnotes are my own.
[2] In the fiftieth year of Henry III, i.e. 1265/66.
[3] *jacent pro uno campo.*
[4] This total does not tally with the preceding acreage.
[5] This term is quite untranslatable; it denotes any area of arable land which is a physically separate unit, within an open field which in turn constitutes a single unit of rotation. *Culture* usually correspond to furlongs.

And the total is 16s. 6d.

And in the aforesaid field it is possible to 'inhok'[1] every second year 40 acres, and the profit thereof in that year is worth 10s.[2]; and thus annual profit can be put at 10s.

Likewise, they say on their oath that in la Leya [there] are 20 arable acres.

And in la Dene [there] are 13 arable acres.

In Willewelande [there] are 8 arable acres.

And in Stallingforlonge [there] are 12 arable acres.

And in Stomdene [there] are 4 acres.

And in la Dounhalf [there] are 6 arable acres.

Total acreage: 63 acres, and [each] acre is worth 7d.

And the total value thereof is 36s. 9d.

They also say that out of the aforesaid 63 acres it is possible to 'inhok' every second year 20 acres, and the profit thereof in that year is worth 11s. 8d.; and thus annual profit can be put at 5s. 10d.

Likewise, they say that in Langethornesforlong [there] are 50 arable acres.

And in Stallingforlonge [there] are 8 arable acres.

And at the head of that field [there] are 7 arable acres.

And on Witehulle [there] are 9 arable acres.

Also, at the head of Witehulle [there] are 9 arable acres.

In Mushulle [there] are 14 arable acres.

In Helinglonde [there] are 9 arable acres.

And in Pikedelonde, next to the road, [there] are 3 arable acres.

And the total thereof is 109 acres, the price per acre 3d.

And the total value thereof is 27s. 3d.

And the sum total of all the arable acres is 411.

And the total of the said acres [in terms] of their worth in money is £9 12s.

Of which, a third part having been subtracted for the field which is lying fallow, to wit, 64s., [there] remain, as the annual net valuation, £6 8s.; and of the profit of the land which can be 'inhoked' each year, 15s. 10d.

Likewise, they say that [there] are there 4½ acres of meadow and they are worth 13s. 6d.

And the pasture *super Dounam* can be sold, on average, for 5s. a year.

And [there] is pasture there for 9 oxen and it is worth 6s. 9d.

And pasture for 6 plough-horses (*affri*) and it is worth 18d.

And pasture for 5 cows and it is worth 2s. 6d.

[1] An 'inhok' is an area temporarily under cultivation within the field which is lying fallow at the time.

[2] This, clearly, should have been 20s.

And pasture for 5 beasts (*averia*) and it is worth 15d.

And pasture for 20 pigs and it is worth 2s. 6d.

And pasture for 400 sheep a year and it is worth 33s. 4d.

Total: 66s. and 4d.

The also say that Roger of Chenne the clerk renders for the land of Radenham 13s. 4d. of free rent a year.

The 'Aid'[1] of the customary tenants is 18s. a year.

Pannage of pigs and [other] animals is worth, in money and ploughing services, 15s. 3d. a year.

The levy of Peterpence is worth 20d. a year.

The profit of the garden, with its grazing and with the profit of the curtilage, is worth 33s. a year.

And the dovecot is worth, on average, 2s. a year.

And the profit of the wood, without waste, is worth 10s. a year.

And a certain customary payment, which is called Schernsilver, is worth, on average, 12d. a year.

Total: £4 14s. and 3d.

[There] are also there in villeinage 13½ virgates of land each of which is let out for a money rent[2] and renders 5s. a year.

And the total is 57s.[3] and 6d.

And of these 13½ virgates of land Mathias of Schottesdene holds 1 virgate of land, and he ought, besides the aforementioned money rent, to plough twice a year for the lord, and this ploughing is worth 4d.

And on those days when he ploughs he shall eat at the lord's expense[4] and he shall give 5¼ bushels of wheat as churchscot, and they are worth 3s. and 3d.

And he ought to harrow the lord's land for the Lent sowing until the whole of the lord's land is sown, and this harrowing is worth 4½d.

And he shall weed the lord's corn for three days and it is worth 2½d.

And he shall lift and carry the lord's hay and it is worth 2d.

And he shall plant beans for one day and it is worth ½d.

Likewise, he shall wash and shear the lord's sheep and it is worth ½d.

And he shall make [one] hay-cock within the manorial compound (*in curia*) and it is worth ½d.

And he owes carrying services (*debet summagiare*) to Andevere and Lutegareshale and it is worth 3d. a year.

And he ought to reap 2½ acres each week in autumn and it is worth, in all, 3s. 2½d.

And he shall make three boon-works in autumn, with two men, eating

---

[1] i.e. tallage.
[2] *posita est ad firmam.*
[3] It should be 67s.
[4] *Comedet in mensa domini*; literally, 'at the lord's table'.

at the lord's expense,[1] and it is worth 3d., subtracting the food of these men.

And he shall carry the lord's corn in autumn and it is worth 4s.

And if he neither reaps nor carries he shall thresh the lord's corn to the same value.

And he ought to gather nuts for half a day and it is worth ½d.

Total [value] of the services of the same virgater, besides the aforesaid money rent: 12s. 2¼d.

Robert Bissop holds 1 virgate and he shall perform the same services, besides the aforesaid money rent, and it is worth 12s. 2½d.

William *de Hegge* holds 1 virgate of land and he shall perform the same services, besides the aforementioned money rent, and it is worth 12s. 2½d.

Robert the reeve holds 1 virgate of land and he shall perform the same services, besides the aforementioned money rent, and it is worth 12s. 2½d.

William Witemon holds 1 virgate of land and he shall perform the same services, besides the aforementioned money rent, and it is worth 12s. 2½d.

Rosa *de la Putte* holds 1 virgate of land and she shall perform the same services, besides the aforementioned money rent, and it is worth 12s. 2½d.

And the total [value] of these six virgates of land, besides the aforementioned money rent, is, in all, 73s. 3d.

Thomas Bonvallet holds half a virgate of land and he shall plough twice a year for the lord and it is worth 2d.

And on those days he shall eat at the lord's expense[2] and he shall give churchscot proportionately to his holding[3] and it is worth 19d.

And he shall harrow and it is worth 4½d.

And he shall weed and it is worth 2½d.

And he ought to make hay (*fenissare*) as [a full] virgate and it is worth 2d.

And he shall plant beans and it is worth ½d.

And he shall wash and shear the lord's sheep and it is worth ½d.

And he shall make [one] hay-cock and is is worth ½d.

And he shall carry (*summagiabit*) and it is worth 1½d.

And he ought to reap as a [full] virgate and it is worth 3s. 2¼d.

And he shall make three boon-works and it is worth 3d.

And on those days he shall eat at the lord's expense,[4] and he shall

---

[1] *Stantibus in mensa domini*; literally, 'staying at the lord's table'.
[2] *Comedet cum domino*; literally, 'he shall eat with the lord'.
[3] *Pro portione sua.*
[4] *Manducabit cum domino*; literally, 'he shall eat with the lord'.

carry the lord's corn in autumn and this same carrying-service is worth 4s., or he shall thresh to the same value.

And he shall gather nuts and it is worth ½d.

And the total [value] of the services of the same [tenant] is 10s. 3d.

Richard King holds half a virgate of land and he shall perform the same services and it is worth 10s. 3d.

John Cuppere holds half a virgate of land and he shall perform the same services and it is worth 10s. 3d.

Robert le Frense holds half a virgate of land and he shall perform the same services and it is worth 10s. 3d.

Geoffrey le Strutere holds half a virgate of land and he shall perform the same services and it is worth 10s. 3d.

Michael of Schottesdene holds half a virgate of land and he shall perform the same services and it is worth 10s. 3d.

Isabella the widow of le Bloware holds half a virgate of land and she shall perform the same services and it is worth 10s. 3d.

John Barnabe holds half a virgate of land and he shall perform the same services and it is worth 10s. 3d.

Walter *de la Mede* holds half a virgate of land and he shall perform the same services and it is worth 10s. 3d.

And the total of these nine half-virgates of land, besides the afore-mentioned money rent, is £4 10s.[1]3d.

Henry Bigge holds ten acres of land and, besides the aforementioned money rent, he shall give three hens and one cock, and churchscot and they are worth 4d.

And he shall harrow and it is worth 4½d.

And he shall weed and it is worth 2½d.

And he shall lift the lord's hay and it is worth 1d.

And he shall plant and it is worth ½d.

And he shall wash and shear the lord's sheep and it is worth ½d.

And he shall make [one] hay-cock in the manorial compound (*in curia*) and it is worth ½d.

And he shall reap in autumn and it is worth 2s. 2½d.

And he shall make three boon-works, with one man, and it is worth 3d.

And he shall thresh, after he shall have reaped in autumn, to the value of the reaping.

And he shall gather nuts for half a day and it is worth ½d.

And total services of the same [tenant] are worth 4s.[2] 7½d.

---

[1] It should be 12s.

[2] 3s. 7½d. by addition; but is possible that the grain which he is, presumably, giving as churchscot, and which is not evaluated above, is worth, on pro rata basis, 1s.

Juliana the widow of Ralph holds ten acres of land and she shall perform the same services and it is worth 4s. 7½d.

John *de la Hurne* holds ten acres of land and he shall perform the same services and it is worth 4s. 7½d.

Emma the widow of William Maideus holds ten acres of land and she shall perform the same services and it is worth 4s. 7½d.

John Maideus holds ten acres of land and he shall perform the same services and it is worth 4s. 7½d.

Robert Aylard holds ten acres of land and he shall perform the same services and it is worth 4s. 7½d.

John Bucke holds ten acres of land and he shall perform the same services and it is worth 4s. 7½d.

John le Paumer holds ten acres of land and he shall perform the same services and it is worth 4s. 7½d.

Total: 32s. 4½d.[1]

William Chicheli holds two acres of land and he shall perform other minor services and they are worth 8d.

And he shall reap in autumn every Monday and Friday and it is worth 16d. for the whole autumn.

And he shall make one boon-work each week, with one man, and it is worth 4d.

And he shall gather nuts and it is worth ½d.

Total: 2s. [2]4½d.

Richard the carpenter holds two acres of land and he shall perform the same services.

Total: 2s. 4½d.

Walter *de cruce* holds six acres of land and his services, besides the 20d. which he renders towards the aforesaid money rent, are worth 5s. 3½d. a year.

And he shall give 1 hen and 1 cock as churchscot and it is worth 2d.

Michael Staymor holds one house with a curtilage and he renders 2s. a year.

And he shall make one boon-work and it is worth 1d.

He shall wash and shear the lord's sheep and it is worth ½d.

And he shall gather nuts and it is worth ½d.

Walter the smith holds one messuage and he renders 12d. a year.

Total: 11s.

And the total of the whole extent of Littleton, at fixed valuation (*in certo valore*), is £28 11s. 2d.

---

[1] This is the total of seven tenants.
[2] *denarii* in the MS.

6

FROM [The Extent of the Manor of Hodsock (Notts.) with Soke,
1324]. Department of Manuscripts, the University of Nottingham,
MS. Clifton, M.92.[1]

The extent of all the lands and tenements of the Manor
of Hodsock made there on Friday, on the morrow of St.
Luke the Evangelist, in the 18th year of King Edward, son
of King Edward,[2] on the oath of Elyas Freman of Oulecotes,
Walter Coke of Holm, Geoffrey Taillour, Henry son of
Thomas, Robert son of Richard, Thomas Anot, Elyas *ad
pontem*, William *in cimiterio*, John of Hermeston, John Proud,
Elyas Pistor, and Elyas *ad capud ville;* who say that [there]
is there a certain Manor, surrounded on all sides with a
moat, in which [there] are: one hall (*aula*), three chambers
(*camere*), a pantry, a buttery, a kitchen, a bake-house, a
granary, two barns, one chapel, two stables, one chamber
above the bridge with portcullis and a drawbridge, one
malt-kiln, [and] two fish-ponds, which are worth nothing
per year beyond their own usefulness (*ultra reprisam*). [There]
is there one garden which is worth, with [its] produce and
grazing, 6d. a year. [There] is there one dove-cote which is
worth 2s. a year. [There] are there, outside the moat, two
stables, [and] one ox-shed, which are worth nothing beyond
their own usefulness. [There] is there one garden whose

[1] There is no proper heading to this document. The document—like so many
documents emanating from lay estates—has been drawn up in a somewhat imperfect
fashion; there are wide blank spaces between the main paragraphs, and frequent
insertions between the lines. In most cases these are obvious corrections to the text
below, though occasionally, they impart additional information. The verso of the
document is badly faded. Two lines at the very top of the document, separated from
the next paragraph by a very wide blank space, are completely illegible, even under
ultra-violet light. The next paragraph is badly faded but can be read without too
much difficulty under ultra-violet light, with the exception of one interlineation, the
reading of which is somewhat uncertain.
[2] i.e. 19 October 1324.

apples, produce, and grazing are worth 2s. a year. [There] is there a certain enclosure, with a fence on the north side, whose grazing is worth 6d. a year. Demesne lands are not being evaluated because they are not measured. And [there] is there one plot of land (*placia*), which is called *Marl(e)*, and it is worth 8d. a year.

Total:
5s. 8d.

[There] is there one plot of meadow which is called *la Stubbynge* and it contains 23 acres, by the perch measuring 20 feet, and each acre is worth 2s. a year. [There] are also there in *Swynwath(e)* 17 acres of meadow, each acre of which is worth 12d. a year. And in le *Holling(e)* [there] are three acres of meadow, each acre of which is worth 2s. a year. In *Langwath(e)* [there] are three acres of meadow, each acre of which is worth 3s. 4d. a year. In *Lokheng(e)* [there] are 27 acres of meadow, by the perch as above, each acre of which is worth 3s. 4d. a year. Total value of the whole meadow a year: £8 9s. It is approved (*probatur*).

[There] is there one park, held in severalty (*separalis*), in which [there] are beasts of chase (*fere*), whose underwood, herbage, pannage and bracken are worth, on average, £4 a year in all the issues. [There] is there one fishery, held in severalty, which extends from the park's fence, towards Carlton, up to a certain place which is called Westcroft, below Holm, which is worth 3s. 4d. a year. [There] is there another fishery, held in severalty, which extends, on the south side, from the bounds made by the boundary above Flixthorp between the water of Billeby and the said fishery, up to Littellond to the north, to wit, to the water of the Prior of Blythe, and it is worth 4s. a year. [There] is there one water-mill in which all men of Hodsock and Hermeston, both free and villeins (*nativi*), ought to grind their grain, to wit, the free to the 20th measure (*ad* 20 *vas*) and the villeins to the 16th measure (*ad* 16 *vas*), and it is worth 53s. 4d. a year. The said jurors, asked as to whether the men of Flixthorp and the chaplains of the Hospital of St. John the Evangelist should grind their grain there as the others above, say that the said chaplains ought to grind their grain there without giving multure to the lord, but whether the men of Flixthorpe ought to grind there they do not know.

[There] is at Holm one water-mill and one cloth-fulling[1] mill, in which all men, both free and villeins (*nativi*), of Holm, Kelesalt and Wodehous ought to grind their grain, to wit, the free and villeins as above, and it is worth 53s. 4d. a year. And [there is] there a certain court from three weeks to three which is worth 20s. a year.

Total: £10 14s.   It is approved (*probatur*).

Services and Rents of the free

Henry Touke of Kelm' and his parceners[2] hold in Kelm' lands and tenements by the service of one knight's fee and he renders 10s. 8d. a year, at the feasts of Christmas and St. John the Baptist, next following, in equal portions[3]; and he shall give suit of court at the next lord's court in Hodsock, from three weeks to three, and he shall perform no other service.[4]

Ralph of Normanville holds in Kedeling and Weston lands and tenements by the service of one knight's fee and renders 10s. 8d. a year at the said feasts, in equal portions, for all the services.

Roger of Cressy of Marcham holds lands and tenements in East Marcham by the service of half a knight's fee [and renders] 5s. a year at the said feasts, in equal portions, and he gives suit of court as the said Henry.

William of Cressy of Melton holds in Melton lands and tenements by the service of half a knight's fee and he renders 5s. a year at the said feasts, for all the service.

Peter of Cressy holds in Kelsalt lands and tenements [but] it is not known by what services.

Robert of Helewelle, the lord of Flixthorp, holds there one half-bovate of land and renders to the lord 2s. a year at the feasts of St. Michael, the Purification of the Blessed Mary, and Pentecost, in equal portions; and he gives suit of court twice a year, to wit, at the court next after the feast of St. Michael and Easter.

Abbot of Wellebeck holds there of the lord lands and tenements [but] it is not known by what services.[5]

---

[1] *Molendinum fullendum pannum.*
[2] i.e. joint tenants with him.
[3] *Equaliter*, throughout the document.
[4] In this section, the description of each new tenant's holdings does not begin a new paragraph, but a blank space is left before each new name.
[5] 'Therefore he is to be distrained' is written above the line.

Prior to Wilhop' holds in Hermeston lands and tenements [but] it is not known by what services.

Henry of Grandon holds one messuage and five bovates of land in Holm, Wodehous and in Hodsock by homage and scutage when it arises, and he renders to the lord 8s. 6d. a year at the feasts of St. Michael, the Purification of the Blessed Mary, and Pentecost, in equal portions; and he shall give suit of court from three weeks to three.

Robert *dyl* Clay holds one bovate of land and one messuage in Hodsock by homage and scutage etc., and he renders 6s. 8½d. a year at the said feasts; he shall give suit of court from three weeks to three etc.

Thomas of Huntingfeld holds there, for the duration of his life, one messuage and one bovate of land for the duration of his life,[1] by the service of one rose a year at the feast of St. John the Baptist, and he owes suit of court twice a year as Robert of Helewell, as above.

William *de elemos(ina)* holds one toft in Hodsock and renders to the lord 3s. a year at the said feasts, in equal portions; and he shall give suit of court as the said Henry.

Peter le Hine holds there one toft and renders to the lord 3s. a year at the said feasts, in equal portions; and he shall give suit of court as the said Henry.

John Ode holds there one toft, to himself and his heirs, and he renders to the lord 4½d. a year at the said feasts; and he shall give suit of court as the said Henry.

John Depreuille holds there one toft and renders 15d. a year at the said feasts, in equal portions; and he shall give suit of court as the said Henry.

John Ode holds one plot of land (*placia*) at the lord's will and renders 4½d. a year at the said feasts, in equal portions.

Alice daughter of Alays(ia ?) holds there one toft and renders 11½d. a year at the said feasts, in equal portions.

John of Harwic holds in Holm one messuage and 1½ bovates of land by homage and scutage, and he renders 7s. 7½d. a year at the said feasts, in equal portions; and he shall give suit of court as the said Henry; and he ought to reap the lord's corn, as if for one day, with 6 men, the lord providing food once a day, and the value of each man's food is 1d., and the work of each one is worth, without food, 1d.; and he shall render to the lord 1 pound of cumin a year, to wit, at the feast of St. Michael.

[1] Repeated in the MS.

Services
and
Customary
Obligations
of the
free[1]

William Ward holds there one messuage and one bovate of
land by homage and scutage and renders to the lord 4s. 7½d.
a year at the said feasts, in equal portions; and he shall give
suit of court as the said Henry.

The heirs of Hugh of Holm holds[2] there one messuage and
half a bovate of land by homage and scutage etc., and renders
to the lord 6s. a year at the said feasts, in equal portions, and
suit of court as the said Henry.

Robert Rouwet holds half a toft in Wodehous and renders
6d. a year at the said feasts, and 2 suits of court at the 2 great
courts.

Alice Perot holds there half a toft and renders 6d. a year as
the said Robert.

Total[3]
76s. 9½d.

William *de elemos(ina)* holds 3 acres of 'forland'[4] and renders
to the lord at the feast of St. Michael 1d.

Elyas Oueryegat holds in villeinage (*in bondagio*) one messuage
and one bovate of land in Hermeston [and] renders to the
lord 10s. a year at the feasts of St. Michael, the Purification
of the Blessed Mary, and Pentecost, in equal portions. And
he shall give suit of court from three weeks to three. And
with his congeners[5] he ought to spread the grass after the
meadows have been mowed [and] to lift, make, and stack
hay thereof, and to receive nothing for [his] work; and they
shall carry all that hay, to wit, in the meadows of *Stubbynge,*
Swynwathe, Hollinge, the meadow of *Langewathe,* and the
meadow of *Lokhenge,* and 2 bovates should make up 1 cart
with 2 men, to count as one carrying-service, the lord providing food once a day; and this food is worth 1½d. a day,
the value of [one] day-work [being] 6d. And he shall weed
all the lord's corn in his demesne lands outside the park,
without food, the value of the work [being] 1d. a day. And
he shall reap, bind, and stack all the said corn of the lord,
the lord providing food once a day; and the food is worth

---

[1] *Servicia et consuetudines.*

[2] Singular in the MS; all subsequent verbs are unextended but I have rendered
them as singular.

[3] There is a note in the margin immediately preceding this total: 'Let it be inquired
into the services and rents of Langwathe'. The information required seems to be that
provided at the foot of the membrane on the same side of it.

[4] *Terre de forlandes,* i.e. newly acquired land of assart, or demesne, origin.

[5] 'Parceners' in the MS. throughout this section, but it is made quite explicit later
on that tenants of the same condition and not joint tenants are meant.

1d., the value of [one] day-work [being] 1d. And with his congeners he shall perform carrying-services, to wit, anyone holding 2 bovates should make up 1 cart with 2 men for the carrying of all the lord's corn, the lord providing food once a day; and the food is worth 1½d., the value of [one] day-work, after deductions (*ultra reprisam*), [being] 6d.

And he shall perform no other service. And with his congeners, to wit, all the villeins (*bondi*) of the soke, he ought to wash and shear the lord's sheep, without food, but they shall receive 12d. towards ale by custom after shearing, and with all his aforesaid congeners 12d. towards ale by custom after hay-making, and 12d. towards ale by custom after the harvest.

Roger Beyewater holds in Hermeston one messuage and one bovate of land there.[1]

Elyas Pister of Hodsock holds there one messuage and 2½ bovates of land.

William Hotow holds 1 messuage and one bovate of land.

Robert son of Richard [holds] 1 messuage [and] 2¼ bovates of land.

Robert Hotowe holds 1 messuage and 2¾ bovates of land.

Hugh Ouerray holds 1 messuage and 1¼ bovate of land.

Alan Oueryegat holds 1 messuage and 2 bovates of land.

Margery the widow of Storteswayn holds 1 messuage and 2 bovates of land.

Geoffrey Cissor holds a fourth part of one bovate of land.

Walter Coke holds in Holm 1 messuage and one bovate of land in Holm.[2]

Henry Godefroi holds there 1 messuage and 1 bovate of land.

John of Farwathe holds in Wodehous 1 messuage and 1 bovate of land.

Henry son of Thomas holds there 2 tofts [and] 2½ bovates of land and a sixth part of one bovate of land.

John Proud holds there 2 tofts and 2 bovates of land.

Emma of Holm holds there 2 tofts and 2 bovates of land.

William *de cimiterio* holds there 2 tofts (and a fourth part of a toft)[3] and 2 bovates (and a fourth part of one bovate)[3] of land.

---

[1] In this section, the description of each new tenant's holdings does not begin a new paragraph, but a blank space is usually left before each new name. The same applies to the section concerned with the 'forlands' on the reverse side.

[2] Repeated in the MS.

[3] Phrases in brackets are inserted above the line in the MS.

John Proud holds there 1 toft and 1 bovate of land.

William son of Agnes holds there 1 messuage (and a fourth part of one messuage)[1] and 1 bovate (and a fourth part of one bovate)[1] of land.

Agnes the widow of Robert holds there 1 messuage and 1 bovate of land.

Agnes the widow of Robert Godfroi holds there 1 messuage and 1½ bovate of land.

William of Holm holds there 1 messuage and 1 bovate of land.

Thomas Anot holds there 1 messuage and 1¼ bovates of land.

Agnes the widow of William son of Henry holds there 1 messuage and 1¼ bovates of land.

John son of Emma holds 1 messuage and 1 bovate of land. Of whom, each one renders for a bovate 10s. a year, at the said feasts, and performs services and customary obligations (*consuetudines*) for a bovate as the aforementioned [Elyas][2] Oueryegate.

And let it be known that all the villeins (*bondi*) of Hodsock render to the lord 20d. a year for the grazing of the pond of the mill of Hodsock.

Henry Houndoc holds 1 messuage and 1 [bovate][2] of land in Holm for the duration of his life, (by the charter of Hugh Cressi)[3] and he renders (*facit*) nothing.

Total of the bovates which are in the hands of the villeins (*bondi*) in Hermeston, Hodsock, Wodehous and Holm: 35½ bovates and a sixth part of 1 bovate.[4] Of which, each bovate renders 10s. a year. Total of money: £17 16s. 8d. And let it be known that of the above-mentioned bovates 1 toft and 1½ bovates of land, which Agnes the widow of Robert Godfroi held in Wodehous, is in the hands of the lord. And 5 tofts and 5 bovates of land in Hermeston are in the hands of the lord on account of the poverty[5] (*paupertas*) of the villeins (*bondi*).

[There][6] is there a certain grassy, boundary track which lies

[1] Phrases in brackets are inserted above the line in the MS.

[2] A tiny piece of the margin is torn out at this point, but it could not have been anything else.

[3] Inserted above the line in the MS.

[4] This total does not tally with the number as counted.

[5] This should have been rendered, perhaps, as scarcity rather than poverty.

[6] This paragraph clearly belongs with the description of the manor at the beginning of the extent, and it is in fact marked with an insertion sign (a cross) but as there are five such crosses scattered throughout the relevant section, it was not possible to insert it in the right place.

on the east side, between demesne lands and the meadow
which is called *Swynwathe*, and which extends from the
gates of the manor, towards the south, up to the small
bridges (*minute pontes*), towards the north; and it is worth
each year 2s. Also, the ditches[1] (*fossata*) around Swynwathe
are worth 6d. a year. Also the ditches around la *Stobbynge*
are worth 6d. a year. Also, [there] is there a certain grassy
track which [extends] from the gates of the manor to the
corner of the park, and it is worth 4d. a year.

Also, the rent of assize in Langwathe and Lettwelle is worth
2s. 2d. a year and 1 ring of silver, value 2d., or, 2d.[2]

3

4   John son of Walter Proud of Wodehous holds there of the
lord one garden and renders 2s. 6d. a year at the said feasts,
in equal portions, as more fully above.

4   [There] are there 19[5] bovates of land of the said bovates in
villeinage above, of which each (bovate of 12)[6] is burdened
with 5½d. of rent at the said feasts for a certain meadow
which is divided among the villeins holding those bovates,
(and each of the remaining ones is burdened with 1d. for
the 'forlands', to wit, one bovate of land renders to the
lord . . .)[6]

Walter Coke of Holm holds there certain 'forlands' (*terre de
forlandes*), which are not measured, for which he renders
15d. a year at the said feasts, in equal portions.

Henry Godfroi holds there certain lands which are called
'forlands', which are not measured, for which he renders 15d.
a year at the said feasts, in equal portions.

Also, the said Walter Coke holds there 1 tenement for which
he renders to the lord 3s. 3d. a year at the said feasts, in
equal portions.

John Ward holds in Hermeston of the lord, for a number of

---

[1] Could be singular; both the noun and the verb are unextended in the MS.

[2] This is the last entry on the obverse side; the reverse side begins with two completely illegible lines at the very top, which are followed, a long way down, by the paragraph concerned with 'forlands'.

[3] A sum ending in 4½d. is written on the margin halfway down the blank space between the two top lines and the paragraph dealing with 'forlands'.

[4] An illegible marginal heading or sum.

[5] 17 is crossed out and 19 substituted.

[6] The words in brackets constitute a single-line insertion; the end part of it: 'renders to the lord . . . ' is uncertain. The missing word at the very end must have been a small sum, and if my reading of the whole sentence is correct, the sense would require it to be 1d.

years, 2 messuages and 2 bovates of land by the lord's demise (*ex dimissione*), and renders to the lord 20s. at the said feasts, in equal portions; and he shall perform services as the aforementioned Elyas Oueryegat on the other side.

Elyas Pistor of Hodsock holds there 4 acres of land and one plot (*placia*) of meadow, which are called 'forlands' and renders to the lord 22½d. a year at the said feasts, in equal portions.

Robert Dytonson holds there 5 acres of land and 1 plot of meadow which are called 'forlands', and renders to the lord 2s. 6d. a year at the said feasts, in equal portions.

Hob Hotowe holds there 3 acres of land and one plot of meadow, which are called 'forlands', and renders 18d. a year at the said feasts, in equal portions.

Huwet Aldonson holds there 3 acres of land and 1 plot of meadow, which are called 'forlands', and renders 18d. a year at the said feasts, in equal portions.

Alan Oueryegat holds there 3 acres of land and one plot of meadow, which are called 'forlands', and renders 18d. a year at the said feasts, in equal portions.

Margery Schorteswayn holds there three acres of land and no meadow, which are called 'forlands', and renders 18d. a year at the said feasts, in equal portions.

Total of the whole Manor of Hodsock apart from Demesne Lands and Works (*Opera*): £46 23d.[2]

Thomas Pincernus holds there three acres of land and one plot of meadow of 'forland' and renders nothing.

Henry Peintour holds 3 acres of land in Hodsock and renders 18d. a year, at the said terms.

Henry son of Thomas renders 2s. a year for the 'forlands' which are not measured.

Robertus Rowe.[1]

Alice Perot renders 12d. a year for a certain house and 1 garden.

Total: 49s. (2½d. ?)[3]

The aforesaid jurors also say that all the villeins in Hermeston, Hodsok, Wodehous and Holm ought to make and repair the ponds (*stagna*) of the mills of Hodsock and Holm, however often, and whenever, may be necessary. And the villeins of Oulecotes,[4] together with the said villeins, ought to repair

[1] Nothing is entered against his name.
[2] This total is somewhat less than the total as counted.
[3] 48s. 8½d. is crossed out and 49s. substituted; 2½d ? seems also to be there under ultra-violet light. This is shown to be correct by addition.
[4] A sub-manor of Hodsock which is surveyed next.

the causeway lying at the head of the pond of the mill of
Hodsock and leading directly up to the ditch abutting on
the lands of Hodsock. And none of the aforesaid villeins
had married his daughter, nor any widow of servile condition had married herself,[1] without the lord's will. And
each shall give merchet of 5s. when the time comes, and for
heriot due from him (*heriettum debitum*) when the time
comes, [he shall give] at the lord's will.

[1] *Et quilibet bondus predictorum non maritavit filiam suam nec aliqua bonda vidua
maritavit se sine voluntate domini.*

7

FROM The Extents of the Lands of the Monastery of St. Edmund [1357]. Br. Mus. MS. Add. 14, 849, f52.

PALGRAVE [Suffolk]¹

[There] are there 146 acres, 2 roods, 25 perches of arable land, whereof,

in² Holm 15 acres, 1½ roods, and a third part of one rood.

In the croft of Henry Le Fled half an acre.

In Hundeshil 4 acres 2½ roods.

In Bullond 4 acres, 3 roods, 10 perches.

In Bergh(e) 14 acres, half a rood.

In Melnefeld 15 acres, 3 roods.

In Thornes 3 acres, 3 roods, 35 perches.

In Hegges 1 acre, 1½ roods.

In Gundeles 1½ acres.

In Halleyerd 3½ roods.

In Corderaisaker 2 acres, 1 rood.

In Bullondbon(saker) 1 rood.

In Palforthe and Saxwelle 7½ acres.

In Sparkes 3½ roods.

In Stakkes and Bullond 2 roods.

Also, next to Bullondbons(aker) 1 acre, 1 rood.

Next to Melnefeld 1 acre, 1½ roods.

In Sparkescroft 2 roods, 10 perches.

Towards (*apud*) the cemetery of St. Andrew 6 acres, half a rood.

Next to Halleyerd 1½ roods.

Next to Northcroft 30 perches.

In Brom 1 rood.

In Palfordehil 4½ acres.

Next to Hegges 1 rood.

¹ I have rearranged the entries so as to start each new item as a separate paragraph.
² *Apud* in the MS.; I have rendered it throughout as 'in'.

L

In Chirchecroft 1 acre, 2 roods, and a third part of one rood.
In Shortegundeles 6 acres.
In Melne 2 roods.
In Merewenes 3 roods.
In Bradelond 2 acres, 3½ roods.
In Melnefeld and Longgegundele 2½ acres.
In Lampet 7 acres.
In Doesaker 1 acre.
In Begh(e) and Palforde 8½ acres.
In Rysenemere 1½ acres.
In le Pom(ere ?) half an acre.
In Longgegundeles 5 acres and a third part of one rood.
In Saxwelle 2½ roods.
In Northcroft 4 acres, 3½ roods.
Next to Blodmere 1 rood.
Next to Dykespond 2½ acres.
In le Doune 1 acre, 2 roods, 30 perches.
In le Busk' 2 acres, 3 roods.

Meadows fit to mow (*Prata falcabilia*)

[There] are there in a meadow called *Estmedwe* 17 acres and two parts
of one rood.

Pasture

[There] are there in *Hallesyke* 2 acres, 2 roods, 10 perches.
And let it be remembered (*memorandum*) that the aforesaid land together with the said meadow and pasture are let out to the men of the
vill (*homagio*) for £6 4s. 8d.
[There] is there 1 wind-mill and it is worth per year[1]

Customary Tenants

Tenement of William Shirreve	The tenement of William Shirreve[2] contains 23 acres, 1 rood of land, with a messuage, whereof, 1 acre, 2½ roods [are] of the suit of the hundred.[3] Whereof, John Shirreve holds 22 acres, 1 rood, 30 perches and the messuage. Richard Shirreve holds of the same [tenement[4]] 3 roods, 10 perches

---

[1] No value is entered against this entry.

[2] The name by which the holding is known; not necessarily that of the current
tenant, but frequently of some past, or even eponymous, holder.

[3] i.e. it is burdened with the obligation of giving suit at the hundred court.

[4] *De eodem;* gramatically this could mean 'of the same tenant', i.e. the tenant who
lends his name to the tenement. It is however quite clear, and is in fact made explicit
under other manors, that the proper extension is 'of the same tenement'.

of land. And it renders[1] 4s. 10¼d. a year, of which 18¼d. [are] for [the commutation of] services.

Tenement of Thomas Seman The tenement of Thomas Seman contains 2 acres, 1 rood of customary land, with one cottage. Of which, Simon atte Syke holds half an acre, John Shirreve 1 acre 3 roods, Thomas Avenant holds the cottage. And it renders 5¾d. a year, of which 1¾d. [are] for services.

Tenement of John Shirreve The tenement of John Shirreve contains 4 acres, 2½ roods of land, with a fourth part of one messuage containing half a rood. Of which, the same John holds 4 acres, 1½ roods, with the said part of a messuage, Richard Shirreve 1 rood of land. And it renders 18½d. a year, of which 6d. [are] for services.

Tenement of Robert Smith The tenement of Robert Smith contains 15 acres, 2 roods, 25 perches of customary land, with a messuage; which messuage, 1 acre [and] 30 perches of the aforesaid land arc of the suit of the hundred. Whereof, the same Robert holds 14 acres, 2 roods, 25 perches of customary land with the messuage. Paulinus Rigge holds of the same [tenement] half and acre. Richard Shirreve holds of the same [tenement] half an acre. And it renders 3s. 10¼d. a year, of which 15¼d. [are] for services.

Tenement of Thomas of Skulton The tenement of Thomas of Skulton contains 20 acres, 1 rood, 20 perches of customary land, with a messuage. Of which, Nicholas of Skulton holds 10 acres, 1 rood and the messuage. Robert Smith holds of the same [tenement] 10 acres, 10 perches. And it renders 4s. 11¾d. a year, of which 20d. [are] for services.

The tenement of Mariota Sandolf contains 13 acres, 2 roods, 30 perches of customary land, with a messuage. Which tenement, Nicholas of Skulton holds and renders 3s. 4¾d. a year, of which, 12¾d. [are] for services.

Tenement of Edward Ernald The tenement of Edward Ernald contains 30 acres, 1½ roods of customary land, with a messuage, [and] with 1½ roods of land of the suit of the hundred. Of which, Reginald atte Cherche holds 14 acres with a part of the messuage. John Boteld holds of the same [tenement] 6 acres 1½ roods, Richard Corderay 2½ roods, Adam Chapman holds of the same [tenement] half a rood, John Odelyn 9 acres with a half of the messuage, John Reynbald 1½ acres, William Barkere 1

---

[1] *Et redd.*, here and throughout the document. This could be extended as 'and they render' but the intended meaning seems to me to be that 'the tenement renders', and I have translated it so throughout.

acre of meadow, John Mous half an acre of meadow and a certain small cottage. And it renders 8s. 7½d. a year, of which 3s. ½d. [are] for services.

. . . . .¹

¹ And so on throughout the remaining customary tenements.

8

FROM *Abstracts of the Inquisitions Post Mortem Relating to Notting-hamshire*, John Standish ed., Thoroton Society Record Series IV, 1914, ii. 145–148.

JOHN DE LONGVILLERS
Writ dated at Westminster, 6 October 25 Edw, I.
[1297] by the King's son

Inquisition made at Tuxford on Monday next after the feast of St. Luke the Ewangelist 25 Edw. I [1297] before J. de Lythegreynes, the King's Escheator beyond Trent, of the lands and tenements which were of John de Longvillers, by Sir William de Beuercotes, knight, Robert de Wlrington of Upton, Roger de Cressy of Marcham, Henry de Sutton in Wylgheby, William de Marcham in Laxton, Simon de Cald-well in the same place, Richard son of Henry de West Marcham, John de Dodington in Tuxford, William de Eyuile of Egmanton, John de Upton, Robert his brother, and William Attepertres of Kirketon. Who say by their oath that

Demesne   The said John of Longvillers
Tuxford held in Tuxford in chief from the King in demesne a certain toft and croft with fruit of the garden and ⅓rd part of a dove-cot, which are worth by the year 5s. And they say that the said John held in demesne in the said vill 143½ acres of arable land, each worth 4d. yearly. And they say that the said John held in the said vill 5 acres of meadow, each worth 18d. yearly. And he held ⅓rd part of a water-mill worth 30s. yearly. And he had 7 tofts which cottars were accustomed to hold and now no one wishes to hold them and they extend altogether to 21d. yearly.

Sum £4 12s. 1d.

Free Also they say that he had 9 free tenants who held freely 13
Tenants oxgangs of land in the said vill of Tuxford, rendering therefor

yearly of rent of assize 38s. 11½d. and ⅓rd part of 1 pound of pepper, payable at feasts of St. Martin and Pentecost.

Sum 39s. 4d.

Bondsmen Also they say that he had there 14 bondsmen (*nativi*) holding 17 oxgangs of land in villeinage, each oxgang renders yearly 8s. of rent of assize. And the said villeins (*villani*) do days' works and customs which extend to 17s. yearly, namely, for each oxgang 12d. And the said bondsmen hold 53 acres 2½ roods of assart land and render therefor yearly 41s. 8¾d.

Sum £10 2s. 8¾d.

Cottars Also they say that there are there 19 cottars holding 9 cottages and 13 acres 3½ roods of land, by divers parcels of assart land, rendering therefor yearly 24s. 9d. And the said cottars do days' works which are worth yearly 18d.

Sum 26s. 3d.

Also there are there 5 tenants who hold 22½ acres of assart land and render yearly 17s. 11½d. for all service.

Also they say that the pleas and perquisites of the Court there are worth yearly 5s.

Sum 22s. 11½d.

Sum of the whole manor £19 3s. 4¾d. Whereof he renders to Richard de Sutton and John Bray 5 marks 15¼d. as appears. All the aforesaid tenements of Tuxford are held in chief of the King by knight service by ⅓rd part of ½ a knight's fee. And the tenant renders therefor yearly to Sir Richard de Sutton of rent of assize 5 marks and to Sir John de Bray 15¼d.

And so the said manor is worth clear £15 15s. 5½d.

Parva Drayton They say also that the said John had in demesne in the vill of Parva Drayton 1 acre 1⅓ roods of meadow worth yearly in the whole 12d.

The sum appears.

Laxton Demesne They say also that the said John held in Laxton 1 toft with garden and close, worth yearly 5s. And he had there in demesne 175 acres of arable, each acre worth yearly 6d. Also he had there 26½ acres of meadow, each worth yearly 18d. Also he had there 5 plots (*placea*) of herbage, each worth 5s. yearly. Also he had there a moiety of 2 parks of which the profit in pasture is worth 9s. yearly and not more, because now there is underwood there. Also he had there a moiety of a windmill, worth 40d. yearly.

Sum £8 9s. 8d.

Free Tenants Also he had there 24 free tenants who hold 16½ oxgangs of land rendering therefor of rent of assize £4 2s. 6¾d.

The sum appears

Bondsmen They say also that there are there 5 bondsmen holding 5½ oxgangs of land in villeinage and they render yearly of rent of assize 50s. 8d. And they do days' works and customs which extend altogether to 37s. 9d. yearly.

Sum £4 8s. 5d.

Cottars Also he had there 12 cottars holding 12 cottages and they render yearly 24s. 6d. And they do days' works which are worth yearly 2s. 7d. And they say that the pleas and perquisites of Court there are worth yearly 5s.

Sum 32s. 1d.

Sum of the whole manor £18 12s. 8¾d.

And they say that the said John held all the said tenements of Laxton of the heir of Robert de Everingham who is the ward of Sir Robert de Tybetoft by commission of the King. And so the King shall have the custody of the lands of the said John as a custody of a custody, and he renders yearly to the said heir of Everingham ½d., and he renders to the Master of the Hospital of Oscington yearly 18d., and to John de Eyuile yearly ½d. and ½ pound of cumin, and to Henry de Lascey Earl of Lincoln yearly 12d., and to the light of the Holy Cross in the church of Laxton half a stone weight of wax, and to a certain perpetual chaplain to celebrate for the souls of the ancestors of the said John 1 quarter of corn yearly, and to a certain Roger ½ bushel of corn yearly.

And so the manor aforesaid is worth clear £18......

Allerton And they say also that the said John had in the vill of Allerton
Demesne in demesne a moiety of a windmill, worth yearly 13s. 4d.

The sum appears

Bondsmen Also he had in the vill of Allerton 3 bondsmen holding 3 oxgangs of land in villeinage, rendering yearly of rent of assize 10s. 6d. And the said villeins do days' works which are worth 3d. yearly.

Cottars Also they say that there are there 4 cottars holding 4 cottages and rendering yearly 4s. 6d., and they do days' works which are worth yearly 4d.

Sum 28s. 11d.

And they say that these tenements of Allerton are held in chief from William son of William by homage only, and the tenant renders to the house of Neusum 7s. yearly.

And so the manor aforesaid is worth clear........

Eton And they say that the said John held in Eton 6 acres of meadow from Robert de Wlpington in chief by homage, each worth 10d. yearly.

Sum 5s.

Carleton   Also they say that the said John held in the vill of Carleton-upon-Trent ... of meadow, each worth yearly 15d.

Sum of the whole extent of........

Also they say upon their oath that Thomas brother of the said John de Longevillers is his next heir, aged 19 years at the feast of St. Ambrose the bishop, next following.

9

Court of Southwik [Hants.] with the View of Frankpledge
[for the term] of Hokeday held on Tuesday next after the feast of
St. Barnabas the Apostle, in the seventh year of King Edward.
[13 June 1279]. Hampshire Record Office, MS. 4M53/C1/2.

Essoins[1]	Richard Fulkelyn had been essoined against William the reeve of Burhunte in a plea of trespass by Thomas Bradewey. John of Kenningeworthe [had been essoined] of the common [suit][2] by Adam Benelewe. Henry le Eir[3] [had been essoined] of the same by Nicholas Wolwyne. Walter Bastard [had been essoined] against John Sloper in a plea of trepass by Richard le Ferur.
Mercy 12d.	Because William Lenggcstocke refused to go to the weight (*ire ad libram*) against the assize,[4] therefore [he is] in mercy.
Mercy 3d.	Because John of Porslonde did not distrain[5] John of Porcesie for numerous defaults, therefore [he is] in mercy. And none the less it is ordered that the aforesaid John of Porcesie, Richard of Steningge, and James le Calewe, be distrained to answer at the next [court] for many defaults.
Mercy 3d.	Because Matilda le Hoppustre did not prosecute [her case] against Joan Fusthilde in a plea of trespass, therefore [she is] in mercy.
It is void (*vacat*) at the next [court]	Because Joan Tribold did not prosecute [her case] against Agnes Lucays.[6] William the reeve of Burhunte [is] the plaintiff in a plea of trespass against Richard Fulkelin [who] essoined himself above and did not come, and so it remains until the next

[1] Excuse for absence at the court presented, on behalf of the person excusing himself, by a named person present at the court.

[2] i.e. he was under an obligation to attend the court as a suitor.

[3] 'Afterwards he came', is added against his name on the margin.

[4] Presumably, the assize of bread is meant; this entry presumably means that he refused to go to have his weights checked.

[5] The usual method of enforcing attendance at court was through distress, i.e. seizure of goods as security for attendance.

[6] This entry is left unfinished and the marginal note makes it clear why.

[court]; pledge for prosecuting Richard Stake, pledge for answering John Wanstede.

Mercy 6d.   Because Richard Stake and Geoffrey Cokerel did not produce Henry Chaplain whom they have pledged in a plea of trespass, therefore [they are] in mercy.

Mercy 3d.   Because Edith le Scarlet did not prosecute [her case] against the aforesaid Henry Chaplain, therefore she, and Adam Herfn her pledge, [are] in mercy.

6s. 8d.   The tithing[1] comes, as summoned, and gives 6s. 8d. for the ancient custom.

distress   The tithingman with his tithing presents that Richard of Steningge [and] John of Porcesie, free tenants, owe suit [of court] and did not come, therefore it is ordered that they be distrained to answer at the next [court]. They also present that Peter Hayron, a villein, made a default and a guarantor had been found (*manuceptus*) for producing [him] at the next [court]. They also present that the hue was raised between

Amerce-   Alice Shonke (6d.[2]) and Agnes Sprot, at the wrongdoing of
ments   the said Alice; pledge, Geoffrey Shonke. Also the hue was raised between Matilda Hosi (6d.[2]) and Matilda le Tannare, at the wrongdoing of the aforesaid Matilda; pledge, Richard Ferur. Also the hue was raised between Cristina Blaunche (6d.[2]) and Edith Calewe, at the wrongdoing of the said Cristina; pledge, Adam Benelewe. Also the hue was raised between Richard atte Forge (12d.[2]) and William atte Brigge, at the wrongdoing of the said Richard; pledges Richard Robekyn and Richard le Ferur. They also present that the said Richard drew blood from the aforesaid Richard, therefore [he is] in mercy (12d.); pledges, Henry le Bator and John Mulcbrigge. Also the hue was raised between Simon Frond (6d.) and Henry le Hayward, at the wrongdoing of the aforesaid Simon, therefore [he is] in mercy; pledge,

at the   Adam atte Felde. They also present that Simon le Frond, a
next   free tenant, owes suit [of court] and did not come, therefore
[court]   it is ordered that he be distrained to answer at the next
distress   [court]. They also present a default of William atte Wolle, a free tenant, and he did not come, therefore he is to be distrained to answer at the next [court].

Inquest   John[3] Crabbe [is] the plaintiff in a plea of trespass and land

---

[1] Or the tithingman; the word in unextended in the MS.

[2] The amount of the individual amercements is written above the name of each person.

[3] Robert crossed out.

against William atte Wolle [who was] not attached,[1] therefore it is ordered that the aforesaid William be summoned to answer the said Robert[2] in the aforesaid plea at the next [court]; pledge of prosecuting, Robert Gruy.

at the next [court]

John Sloper [is] the plaintiff in a plea of trespass against Walter Bastard essoined above, and so it remains until the next [court]; pledge of prosecuting John Legge, pledge of answering Richard Stake.

3d.

Cristina Blaunche for a trespass against Edith Calewe [is] in mercy, and she pledges to the aforesaid Edith 6d., as has been decreed by an inquest; on the surety of Roger Oysel and Adam Benelewe.

3d.

Edith Calewe for her false complaint against the same Cristina [is] in mercy.

3d.

Nicholas Wolwyne [is] in mercy for sheep in the lord's corn.

6d.

Richard atte Barre [is] in mercy for the same, ward having been made.[3]

12d.

Nicholas Wolwyne habitually brewed [ale] and broke the assize, therefore [he is] in mercy.

2s.

Richard le Tavernir habitually [brewed ale, therefore he is] in mercy.

3d. Henry le Hayward once,[4] in mercy.

3d. Henry le Frond once, in mercy.

3d. Richard le Boyn once, in mercy.

3d. The widow of Bruse once, in mercy.

3d. Gilbert atte Halle once, in mercy.

3d. The widow of Tribold once, in mercy.

forgiven Walter Cocus once, in mercy.

3d. Matilda Ronke once, in mercy.

3d. Joan daughter of John le Bacare once, in mercy.

6d. Richard le Ferur twice, in mercy.

6d. Emma Shonke twice, in mercy.

6d. Thomas Colmere twice, in mercy.

12d. Geoffrey Chapman habitually, in mercy.

3d. Margery le Tannere once, in mercy.

12d. John atte Bere habitually, in mercy.

3d. Joan le Hore once, in mercy

6d. John Sloper twice, in mercy.

forgiven William Dormal many times, in mercy.

3d. Danyel Mayle once, in mercy.

---

[1] i.e. not distrained by seizure of goods.

[2] This should also have been changed to John.

[3] i.e. the particular part of the field having been declared closed to animals.

[4] The entries in the two parallel columns all refer to breaches of the assize of ale, I have not supplied the implied phrase 'brewed . . . therefore he is . . . ' in subsequent entries.

3d. Richard Rous once, in mercy.

6d. Roger Oysel twice, in mercy.

3d. Geoffrey Shonke once, in mercy.

3d. Roger le Beir once, in mercy.

3d. Margery le Doit once, in mercy.

3d. Stephen atte Hulle once, in mercy.

3d. Peter Hayron once, in mercy.

3d. William Lucays once, in mercy.

3d. Peter Tomberel once, in mercy.

3d. William Lengestocke once, in mercy.

forgiven Philip Tranchemeir once, in mercy.

3d. William le Cartere once, in mercy.

2s.   Because John Sloper felled without permission 14 oaks on the tenement which he holds of the lord Prior, therefore [he is] in mercy, and let the said tenement be seized into the hands of the lord.

at the next [court]   It is ordered to distrain William Visekyn to show and demonstrate at the next [court] by what right, and by what title, he holds his tenement of the lord.

Total of tithingpenny:	6s. 8d.
Total of perquisites:	22s. 3d.
Sum total:	28s. 11d.

10

FROM *Select Pleas in Manorial and Other Seignorial Courts*,
F. W. Maitland ed., Selden Society, London, 1889, i, 178–182.
[Pleas in the Courts of the Hundred of Whorwelsdown (Wilts.)
and the Manor of Ashton].
Arrear[1] Hundred Court for Hokeday held on Friday before the
feast of S. Barnabas in the forty-sixth year of King Henry III
[A.D. 1262].[2]

Essoins	John Mediciner essoined of the common summons by John Foke. He comes, so his name is struck out.
	Roger the Theign essoined of the common summons by Reginald Griffin.
	Peter son of Peter Mead essoined against Cristina daughter of John Sewald by Stephen of Mudwortley in a case of battery and raising the hue.
Appear-ance	Ralph of Garston appears against Roger le Bole [who] does not appear when called, so by judgment of the hundred let him be distrained to come to the next hundred [court] to answer both as to his default, and as to the main action,
distress	and let his pledges likewise be distrained.
distress note	Thomas Seliit and Walter de la Splotte tithingmen of Keevil must be distrained for their default.
	Hugh Burel and [the tenants of] Franklain's tenement must be distrained for their default.
Memoran-dum distress	Be it remembered that the tithingmen of Southwick say that William of Southwick and Thomas Cook are received at the house of John Uphill of Bradley, so let John be distrained to come to the next hundred [court] and let William and Thomas be attached if they be found.
	Emma the widow of West Ashton is in mercy for withdrawing herself from the plaint that she made against William the tithingman; pledges [for the amercement], John

[1] As Hokeday was on 18 April, and S. Barnabas does not occur until 11 June, I take it that this court is held by adjournment, and so is an 'Arrear Hundred'.

[2] Text and footnotes as given by Maitland, but I have added the marginal headings which Maitland gave only against the parallel Latin text.

6d.   Shiregreen and William the tithingman: she makes fine (6d.). Let inquiry be made as to her pledges to prosecute.

Appear-   Cristina Sewald plaintiff appears against Peter son of Peter
ance   Mead; pledges to prosecute, John Burgess and John Sewald. The same Peter is attached to answer John Burgess and Peter Mead.

distress   Walter of Dunstanville and Robert le Busic his pledge and Richard le Hyrtis Walter's pledge must be distrained to come to the next hundred [court] to hear their judgment and to answer for their default.

Appear-   Alice wife of John of Scales plaintiff appears against Elias
ance   son of Richard El'; pledges to prosecute, Roger Jagard and John of Scales. The said Elias is attached to answer the said
6d.   Alice; pledges, John Shiregreen and Roger Jagard.

2s.   Humphrey of Bradley is in mercy for a tort done to William Cantelow; pledges, Sampson and William Blanchard; he makes fine (2s.).

6d.   Thomas Alis is in mercy for not producing Gilbert Miller and Thomas Scardi whom he undertook to produce.

6s. 8d.   From Gilbert Grasenoil 6s. 8d. for all complaints and disputes; pledge, Laurence Wood.

Peter Chaffinch complains of Robert son of Robert of Tilshead. Upon this comes Richard of Tilshead and craves [cognisance of the action for] the court of his lady[1] and this is granted to him by assent of the hundred [court]. He has a day on Monday next after the Nativity of the Baptist.

Present-   Richard Blundet tithingman of Tilshead comes and says that
ments of the he knows nothing and offers to prove this.
tithing-   Thomas Alis tithingman of Coulston comes and makes
men   mention of a man wounded in the court of the lord of Baynton on Wednesday in Whitsun week. Adam son of John Simon has broken the assize.[2] William Cobbler and William Pain are received into his [Thomas's] tithing. Nothing more etc. Robert Abram tithingman of Tinhead comes and mentions that wool has been pulled off his sheep in the fold and stolen by the men of Tinhead. And Ralph Reaper is in mercy for he is convicted, and let inquiry be made for the names of the other men by Richard Corbin. Also Robert is in mercy
6d.   (6d.) for not producing Hugh of Scales whom he undertook to produce (Hugh Scales is quit because his summoner has

---

[1] The Abbess of S. Trinity at Caen held the manor of Tilshead; see Hoare's *Wiltshire*, ii. 42. Part of it seems to be within this hundred, part in another hundred.
[2] The assize of beer or the assize against receipt of strangers.

distress

12d.

6d.

12d.

not come) and David servant of William Sprakling whom he undertook to produce. Nothing else etc. Thomas Alfred and Osmund Busic have made default.

William Sprakling is in mercy for not producing David his servant whose pledge he was (12d.). Thomas Dunstan and Robert Abram are [William's] pledges.

Richard Charke in mercy for speaking ill for William Sprakling; pledges, Robert Abram and William Sprakling; he makes fine. He is again in mercy for saying that Walter Pandolf was his fourth man. Respited because [there is an entry about this] elsewhere.[1]

Richard Charke tithingman of Tinhead comes and says that William Wilan (amerced 6d.) and Walter Blache (6d.) have broken the assize. He has undertaken [for their amercements]. Nothing else etc. He makes no mention of the hue raised in his tithing by Cristina Sewald, therefore he is in mercy; the amercement is respited.

John Olen' tithingman of Edington came and made mention of the hue raised by Peter Mead against Walter servant and dependant of Ralph of Edington on Trinity Sunday at the hour of vespers. And he made mention of the hue raised by Cristina Sewald against Peter son of Peter Mead. Nothing else, etc.

John Burgess tithingman of Edington comes and says that the house of Alice Hethewey was broken on the night of Whit-Tuesday and a mantel of burnet and a coverlet were carried thence.

Richard Hordy tithingman of Southwick comes and says that the house of Lucy Hogeman was broken on Tuesday next after the feast of S. John before the Latin Gate and thence were carried off a coverlet and a linen garment and a sheet and a towel, bread and corn. On being asked whether he suspects anyone, he says, No. And on the night of Thursday in Whitsunweek a beehive was stolen from Ducie widow of Richard Miller. And he made mention that the house of Hugh Bokel was burnt and he [Hugh] inside it.

Thomas Heribit tithingman of Southwick comes and says that Alexander Prior (pardoned) and Nicholas Burdun (6d.)

[1] This passage is obscure. Richard's first offence seems that of mispleading, 'miskenning' on behalf of William. His second offence may be connected with the representation of each tithing by the tithingman and four men; but the text as it stands seems untranslatable.

have broken the assize. Thomas is pledge that this be amended. He says nothing else.

John Hoper tithingman of Southwick comes and says that a certain man came to the house of John Uphill on the night of Saturday after the Invention of Holy Cross and carried off clothes. The same John is to be distrained to come to the next hundred [court] to answer those things that shall be charged against him.

distress

William tithingman of West-Ashton comes and says that William of Southwick was very often received in the house of Cristina Walcock on the tenement of Roger Agard. Also he made mention of the fire that took place at Bradley and of wool plucked from the sheep of Juliana Sauser and of three great fleeces of wool stolen in the bakehouse of John Shiregreen. Also he makes mention of a medley between Elias son of Richard Ile and Walter son of Walter the Theign on Trinity Sunday after dinner, about which the hue was raised. The same William is charged with the receipt into his tithing of Hugh le Duc; he denied the charge; therefore let him make his law.

Walter Nel is made tithingman and says that the chest of Emma Waters was broken and her goods were carried off in [to] the courtyard of Adam Doget. And he makes mention of a coffer broken open in the house of Dua Waters and one bushel of wheat carried off. On being asked whether they suspect anyone, they say, No. Nothing else.

Walter Maries tithingman of Littleton comes and says that he knows nothing and offers to prove this. Thomas Stikeb' has made default.

Adam Taleman tithingman of Hinton comes and says that he knows nothing etc.

John Goin and William Shepherd tithingmen of Easton[1] came and said that Jamie Bus, Walter Gopill, Robert Ailrich, and Isabella Hall have broken the assize and that a certain gallon measure was pledged by Lucy servant maid of Walter Tailor.

6d.

Thomas Benuit in mercy for a tort done to Gilbert Fore; fine 6d.

Mercy 6d.

William Hody in mercy for a tort done to Adam Clerk; pledge[2]

John son of Ralph of Edington, Robert of Warminster and

[1] Seemingly a hamlet of Ashton.
[2] The pledge is not named.

Walter son of Ralph of Edington are to be attached to answer Peter Mead. Peter's pledges to prosecute, Roger of Codridge and Robert Already.

Defaults   John of Tinhead, Thomas of Cheney, Hugh Burel, the tenement of John Franklain, Ralph of Tresborough, William of Huthe.

Sum total: 14s. 6d. plus 2d.

From the widow of Richard of Gaysford as a fine for land 20s.; pledge for the money and for the services due from the land, Laurence Wood and William Noldeken. But this belongs to the hallimoot.

William Ailrich and Adam Shepherd are to be distrained to come to the next hundred [court] for not producing Nicholas Young whom they replevied in the matter of the wounding of Geoffrey Cobbler by the said Nicholas, Elias Juvenet and Walter Gopill.

Thomas Benuit, William of Morheath, Ducie Dyer, Walter Norais, John Palmer have broken the assize.

M

11

FROM [Court Rolls of the Manor of Brambelshute][1] Hampshire Record Office, MS. 4M. 61/2.

Court of Brambelshute [Hants.] held there on Monday next after the Purification of the Blessed Mary, in the Seventh Year of King Edward III [8 February 1333].

Merch	6d.	Robert atte Downe puts himself in mercy for 15 sheep in the lord's wood; by surety (*per plevinum*) of William Voghel.
Mercy	4d.	Robert atte Lee [puts himself in mercy] for 30 sheep in the same place; by surety of William le Voghel.
Forgiven		William le Voghel [puts himself in mercy] for 50 sheep in the lord's wood; by surety of Robert atte Lee.
Mercy	6d.	Alice of Iwschote puts herself in mercy for 15 sheep in the lord's wood; by surety of Robert atte Downe.
Mercy	3d.	Peter atte Hole [puts himself in mercy] for 5 pigs in the lord's wood; pledge, Henry atte Synderhupe.
Mercy	6d.	Lord Richard of Stone [is in mercy] for 10 pigs in the lord's corn; pledge, Ralph Consond. The same Richard [is in mercy] for 5 cows and 1 horse, with a colt, in the lord's pasture; pledge, Ralph Consond.
Mercy	1d.	Robert le Dow puts himself in mercy for unjustly impounding the horse of Henry Gasse.
Mercy	6d.	Robert Faber puts himself in mercy for 1 mare with [its] foal in the lord's corn; by surety of Robert le Downere.
Mercy	2d.	Reginald atte Hacche [puts himself in mercy] for 1 colt in the lord's corn; pledge Robert Faber.
Mercy	2d.	Robert Faber [puts himself in mercy] for 3 pigs in the lord's pasture; by surety of Reginald atte Hacche.
Mercy	3d.	Peter atte Valghe puts himself in mercy because he failed to perform autumn services according to what he owed.

[1] The roll from which this extract is taken has no collective heading.

Mercy 6d. Robert atte Downe puts himself in mercy for a trespass against the lord at the mill; surety of Robert le Queynte.

Mercy 3d. Robert Faber puts himself in mercy for defaming William Cissor by falsely accusing him of theft.

Fine 8s. Simon atte Eldemelle who held of the lord one messuage and one fardel of land has died, by reason of whose death the lord had 1 ox as heriot, value 7s. And to this court comes Agnes, who was the wife of the aforesaid Simon, and gives the lord 8s. as a fine for having ingress therein, by surety of William le Voghel and Robert atte Lee, to hold according to the custom of the manor; and she has done fealty. And the aforesaid pledges have undertaken on behalf of the aforesaid Agnes that she would hold the aforesaid holding in as good a state as she has received it in, by the inspection of the whole homage.

Election of the tithing man Henry atte Synderhupe has been elected to the office of tithingman and sworn in.

An inquest [was] held by the whole homage as to whether anyone of the homage has done damage to his tenement, who say on their oath that Peter atte Valghe has impoverished (*deterioravit*) his tenement, as in ditches, buildings and the garden, to the value of 20s., whereby it is decreed that the aforesaid Peter shall make good the aforesaid defaults under the penalty of having to pay the lord 20s. between next Easter and the Easter next following after that.

Affeerers[1] { Robert atte Lee / William le Foghel } Total, with the fine, 12s.

[1] Assessors of fines.

12

FROM [Court Rolls of the Manor of Brambelshute][1] Hampshire Record Office, MS. 4M. 61/3.

Court of Brambelshute [Hants.] held there on Saturday next after the feast of St. Richard the Bishop, in the Eleventh Year of King Edward III [5 April 1337].

Mercy 2d. Henry Mayhyw puts himself [in mercy] for 1 mare in the lord's pasture.

Mercy 2d. John le Carpenter puts himself [in mercy] for 2 cows in the lord's pasture.

Mercy 2d. John le Carpenter [puts himself in mercy] for 10 sheep in the lord's pasture.

Mercy 2d. Ralph Consond [puts himself in mercy] for 2 bullocks in the lord's pasture.

Mercy 2d. Robert Faber [puts himself in mercy] for 2 piglets in the lord's mast.

Mercy 2d. William of Chiltely [puts himself in mercy] for 5 cows and bullocks in [the lord's] pasture.

Mercy 2d. William Stragard [puts himself in mercy] for 1 cow and 1 bullock in the lord's pasture.

2d. Robert atte Lye [puts himself in mercy] for 3 horses (*affri*) in the lord's pasture.

2d. John atte Downe [puts himself in mercy] for 7 oxen and cows in the lord's pasture.

2d. Robert Faber [puts himself in mercy] for 9 sheep in [the lord's] pasture.

2d. Reginald atte Hache [puts himself in mercy] for 2 piglets in the lord's mast.

2d. John de Haselmere [puts himself in mercy] for 2 piglets in the lord's mast.

2d. Agnes atte Hole [puts herself in mercy] for 4 piglets in the lord's pasture.

2d. Matilda atte Lhupe [puts herself in mercy] for 1 sow in the lord's pasture.

[1] The roll from which this extract is taken has no collective heading.

Mercy 2d. Richard Consend [puts himself in mercy] for 4 piglets in the lord's pasture.

3d. Nicholas of Chudhurst for permission to come to an agreement with Robert atte Lye in a plea of trespass.

Mercy 1d. Robert le Queynte [puts himself in mercy] for the default of services at the mill.

2d. Peter atte Valghe for the same.

Mercy 2d. Thomas le Fre [puts himself in mercy] for the default of carting hay from Lowsly.

2d. Robert atte Lye for the same, to wit, for making hay.

Mercy 2d. John atte Downe [puts himself in mercy] for the default of hay-making.

2d. Thomas le Fre [puts himself in mercy] for the default of carrying wood.

Mercy 2d. Robert atte Downe [puts himself in mercy] for the default of carrying wood.

2d. Robert atte Lye [puts himself in mercy] for carrying away the lord's wood.

Mercy 2d. Henry Maihew [puts himself in mercy] for a trespass against Robert atte Lye.

12d. Robert atte Lye [puts himself in mercy] for having paid 42d. to the Chapel at Aulton for hay.

at the next [court]

The homage presents that Robert of Falstowe [and] Robert atte Towne have removed themselves (*extraneati sunt*) outside the lord's domain, therefore it is ordered that they be summoned to present themselves here at the next [court].

Mercy 6d.

The whole homage puts itself in mercy for the concealment of 1 cart-load of wood removed by William le Foghel (3d.), therefore he is in mercy.

Affeerers   Robert atte Lye
            Robert Faber   } Total: 5s. 11d.
            Robert le Queynte

The Court held there on Friday on the morrow of St. Edmund the King in the Eleventh Year of King Edward III [21 November 1337].

Amercements 2s. 5d.

Reginald atte Hole (2d.)[1] puts himself in mercy for 12 sheep in the lord's pasture. Ralph Consond (2d.) for 4 pigs in the lord's pasture. Reginald atte Hecche (2d.) for 4 piglets in [the lord's] pasture. John le Sopere (1d.) for 1 pig in [the lord's] pasture. Robert Faber (2d.) for 2 piglets in [the lord's] pasture. John le Taillor (1d.) for 2 piglets in the lord's pasture. Roger le Sontere (1d.) for 2 piglets in the lord's pasture. John le Kembere (2d.) for 1 pig in [the lord's] pasture. John le Carpenter (2d.) for 2 pigs in [the lord's] pasture. The same John (2d.) for 8 sheep in [the lord's] pasture. Peter of Hundesham (2d.) for 4 pigs in the lord's pasture. Robert atte Lye (2d.) for 1 horse in the lord's pasture. Robert atte Synderhupe (2d.) for 16 sheep in [the lord's] pasture. Roger le Sontere (3d.) for 1 colt in the lord's pasture. John of Weston (3d.) for 4 bullocks in the lord's patuure.

at the next [court]

Peter of Hundesham (he is not present[2]) the plaintiff, appears through his pledge Robert atte Synderhupe against William le Coupere in a plea of debt; he was attached in 6 ells of russet and it is ordered that he be better distrained by the next (court).

at the next [court] Amercements 2s. 10d. distress

The homage presents that the lord's corn was badly guarded in autumn through the default of John of Rogace the *messor*, the damge being assessed (*ad dampnum*) at 1 quarter 4 bushels of oats (21d.[2]) and 2 bushels of rye (9d.[3]). It also presents that Robert atte Lye, Robert atte Downe, [and] Thomas le Fre had devastated (*devastaverunt*) their tenements, therefore it is ordered that each one of them repairs the aforesaid tenements by the next [court] under the penalty of half a mark. It also presents that Walter le Stamere made a breach (*fregit*) in the lord's close, therefore it is ordered that he be distrained by the next [court] to answer for [this] trespass to the lord.

Mercy 2d.   Robert atte Downe puts himself in mercy for a trespass against William le Voghel. And it is ordered to levy 10d. from the same Robert for the benefit of the said William.

Total: 5s. 3d.

[1] The sums in brackets are written above the names of the person amerced in the MS. I have not supplied the implied phrase 'puts himself in mercy' in subsequent entries.

[2] The phrase in brackets is written above his name in the MS.

[3] The sums in brackets are written above each amerced person in the MS.

13

FROM The Account Roll of the Manors of the Bishopric of Winchester for the Eleventh Year of the Consecration of John of Pontoise. Hampshire Record Office, MS. Eccl. Comm. 2/159286 [1291/2].

STAPLEGROVE in TAUNTON [Somerset]

Entry and Marriage Fines

Likewise, they render account for 4s. from Robert le Muchele for marrying his daughter Alice. And for 60s. from Adam Cole to have Emelota the widow of Folkemer with half a virgate of land. And for 12d. from William son of Adam Cole to have one acre of land, by his father's concession. And for 60s. from Thomas son of Walter Folkemer to have half a virgate of land, by the concession of Adam Cole. And for 40s. from Simon Glide to have one half of a half-virgate of land, which was Stephen Glide's, for he has paid a fine for the other half some time ago (*temporibus retroactis*). And for 20s. from William Kynth' of Coddesheye to have 5 acres of land, by the concession of John of Chilewardeswode. And for 12d. from Robert Wynter to have one half of one messuage and one curtilage, by the concession of Walter Colling. And for 4s. from Thomas Kyng the baker to have one house and curtilage, by the concession of Walter Carter. And for 6d. from Alice Colling for getting herself married. And for 12d. from John son of John Warman to have a part of a house, by the concession of Margery of Ak'. And for 6d. from the same John to have one house with a curtilage, by his father's concession. And for 13s. 4d. from Agnes the widow of William *longus* to retain 1 fardel of land which was her husband's. And for 10s. from Adam Kempe and Richard Sprut to have 3 acres of land in Wodelond, by the concession of Richard le Palmer. And for 30s. from the communal fine at Hockeday (*de Hockedayeswyte*).

Total: £12 5s. 4d.

Perquisites

Likewise, they render account for 6d. from Thomas Trot for a breach of an agreement. And for 6d. from Robert Tolle for a concealment. And for 6d. from Nicholas Colling for a transgresion (*delictum*) of pasture. And for 12d. from William Pirelond and Benedict of Witemore for a transgression of pasture. And for 6d. from William of Pirelond for breaking the pinfold. And for 6d. from William *de ecclesia* for a transgression of pasture. And for 6d. from Walter Shirreve for damage to the corn (*delictum bladi*). And for 12d. from Robert Uppehille and William *de aqua* for breaking the pinfold. And for 12d. from Nicholas de la Witeghe and William Kene for bad ploughing. And for 6d. from William Kene and Walter Colling for a transgression of pasture. And for 3d. from Adam Colling for the same. And for 12d. from John Warman to have one acre of land, which is called Hevedlond, for the term of sixteen years from Robert Uppehille. And for 2s. from William of Pirelond for the recovery and custody (*warda et forfengium*) of 9 lambs. And for 2s. from John *de la stone* for a concealment of pannage. And for 12d. from Gilbert Bosse, and William le Pour, and others, for a default. And for 3d. from Benedict of Witemore for a transgression of pasture. And for 3d. from William of Pirelond because he was convicted. And for 6d. from Robert le Mochele for a false complaint (*querela*). And for 12d. from Roger Dolling and John le Noreys for threshing. And for 12d. from Benedict of Witemore for receiving. And for 3s. from the tithing of Pirelond for a concealment. And for 12d. from John Carpenter to have 1 croft, which is called Pyredowne, for the term of fourteen years from Simon Glide. And for 6d. from Benedict of Witemore and Richard Wynter for damage to the corn. And 3d. from Adam Cole for a transgression of pasture. And for 6d. from Emma the widow of Benedict But [and] Adam Bouker for damage to the wood (*delictum bosci*). And for 6d. from William of Pirelond for a transgression against Thomas *de angulo*. And for 6d. from John Warman for a false complaint. And for 6d. from Richard Austyn for receiving. And for 3d. from Edith Ak' for the same. And for 6d. from Richard Wollere for the same. And for 6d. from Robert le Mochele for contempt. And for 6d. from the ploughmen of Staplegrove for a transgression. And for 12d. from Robert le Mochele to have an inquest. And for 6d. from Richard atte Witeghe for bad ploughing. And for 3d. from William Colling for a default. And for 12d.

from Thomas Trot and Adam Colling for damage to the corn. And for 6d. from William Borde and Adam Chek' for an affray and other transgressions. And for 6d. from Thomas Harde for threshing. And for 12d. from John *de cruce*, and others, for a default in respect of their obligation to make enclosures.[1] And for 6d. from William *de ecclesia* for obstructing a certain road. And for 6d. from Robert Glide for a transgression against Agnes of Tobrigge. And for 12d. from Adam Cole and Roger Cole to have, and marl, 2 acres of land for the term of 12 years from William Cole their father. And for 6d. from Robert the dyer to have a half of $1\frac{1}{2}$ acres of land from William Cole until he has nine crops thereof. And for 3d. from Robert le Mochele for a transgression of pasture. And for 2s. from Gilbert Bosse to have, and marl, one acre of land for the term of sixteen years from William *longus*. And for 6d. from Emma the widow of Burlond for damage to the wood. And for 6d. from Mariota of Holeford because she did not come. And for 6d. from Peter le Pottere to have one acre of land and one small plot of meadow for the term of seven years from Cristina the widow of William Wyte. And for 12d. from William le Turnur for a false complaint. And for 12d. from Hugh Pour to have one plot of land, which is called Sufforlong, for the term of five years from Agnes the widow of William le Lung. And for 6d. from Robert Glide for a false complaint. And for 6d. from Nicholas le Turnur for a default. And for 6d. from Adam Cole for a transgression of pasture. And for 6d. from William Loverich for threshing. And for 6d. from Mariota of Holeford to have an inquest. And for 2s. from Thomas Kyng, William Knyt, Adam Loverich and others, for a default in respect of week-work.[2] And for 23s. 3d. from those who brewed ale (*de braciatoribus*)[3] for breaking the assize.

Total: 64s. 9d. Total of both: £15 10s. 1d.

---

[1] *Pro defectu clausture.*
[2] *Pro defectu operum.*
[3] These were not professional brewers but ordinary peasants brewing ale at home as a side-line; in fact, this was usually done by the wives.

14

FROM [Various Account Rolls of the Bishopric of Winchester[1]].

[Provenance of a one-virgate holding in Bishop's Waltham (Hants.) 1227–1500.[2]]

1227 (159281) 20s. from Philip of Hoo for an entry fine (*finis terre*). NB. In the Custumal of 1259/60 (British Museum, MS. Egerton 2418) he is credited with 1 virgate in Southwaltham (= Hoo), 1 meadow and 2½ acres of purpresture. The entry fine in 1227 must be for the virgate, for entry fines for his other land exist.

1269 (159450A) 13s. 4d. from Germanus of Hoo for an entry fine for half a virgate of land of which Philip, his father, died seised and invested (*seisitus et vestitus*); for he had paid a fine previously for the other half.

1286 (159307) 4s. from William le Wyte, William Serle and Robert Wodelock to have the land of Germanus of Hoo for the term of 13 years. NB. The holding of Germanus of Hoo must have gone eventually to William Germayn (or Jermayn), probably, his son.

1328 (159340) £4 from Andrew of Bodenham and Isabella his wife to have 1 messuage and 1 virgate of land in Hoo, by the

---

[1] Reference numbers are given in brackets with each entry following the date; the dates do not, of course, appear in the original documents. All the documents are at the Hampshire Record Office and are in two series: Eccl. Comm. 2/159 . . . , being the composite account rolls for the whole estate, and BW.1– series, being the individual account rolls for Bishop's Waltham.

[2] This is one of some 200-odd provenances which I have reconstructed for Bishop's Waltham; this provenance ignores any other land transactions the tenant may have been involved in, and is based on an index of entry fines, marriage fines, and heriots, for the period 1208–1500, grouped alphabetically around the person they refer to. Similar reconstructions could, of course, be attempted for other manors of the Winchester estates as well, but the task is beyond the possibilities of one person; my Waltham index alone runs to 1147 foolscap pages of typescript.

surrender of William Jermayn for the use of (*ad opus*) the said
Andrew and Isabella.

NB. Isabella seems to have been the heiress to the holding.
Andrew of Bodenham is clearly the same person as Andrew
Germayn (or Jermayn) later on.

1331 (159343) 40s. from Richard Hughe to have 1 messuage and 1
virgate of land in Hoo, which he had recovered (*recuperavit*),[1]
from Andrew Germayn and Isabella his wife, as his right.

1333 (159345) 20s. from Andrew of Bodenham and Isabella his wife
to have 1 messuage and 1 virgate of land in Hoo, which they
have recovered, from Richard Hughe, as their[2] right.

1338 (159451) 20s. from Isabella who was the wife of Andrew of
Bodenham to retain 1 messuage and 1 virgate of land in Hoo,
which were the said Andrew's, her husband.

NB. At the same time Isabella bestowed 1 cottage with a
curtilage and an annuity of 1 quarter 5 bushels of wheat,
and 1 quarter 5 bushels of barley, on her mother, Alice
Jermayn, for life.

1341 (159351) 20s. from John le Spencier to have Isabella Germayn
with her land, namely, 1 messuage and 1 virgate of land in Hoo,
1 messuage with 1 curtilage in Waltham.

NB. John le Spencier must be the same person as John le Parker
later on.

1361 (159371) 30s. from Alice daughter of Isabella Bodenham to
have 1 messuage and 1 virgate of bond land (*terre native*) and
8 acres of purpresture (*terre purpresture*) in the tithing of Hoo,
which belonged to the said Isabella her mother, and which John
le Parker, who had married the said Isabella, held for the term
of his life.

1361 (159371) 40s. from Roger le Clerk of Upham to have Alice
daughter of Isabella Bodenham with her land, namely, 1
messuage and 1 virgate of bond land, and 8 acres of purpresture,
in the tithing of Hoo.

1364 (159374) 50s. from William Hughe to have 1 messuage and 1
virgate of bond land, and 8 acres of purpresture, in Hoo, which
belonged to Alice Germayn his niece who had married Roger
of Upham, who survived her; and he has forfeited this holding
according to the custom of the manor for he had accepted
another wife.

NB. William Hughe must have surrendered his holding to his
son Thomas before 1385, since he died in 1385 and the

---

[1] i.e. through legal action in the manorial court.
[2] Singular in the MS.

holdings which his widow paid to retain do not include it. Since the only missing account roll in this period is that of 1381 it can be safely assumed that Thomas got his holding in 1381.

1438 (BW.62) 10s. from William son of Thomas Hughe to have 1 messuage and 1 virgate of bond land, and 8 acres of purpresture (*terre borde*), in the tithing of Hoo, which were Thomas', his father, and for which Joan, who was the wife of the said Thomas, refused to pay a fine.

NB. His holding must have gone to Alice Hughe (his daughter or widow), probably in 1440 or 1444.

1449 (159440) 10s. from George Motelle to have Alice Hugh with her land, namely, 1 messuage and 1 virgate of bond land, and 8 acres of purpresture (*terre borde*), in the tithing of Hoo.

1451 (BW.72) 6s. 8d. from John Aylerygge to have 1 messuage and 1 virgate of bond land, and 8 acres of purpresture (*terre borde*), in the tithing of Hoo, by the surrender of George Motelle and Alice his wife, who has been examined concerning this matter.[1]

1466 (BW.89) 8s. 4d. from Robert Legate to have 1 messuage and 1 virgate of bond land and 8 acres of purpresture (*terre borde*), in the tithing of Hoo, by the surrender of John Aylerygge.

NB. In the Rental dated 1464 (Eccl. Comm. $158819\frac{10}{10}$) Robert Legate is already credited with this holding. It is quite likely that he took possession some time before the payment of his fine; this laxity is fairly frequent in the fifteenth century. The heriot of John Aylerygge was recorded in 1465.

Some time between 1466 and 1501 his holding went to William Payne.

1501 (BW.127) 10s. from Robert Wodman to have 1 messuage and 1 virgate of bond land which was formerly Robert Legate's, by the surrender of William Payne.

---

[1] *Super hoc examinate;* since the holding was her inheritance, her views on the matter were investigated by the court.

15

FROM *Historia et Cartularium Monasterii Sancti Petri Gloucestrie*, William Hart ed., London 1867, III, 221–222.

Articles of Enquiry by the Frankpledge

First, let it be enquired about those who are in breach of the peace of the Lord King
About blood drawn,
About treasure found,
About hue and cry raised and not followed,
About clipping of new and old coins,
About women oppressed by force,
About goods and other things seized in distraint against security and pledges,[1]
About waters diverted or obstructed,
About public roads or paths obstructed or restricted,
About purprestures made on the king's or the lord's land,[2]
About those who had run away before the arrival of the justices and afterwards returned, without warranty,
About the harbourers of thieves,
About those who are well-off but neither have anything, nor work, nor are merchants, but are inn-keepers,
About tanners of hides of horses or oxen in rural settlements (*villa rurali*),
About strays not claimed after three days,
About those who are of twelve years of age and are not in a tithing,
About those who had been in a tithing and have withdrawn themselves without permission,
About those who gave hospitality to strangers without permission,

[1] *De namio et aliis rebus vetitis contra vadium et plegios.*
[2] *De purpresturis factis contra regem vel dominum.*

unless they came in broad daylight on one day and left in broad daylight the next day.[1]

About Christian usurers,

About bakers selling bread contrary to the assize,

About brewers selling ale contrary to the assize,

About false gallons or pottles[2] or those who have duplicate gallons or pottles (*duplicem gallonem vel potellum*),

About false or duplicate bushels,

About false ell rods,

About false weys or pounds,

About false 'toll-hoops' (*tolhopum*)[3] at the mill,

About those who have withdrawn themselves from following the tithing,

About all of twelve years of age whether they are present as they had been summoned to do,

About all things touching the Crown or the liberty of the lord,

About the court (*halimotum*) whether it is present in full as it had been summoned,

About the chief [manorial] officer (*capitalis serviens*) whether he is suitable or not,

About other manorial servants (*famuli curie*) whether they are suitable or not,

About manorial animals whether they are well looked after,

About the land, whether it is well cultivated,

About meadows, fields [and] woods, whether they are well taken care of,

About those who make their sons into clerks (*ponunt ad clerimoniam*) without permission,

About those who cut down free trees (*libera ligna*) without permission,

About those who overburden the common pasture of the village with animals of strangers, without permission,

About those who marry their daughters without permission,

About those who permit their buildings (*domus*) to fall down on account of poverty (*per paupertatem*).

---

[1] *nisi per unum diem clarum veniat et per clarum diem vadat.*

[2] A liquid measure, of 2 quarts (?).

[3] A grain-measure by which multure was received.

16

FROM The Account Roll of the Manors of the Bishopric of Winchester for the Eleventh Year of the Consecration of John of Pontoise. Hampshire Record Office, MS. Eccl. Comm. 2/159286 [1291/92].

THE FAIR OF ST. GILES [in Winchester]

East
Gate

EAST GATE. The first, second, third, fourth, fifth day he responds[1] [for] 19s. 10d. The sixth day 12d., the seventh 11s. 10d., the eighth 10s. 4d., the ninth 8s. 10½d., the tenth 18d., the eleventh 3s. 1d., the twelfth 7s. 2d., the thirteenth 11s. 9d., the fourteenth 7s. 3d., the fifteenth 4s. 10d., the sixteenth 8s. 5½d., [and] the seventeenth, eighteenth, nineteenth, twentieth, [and] twenty-first nothing this year. Total £4 15s. 11d.

South
Gate

SOUTH GATE. The first, second, third, fourth, and fifth day he responds[1] [for] 15s. 4d. The sixth day 4s. 11d., the seventh 12s. 5d., the eighth 26s. 10d., the ninth 16s. 10d., the tenth 7s. 0½d., the eleventh 2s. 7d., the twelfth 2s. 10d., the thirteenth 5s. 5d., the fourteenth 4s. 2½d., the fifteenth 3s. 6d., the sixteenth 3s. 2d. Total: 105s. 1d.

West
Gate

WEST GATE. The first, second, third, fourth, fifth day he responds[1] [for] 2s. 2d. The sixth day 13d., the seventh 18d., the eighth 17d., the ninth 18d., the tenth 5d., the eleventh 11½d., the twelfth 15d., the thirteenth 2s. 2½d., the fourteenth 3s. 2d., the fifteenth 22d., the sixteenth 3s. 2d., also 12d. for a certain toll. Total: 21s. 8d. Total of all the gates: £11 2s. 8d. Let it be remembered that immediately after the sixteenth day the fair was seized into the hands of the lord King and the money collected placed in custody of the lord Bishop, in a certain chest under the seal of the sub-escheator and the sheriff, and no mention has been made in this account of the receipts after that day.

---

[1] Unextended capital 'R' in the MS., i.e. the person rendering account accounts for.

Payments for weighing (*Magnum Pondus*)[1] for the whole duration of the fair: £4 2s. 4d. Total as shown.

From ground-rents (*de terragio*) this year, £25 15s. 8d.

From toll on cattle (*de boagio*)[2] this year 50s. 6d.

From stall-rents (*de seldagio*) of Ireland this year, to wit, for 31 windows[3] each 2s. 6d., 77s. 6d.

From stall-rents of York this year 38s.

From stall-rents of burellers[4] of London this year £4 2s. 0d.

From stall-rents of Lincoln this year 6s. 8d.

From stall-rents of the French this year, to wit, for 40 windows each 3s., £6. Total: £44 10s. 4d.

From the entry of the fair (*de introitu ferie*) this year 4s. 4d.

From [the toll of] Romsey, Rudbrugge, Hursley, and Crawley roads 44s. 1½d.

From [the toll of] Cheriton and Alresford roads 5s. 6d.

From the office of reeve of the city (*prepositura Civitatis*), namely, from the petty tolls of those passing through £6.

From traders in[5] saddles and ladders 30s.

From traders in burel 13d.

From traders in teasels 12d.

From traders in wheels 7d.

From the officer in charge of[6] animals in meadows and fields 46s. 8d.

From the officer in charge of[6] animals at the fair 15s.

From pleas and perquisites £4 17s. 7d.

For the favour (*gracia*) of entering the fair with diverse merchandise after the day of the Nativity of the blessed Mary,[7] 118s. 6d.

From the roofing of the toll-house sold, together with the timber of the same house, for it was all rotten, with 1 small hedge next to the east gate and a certain other hedge next to the house of Laurence Parmentarius, 7s. 8d. Total: £24 12s. 0½d.

---

[1] i.e. Payment for the use of the tron—the great weigh-beam provided by the authorities. In other documents it is called tronage.

[2] Almost certainly a variant spelling of *bovagium*.

[3] Individual merchants were allocated windows in long shops erected on the site of the fair; the shutters opened vertically downwards—like so many modern cocktail cabinets—and the goods were displayed on them.

[4] i.e. sellers of coarse woollen cloth known as 'burel'.

[5] This is given throughout as *de ministerio* + the object involved in the genitive. Traders seem to have been divided into sections each forming an 'office' (*ministerium*), for the purpose of collecting dues, etc.

[6] *De ministerio animalium* . . .

[7] 8 September.

Amerce-
ments

Also, he accounts[1] for 2s. 9d. of amercements which could not be levied in the preceding year. And [for] 5s. 6d. from 2 small carpets (*tapete*) (4s.[2]), 1 saddle-cloth (*hucia*) (12d.), and 1 deer-skin (6d.) assessed in the court of the soke and sold; these same objects having been seized as security for inspection at the fair of St. Giles the previous year.[3] Total: 8s. 3d. Sum total of receipts: £84 15s. 7½d.

Keeper (*custos*) of the East Gate: Nicholas of Anne, William of Stoke, for 20 days.

Keeper of the South Gate: Arnald of Burle for 20 days.

Keeper of the West Gate: John of Botes for 20 days.

Keeper of saddles and ladders, farmed out (*ad firmam*): John Franceys.

Keeper of animals at the fair, farmed out: Walter Crude.

Keeper of animals in meadows and fields, farmed out, Hugh Balehorn.

Keeper of the office of reeve of the City (*prepositure Civitatis*), farmed out: Roger Bunfray.

Keeper of Romsey, Rudbrugge, (and) Crawley roads, farmed out: Ralph *de la stone* and Gilbert the *messor* of Mardon.

Keeper of Cheriton and Alresford roads, farmed out, Hugh the forester.

Keepers of the shops of traders[4] in burel, not farmed out: John of Welewe, William of Sarr (um ?).

Keepers of the shops of traders in teasels, not farmed out, John Randolf, Richard Faler of Spakeford, John Wade.

Keeper of the shops of traders in whecls, not farmed out; Adam Sombourne, canon.

And [let it be remembered[5]] that none of the aforementioned expenses are entered this year because all these expenses were taken from the chest before it had been sealed.

Keepers of the tron (*magni ponderis*): Nicholas Wodelock, William of Waltham, 6s. 8d.

Doorkeeper at the pavilion (*hostiarius papillionis*): Robert Pore for 20 days.

Chamberlain at the Pavilion (*camerarius papillionis*): John of Anne for 20 days.

---

[1] *Idem r. de . . .*
[2] The sums in brackets are entered above the appropriate items in the MS.
[3] *que quidem vadia capta erant anno preterito pro scrutinio in feria St. Eqidii.*
[4] *Custodes ministerii* + the goods in the Genitive, throughout this section.
[5] The margin is damaged at this point; *memorandum*, or, *sciendum* is clearly required by the sense.

Crier of bans (*clamator bannorum*) at the fair and in the city: Walter.

Guardians (*custodes*) of the pass of Alton:[1] Hugh of Solrigge, William of Abinton, John of Forton, Alexander of Solrigge, Ralph of Alresford, William Boammund, John Manz, John of Torsaghe, for 16 days, 44s., each 6d. a day.

Guardians of the same pass on foot: John Dunnyng, Nicholas of Hursley, William Beste monk, Gilbert of Sutton, William of Torsaghe, John of Kanynges, Thomas le Hende, William Staleworthe, to wit, for 16 days 24s., each 2d. a day. Total: as shown. Total of the three preceding sums: £4 14s. 8d.

Minor MINOR OFFICIALS (*Parvi servientes*): William Wayte,
Officials Adam the clerk, Daynel, Walter Sutor, the cobbler (*sutor*) of Hursley, John of Alton, from the first day for 20 days.

Minor officials continued: John Tecle, John Sone, Hugh of Farnham, Adam of Aldewyke, William of Bello Alneto, William Swift, from the eve [of the Nativity] of the blessed Mary, to wit, for 12 days.

Collectors of ground-rents and tolls on cattle: Geoffrey of Wolvesey, Richard of Frilond.

Armed guardians (*custodes cum armis*)[2] of the fair and pavilion: Roger Everard, John of Benstede, Peter of Porteslade, Richard Frilond, William Chiddene, Peter Doffel, Philip of Exton, William de la Dene.

Expenses. In expenses of the same officials guarding the pass and fair, with the minor officials at the pavilion, as is shown in the account of the chamberlain, 38s. 7d. In hiring a house (*conducta*) at the West Gate for collecting tolls there, 2s. In erecting 1 toll-house at the South Gate, making daub walls (*wallanda*), collecting straw, and thatching the said house, 4s. 8d. In expenses of the household at Wolvesey at the time of the fair because the lord Bishop was present [there] and nothing was expended during that time [on the household] except oats,[3] £13 7s. 2d. Given, as their stipend, to 4 grooms (*garciones*) staying [behind] for 3 days after the inspection in the pavilion, and to William Swift, as his stipend, for 6 days, 2s. In stones and sand bought for the repairs of the shops 6d.

---

[1] In the MS. the heading is contained entirely within the margin, and is not repeated in the text itself. Other account rolls have: 'guardians of the pass of Alton, mounted, armed, and with their own servants'.

[2] Other account rolls have: 'armed guardians of the fair and pavilion, day and night'.

[3] I take this to mean that nothing was delivered free except oats.

Cash
Deliveries

Total: £15 14s. 11d. Total of all the expenses: £20 9s. 7d. And £64 6s. 0½d. are outstanding. CASH DELIVERIES. Delivered to lord Paganus, the treasurer at Wolvesey, by 1 tally, £64 6s. 0½d. And he is quit.

17

FROM Wiltshire Taxation Account for a 15th of Certain Religious Houses and of the Tenants on Manors Belonging to Them.[1] P.R.O. MS, E. 179/242/47.

THE MANOR OF BERWICK OF THE ABBEY OF WILTON [1225]

From John son of Peter. From 6 oxen 18s. From 2 cows 5s. From 5 *bovetti*[2] 10s. From 105 sheep 35s. Total: 68s. Total of the 15th: 4s. 6½d.

From Richard son of Peter. From 6 oxen 18s. From 5 cows 12s. 6d. From 3 *bovetti* 4s. 6d. From 2 calves, more than a year old, 2s. From 20 wethers (*multones*) 10s. From 80[3] ewes and hoggs[4] 26s. 8d. From 1 quarter of wheat 2s. 8d. From 2 quarters of barley 4s. From 2 quarters of oats 2s. Total: £4 22d. Total of the 15th: 5s. 5½d.

From Richard of Berwick. From 15 oxen 45s. From 1 cow 2s. 6d. From 4 *bovetti* 5s. From 8 pigs 4s. From 2 bee-hives 12d. From 176 sheep 58s. 8d. From 5 quarters of wheat 13s. 4d. From 2 quarters of barley 4s. From 4 quarters of oats 4s. Total: £6 17s. 6d. Total of the 15th: 9s. 2d.

From John Cuti. From 6 oxen 18s. From 60 sheep 20s. Total: 38s. Total of the 15th: 2s. 5½d.

From Nicholas of Wiltshire. From 16 oxen 48s. From 178 sheep 58s. Total: 106s. Total of the 15th: 7s. ¾d.

From Nicholas Riehel. From [1] *juvenca*[5] 2s. From 5 sheep 20d. Total: 3s. 8d. Total of the 15th: 3d.

From Matilda the widow 3s.[6] From 2 cows 5s. From 1 *juvenca* 2s.

---

[1] This heading comes not from the document itself but from its outer cover. The document is the taxation return for 1225.
[2] A bullock between one and two years old.
[3] 'four times 20' in the MS.
[4] Hogastri, i.e. sheep of either sex between one and two years old.
[5] A heifer between one and two years old.　　[6] Must be for an ox or a horse.

From 2 calves, more than a year old, 2s. 6d. From 25 sheep 8s. 4d. Total: 20s. 10d. Total of the 15th: 16½d.

From Roger Nuce. From [1] mare 3s. 4d. From 2 cows 5s. 6d. From 1 *bovettus* 18d. From 15 sheep 5s. Total: 15s. 4d. Total of the 15th: 12¼d.

From John Croc. From 1 cow 2s. 8d. From 21 sheep 7s. Total: 9s. 8d. Total of the 15th: 7¾d.

From John Franceis. From 2 cows 5s. 6d. From 3 sheep 12d. Total: 6s. 6d. Total of the 15th: 5¼d.

From Osbert. From 2 cows 5s. 6d. From 40 sheep 13s. 4d. From 1 bee-hive 6d. Total: 19s. 4d. Total of the 15th: 15½d.

From Jordanus. From 1 cow 2s. 9d. From 1 *bovettus* 15d. Total: 4s. Total of the 15th: 3¼d.

From Robert Prust. From 1 cow 2s. 8d. Total of the 15th: 2d.

From Robert Pope. From 1 feeble (*debilis*) mare 2s. From 1 cow and calf 4s. From 4 sheep 16d. Total: 7s. 4d. Total of the 15th: 6d.

From Godelwa the widow. From 1 cow 2s. 8d. Total of the 15th: 2d.

From Odo. From 2 cows 5s. 6d. From 1 *bovettus* 18d. Total: 7s. Total of the 15th: 5½d.

From Juliana the widow. From 1 cow 2s. 6d. Total of the 15th: 2d.

From Robert Popa. From 1 mare 3s. From 2 cows 5s. From 14 sheep 4s. 8d. Total: 12s. 8d. Total of the 15th: 10d.

From Walter *de gardino*. From 1 cow 30d. From 5 sheep 20d. Total: 4s. 2d. Total of the 15th: 3½d.

From Alan Sopere. From 6 sheep 2s. Total of the 15th: 1½d.

From Simon. From 1 cow and [1] *bovettus* 4s. Total of the 15th: 3¼d.

From John Vader. From 1 mare 2s. 8d. From 2 cows 5s. From 10 sheep 3s. 4d. Total: 12s. Total of the 15th: 9d.

From Richard Cukeman. From 1 mare 3s. 4d. From 1 cow and [1] *bovettus* 4s. From 8 sheep 2s. 8d. Total: 10s. Total of the 15th: 8d.

From Agnes the widow. From 1 *juvenca* 2s. From 3 sheep 12d. Total: 2¼d.

From Geoffrey *albus*. From 1 mare 2s. 8d. From 2 cows 5s. From 8 sheep 2s. 8d. Total: 10s. 4d. Total of the 15th: 8¼d.

Total: 39s. 3d.

18

FROM [Various Account Rolls of the Manors of the Bishopric of Winchester]. Hampshire Record Office, MS. Eccl. Comm. 2/159447, 159291A, 159291B.

DOWNTON [Wilts.]: EXPENSES IN THE NEW ASSART [1251/52][1]

In [digging] 17 furlongs (*quarentene*), 2 perches[2] of ditches around the new purpresture at *Loshangre* £7 2s. 1d., 2½d. per perch which was 7 feet in width and 6 feet in depth.

In planticia eiusdem[3] 18s. 11d., to wit, for 3 perches 1d.

In [digging] 33 perches around the farm-yard (*bertona*) of the same [purpresture] 6s. 10½d., to wit, 2½d. per perch.

In planticia eiusdem 11d., to wit, for 3 perches 1d.

In 8,400 stakes for the hedge around the same purpresture 14d.,[4] to wit, 20d. for a thousand.

In making 16½ furlongs of enclosure around the same, and 31 perches around the farm-yard, together with gathering and carrying brushwood (*claustura*) [for it], 51s. 9½d., to wit, 3s. for a furlong.

[1] A new assart was carved out for arable cultivation on the manor of Downton in 1251–1252 and developed over the subsequent years; the first two years are translated here. It must be pointed out, however, that considerable additional expenditure, mainly on stocking the place with animals and implements, was debited against the manor itself. The new assart was at first called *Loshangre* but this was later changed to Cowik. As I have no special knowledge of the technicalities of medieval farm-buildings I have shown my translation of this document, and of Doc. 19, to Mr M. Barley, of Nottingham University, who was kind enough to suggest a number of improvements.

I have rearranged the entries so as to start each new item as a separate paragraph; this applies to all the extracts in this document.

[2] At 40 perches to a furlong and 16½ feet to a perch this = 3,751 yards.

[3] This is referred to later on as *planticia eiusdem fossanda*. I was not sure what the exact nature of this operation was but, as Dr Rogers has pointed out to me, it must have meant cutting reeds and other growth on the edges of the ditch.

[4] This should have been 14 shillings.

In digging up 107 trunks (*lignis fodiendis*) for new buildings in the said farm-yard, and for stakes for the hedge round the same, [and] digging up 254 stumps to make way for the ploughs, £6 4d., to wit, for each trunk and stump 4d.

In levelling old ditches and digging up thorns (*spine*) to make the ground level for the ploughs 16s. 4d.

In making two new ploughs for the assart 6d.

In binding them with new iron 10d.

In 2 new shares and coulters bought 3s. 6d.

In steel for repairing the said iron-work (*ferramenta*) 12d.

In wages of the smith for making them 12d.

In 2 plough-irons (*pedes ferrei*) for the same [ploughs] 6d.

In repairing the said irons, as need arose, whenever they broke, 12d.

In mending the wood-word (*carpenteria*) of the ploughs 3d.

In wood-work of the harrows, and yokes, for the same purpresture 18d.

In harrowing the land 2s.

In weeding 47 acres in the same assart 3s. 11d.

In expenses of 1 boon-work in autumn for the reaping of oats in the same 4s.

In carting the same oats 10d.

In the carpentry of the gate of the same farm-yard 2s.

In nails for it 2d.

In hinges (*gunphi et vertenelli*) for it 8d.

In making a pinfold 2d.

In the carpentry of 1 ox-shed, with stalls for oxen, and other things pertaining to it, 30s. 8d.

In wattling (*waldura*) of the same 2s. 6d.

In gathering twigs (*virge*) for the sheep-house, and gathering twigs for wattling, 8d., with carriage.

In straw bought for thatching 12s. 5d.

In the carting of the same straw 4s. 2d.

In wages of the thatcher (*coopertor*) 6s. 4d.

In making daub walls (*plastura murorum*) of the same 4s. 6d.

In cutting boards for 3 gates, and for the timber of the ox-stalls, 2s.

In 2 pairs of hinges and nails for gates 16d.

In 1 lock for the same, 8d.

In the carpentry of the barn there, together with covering it with laths £6.

In making 9,000 laths 7s. 6d., to wit, 10d. for a thousand.

In 23,000 lath-nails for the same 15s. 4d.

In 1,250 large nails (*magni clavi*) for attaching planks to walls and rafters 2s. 10d.

In the carting of straw for the thatching of the same 8s. 7d.
In wages of the thatcher 16s.
In making a daub wall (*muro plastrando*) 10s.
In hinges for the gates 5s. 6d.

Total: £32 6s. 2d.

EXPENSES OF *LOSHANGRE* [1252/53]

In the iron-work of 2 ploughs together with 1 new share, and 1 coulter, and plough-irons, bought 5s. 5d.
In wages of the smith 3s.
In repairing the wood-work of the same ploughs 6d.
In 2 pairs of wheels for the ploughs 4d.
In sowing and harrowing 26 acres of wheat and rye 2s. 2d.
In sowing and harrowing 52 acres of oats 2s.
In digging up stumps and thorns within the close 16s. 8d.
In weeding the said acres 5s. 3½d.
In [digging] 44 perches of ditches around the farm-yard, for the enlargement of the yard (*ad curiam elargandam*), which was 7 feet in width and 6 feet in depth, 9s. 2d., to wit, 2½d. per perch.
In planticia eiusdem fossanda 18d.
In digging up 5 trunks in the same ditch 15d.
In the carpentry of 2 new gates 3s.
In 4 iron hangers (*pendentes*) for the same gates, with hinges (*gunphi*), staples (*stapelle*), and hasps (*haspe*), 18d.
In gathering and carrying brushwood (*claustura*) for the farm-yard hedge 2s. 3d.
In making (*claudendo*) the same hedge 16d.
In remaking and extending (*renovando et aumentando*), by carpentry, one building which was previously an ox-shed, 7s.
In mending its wattling (*waldura*) 12d.
In making a daub wall (*murus de plaustro*) 3s. 10d.
In thatching (*coopertura*) the same 6s. 8d.
In digging up stumps within the farm-yard, and levelling one ditch, and levelling up in [various] places (*placiis dirigendis*), including the floor (*aer*) of the barn and other buildings, 5s. 4½d.
In 1 bolt for the gate 2d.
In 2 autumn boon-works of 160 men who reaped all the corn within the close, in ale, 3s.
In 8 pairs of cart-wheels bought for marling 7s.
In making 2 pairs of wheels for the waggons[1] (*plaustrum*) 2s. 4d.
In the carpentry of all the [wooden] parts (*omni apparatu*) of 8 carts,

[1] or singular.

together with fitting 2 waggons with axles (*axandis*), 4s. 9½d., together with cutting boards for the gates.

In 8 seats for the carts for marling 16d.
In 8 swingle-trees with 'bases'¹ 4s.
In fitting axles to carts and waggons² 12d.
In clouts (*cluti*) for the same 3s. 8d.
In tallow 12d.
In ropes, girths (*sengulis*), and crupper-straps (*caudaris*), 6d.
In 3 pick-axes for marling 15d.
In making 3 shovels (*tribula*) and binding them with iron 12d.
In shoeing 10 horses, from the manor, going to the marling 3s. 6d.
In sending 3 men for 83 days to dig up marl 31s. 2½d., each 3⅛d. a day.
In expenses of 5 grooms (*garciones*) who came from the manor, with 10 horses, to marl for 43 days 26s. 10½d., each 1½d. a day.
In spreading 2,040 heaps of marl 4s. 3d., to wit, for a hundred 2½d.
In the carpentry of 1 ox-shed at *Loshangre*, 140 feet in length, 60s.
In the carting of timber for the same 6s.

Total: £12 2s. 0½d.

BILLINGBEAR³ [1252/53]

For [digging] 1050 perches⁴ of ditches at Billingbear £6 11s. 3d., the price per perch 1½d.
And for 5,700 willows bought for the hedge there 20s. 6d.
And for planting the same 3s. 1d.
And for enclosing (*claustrandis*) 570 perches 23s. 9d.
And for the carpentry of a building there, to serve as a dairy, 7s.
And for making walls 2s.
And for 450 laths bought 2s. 7½d.
And for 2000 nails bought for the same [laths] 18¼d.
And for hinges (*gunphi et vertenelli*) and nails for doors and windows 8d.
And in stipend of the thatcher (*coopertor*) 1s.
And for 1 lock bought 3d.
And for making 1 gate to the meadow, and 1 gate to the purpresture, 2s. 4d.

¹ *In 8 paronis, paronellis cum basonibus.*
² or singular.
³ Billingbear in Wargrave. A very sizeable assart was carved out there in 1252/3 for the purpose of arable, and dairy, farming and it was extended in subsequent years. The cost of stocking the place was borne by the manor.
⁴ At 16½ feet to a perch = 5,775 yards.

And for 2 bolts for the same 6d.
And for the great gate, at the entrance to Billingbear, bought 4s.
And for repairing, and making fast, the same 2s.
And for nails bought for the same 5½d.
And for mowing the meadow and making, and carting, hay 4s.
And for making a ditch for watering cows 9s. 1d.

Total: £10 16s. 0½d.

BILLINGBEAR [1253/54]

For [digging] 311 perches[1] of ditches between *Benefeld* and Billing-
bear 64s. 9½d., the price per perch 2½d.
And for 2,900 willows bought to be planted there 9s. 8d.
And for planting them 2s.
And for making a hedge thereon 19s. 5d., the price per perch ¾d.
And for [digging] 60 perches of ditches around the farm-yard (*bertona*)
of Billingbear 7s. 6d., the price per perch 1½d.
And for willows bought for the same 12d.
And for making a hedge thereon 3s. 9d.
And for [digging] 69 perches of ditches at the head of the western
purpresture 14s. 4½d., the price per perch 2½d.
And for [digging] 169 perches of ditches around the same purpresture
21s. 1½d., the price per perch 1½d.
And for 2,800 willows bought for the same 9s. 4d.
And for planting them 20d.
And for making a hedge thereon 19s., the price per perch 1d.
And for [digging] 68 perches of ditches around the eastern purpresture
14s. 2d., the price per perch 2½d.
And for [digging] 166 perches of ditches on the other side of the
same 20s. 9d., the price per perch 1½d.
And for 2,600 willows bought for the same 8s. 8d.
And for planting them 17d.
And for making a hedge thereon 19s. 6d., the price per perch 1d.
And for cleaning and enlarging the old ditch, in places, 28s. 9½d.
And for emending, similarly, the old hedge, in places, (?)s.[2]4d.
And for (? ?)[3], in places, 8s. 4½d.
And for making 4 gates within, and outside, the purpresture 3s.

Total: £14 16s. 5½d.

---

[1] The total length of the ditches in this account is: 4,306¼ yards.
[2] The shilling part is damaged.
[3] The description is damaged.

19

FROM The Account Roll of the Manors of the Bishopric of Winchester for the Sixth Year of the Consecration of *Dominus* Henry of Marwell. Hampshire Record Office, MS. Eccl. Comm. 2/159325 [1309/10].

IVINGHOE [Bucks.]: The Cost of a New Barn[1]

In timber bought anew £33 1s. 3d., £6 4s. 7d. having been subtracted from the original purchase [price] for the top, lop and branches (*rami, coperones, et cortices*) accruing from the said timber, as is shown in [the roll of] the particulars (*per particulas*).

In felling the said timber 16s.

In expenses carting the said timber, as boon-work, 70s. 11½d., as is shown in [the roll of] the particulars.

In hiring (*conductis*) carts to cart timber and laths 54s. 10d., as is shown in [the roll of] the particulars.

In 65 stones bought at Eglomount for underpinning the posts and making the foundations 9s 7d.

In 12 quarters of lime bought 6s., the price per quarter 6d.

In making the said foundations, on piece-work basis (*ad tascham*) 26s. 8d.

In 7,500 laths bought for the said barn 40s. 6d., whereof 4,800 the price per thousand 5s. 10d., and 3,500 the price per thousand 5s.

In 1,800 laths bought at St. Albans 17s. 5d., the price per hundred 11d. Also, in 900 laths bought at Dunstaple 9s., the price per hundred 12d.

In 52,800 tiles, together with lime, bought for the said barn £6 8s. 5½d., whereof 15,800 the price per thousand 2s. 8d., and 37,000 the price per thousand 2s. 4d.

In 13,500 tiles bought 45s. 6d., the price per thousand 3s.

In 700 hoop-tiles (?) (*hupetighels*) and ridge-tiles bought 16s. 4d., the price per hundred 2s. 4d.

Also, in 50 hoop-tiles and ridge-tiles bought 18d.

In 70,000 pegs (*keville*) bought for the said tiles 10s. 8d., whereof 24,000 the price per thousand 1½d., and 46,000 the price per thousand 2d.

In gathering moss 1s. 8d.[2]

[1] I have started each new item as a separate paragraph.

[2] I am grateful to Mr Barley for pointing out to me that this was needed for waterproofing the tiles.

Also, in laying 65,000 flat tiles, 750 hoop-tiles and ridge-tiles, on the said barn 36s. 4½d., to wit, for a thousand flat tiles 6d., and as much for a 100 hoop-tiles and ridge-tiles.

Also, in expenses of carting tiles and laths, together with hiring (*conductus*) one man to level up the site of the said barn, as is shown in [the roll of] the particulars, 21s. 3¼d.

In 200 great nails (*grossi clavi*)[1] bought for affixing great timbers (*grossum meremium*) and rafters (*cheverones*) onto the barn 5s.

In 4,000 great nails for affixing great timbers and rafters, and for affixing timbers and tiles, 13s. 7d., whereof 600 the price per hundred 4½d., and 3,400 the price per hundred 4d.

In 63,500 nails bought for affixing laths 47s. 7½d., the price per thousand 9d.

In 4 hinges (*gunphi et vertenelli*) bought for the smaller gates of the same barn 16d.

In 11 pieces of iron bought for hoops, plates, gudgeon-pins, and nails[2] for the greater gates of the barn, 6s. 5d., the price per piece 7d.

In stipend of the smith for manufacturing the said pieces for the aforesaid gates, 6s. 5d.

In the carpentry of the said new barn, together with 2 porches, on piece-work basis, £14 6s. 8d.

In fixing (*ponendis*) laths onto the said barn and its walls, on piece-work basis, 13s. 4d.

In sawing timber and boards, on piece-work basis, 55s. 6d.

In 2 thick hempen ropes to lift up large timbers 3s.

In 6 bushels of wheat bought and made into bread (*furniti*), for the expenses of the carpenter and other men helping to erect the great timbers of the said barn 6s. 4½d.

In ale [for them] 9s. 1d.

In meat, herrings, fish, eggs, and cheese bought for the same 7s. 11½d.

In hiring (*conductis*) 19 men, as if for one day, to help erect the great timbers of the said barn, 19d. and food provided.[3]

In 11 ash boards bought for the gates of the said barn 7s. 4d., the price per board 8d.

In 2 bolts, with nails, bought anew for the gates of the said barn 1s. 2d.

In making daub walls (*muro plastrando*) of the said barn, on piece-work basis, 26s. 8d.

Total: £83 8s. 0¼d.

[1] I am grateful to Mr Barley for pointing out to me that these, though referred to as 'nails', could not have been anything else but wooden pins.

[2] *Pro circulis, platis, goionis, haspis et clavis.*

[3] *Et mensam domini*, literally, 'and the lord's table'.

20

FROM *Statutes of the Realm,* London, 1810, I, 2–3.

THE PROVISIONS OF MERTON [1236], SECTION IV.

Also, Because many great Men of England, who have infeoffed Knights and their Freeholders of small Tenements in their Great Manors, have complained that they cannot make their Profit of the residue of their Manors, as of Wastes, Woods, and Pastures, whereas the same Feoffees have sufficient Pasture as much as belongeth to their Tenements; It is provided and granted; That whenever such Feoffees do bring an Assise of Novel Disseisin for their Common of Pasture, and it is knowledged before the Justicers, that they have as much Pasture as sufficeth to their Tenements, and that they have free [Egress and Regress] from their Tenement unto the Pasture, then let them be contented therewith; and they on whom [it was complained] shall go quit [of as much as] they have made their Profit of their Lands, Wastes, Woods, and Pastures; And if they alledge that they have not sufficient Pasture or sufficient Ingress and Egress according to their Hold, then let Truth be inquired by Assise; And if it be found by the Assise, that the same Deforceors have disturbed them of their Ingress and Egress, or that they had not sufficient Pasture, as before is said, then shall they recover their Seisin by view of the Inquest so that by their Discretion and Oath the Plaintiffs shall have sufficient Pasture, and sufficient Ingress and Egress in form aforesaid; And the Disseisors shall be amerced, and shall yield Damages, as they were wont before this Provision. And if it be certified by the Assise, that the Plaintiffs have sufficient Pasture with Ingress and Egress as before is said, let the other make their Profit of the residue, and go quit of that Assise.